BEFORE WE LOST THE LAKE

02 03 04 05 06 24 23 22 21 20

Caitlin Press Inc.
8100 Alderwood Road
Halfmoon Bay, BC V0N 1Y1
www.caitlin-press.com

Text and cover design by Vici Johnstone
Printed in Canada

Caitlin Press Inc. acknowledges financial support from the Government of Canada and the Canada Council for the Arts, and the Province of British Columbia through the British Columbia Arts Council and the Book Publisher's Tax Credit.

Library and Archives Canada Cataloguing in Publication

Reimer, Chad, 1963-, author
        Before we lost the lake : a natural and human history of Sumas Valley / Chad Reimer.

Includes bibliographical references and index.
ISBN 978-1-987915-58-7 (softcover)

        1. Sumas Lake (B.C.). 2. Abbotsford (B.C.)—History.
3. Abbotsford (B.C.)—Historical geography. 4. Sumas Prairie (B.C. and Wash.)—History. 5. Sumas Prairie (B.C. and Wash.)—Historical geography. I. Title.

FC3845.S92R45 2018   911'.71137   C2018-903398-3

BEFORE WE
LOST
THE LAKE

A Natural and Human
History of Sumas Valley

CHAD REIMER

CAITLIN PRESS

CONTENTS

To Shannon

ACKNOWLEDGEMENTS

I have lived with this book for well over a decade—from posing the first simple questions, through chipping away at the mountain of primary material, to the struggle of making sense of it all in writing. Along the way, I have benefitted from the professionalism and hard work of archivists and librarians from Victoria to Washington DC, for which I am greatly indebted. The reference staff at the BC Archives listened to my endless requests patiently and filled them promptly. The interlibrary loan department and Chilliwack circulation desk of the University of the Fraser Valley always delivered, no matter how large or obscure my request. It was an absolute delight to work in the National Archives and Records Administration in Washington, and the staff of the map department went above and beyond the call of duty.

Closer to home, I want to thank the following individuals for their help: Tia Halstead at Sto:lo Nation Archives; Kris Foulds at Reach Gallery and Museum; Paul Ferguson of the BC Archives; Shannon Bettles of Ft. Langley National Historic Site; and Calvin Woelke at the Land Titles and Survey Vault. Vici Johnstone and the crew at Caitlin Press have been a joy to work with; their energy and courage know no bounds. My biggest debt is to my wife, Shannon, who never stopped believing this book would see the light of day.

INTRODUCTION

Driving east from Vancouver along the Trans-Canada Highway, past the monotonous stream of malls, box stores and subdivisions that is suburban sprawl, you reach the crest of an escarpment on the edge of Abbotsford. Looking below you see miles of flat prairie, framed between the towering Cascade Range to the south and Sumas Mountain to the north. The land is divided into a checkerboard of country roads, green fields and clutches of tidy farm buildings. For British Columbia—with its sea of mountains and arid interior plateaus—it is a rare sight, more reminiscent of the Prairies than the far west coast.

In need of a stretch, you exit at Whatcom Road, famed as the route taken by miners during the great Fraser River gold rush. A rest stop nestled along Sumas River appears; you pull in and, drawn by the glint of sunlight from a bronze plaque mounted on a pole, walk over to take a look. In the boosterish language of such things, the historical marker celebrates an engineering feat from a century ago: "In 1924, by a system of stream diversions, dams, dykes, canals and pumps, 33,000 acres of fertile land were reclaimed from Sumas Lake." Only then do you realize that what you took as natural prairie was the bed of an extinct lake. And as you head back onto the freeway, you cannot shake a feeling of unease that the dry road stretching out ahead should be under water.

A century and a half ago, in early summer 1859, another visitor encountered the "low and comparatively flat land" of Sumas Valley, but it looked very different. After an exhausting journey by canoe and foot, veterinary surgeon John Lord pitched his tent alongside other members of the Northwest Boundary Survey. He recorded his impressions of the scene before him:

> Our camp was on the Sumass prairie, and was in reality only an open patch of grassy land, through which wind numerous streams from the mountains, emptying themselves into a large shallow lake, the exit of which is into the Fraser by a short stream, the Sumas river.

In May and June this prairie is completely covered with water. The Sumass river, from the rapid rise of the Fraser, reverses its course, and flows back into the lake instead of out of it. The lake fills, overflows, and completely floods the lower lands. On the subsistence of the waters, we pitched our tents on the edge of a lovely stream. Wildfowl were in abundance; the streams were alive with fish; the mules and horses revelling in grass kneedeep—we were in a second Eden![1]

Few people today are aware that a sprawling lake once covered Sumas Valley, reaching all the way from Sumas to Vedder Mountain. Every spring, the lake's shores expanded even farther. In exceptional years, during high flooding, the waters stretched from Chilliwack into Washington State, forming a veritable inland sea. Sumas Lake and its surrounding wet prairies were rich with life, home to a dizzying array of plant and animal species. Natural grasslands spread out for miles on either side of the lake, massive sturgeon and runs of salmon prowled its waters, and countless waterfowl darkened its skies.

Yet the life story of Sumas Lake has never been told. The handful of historical works that have dealt with the topic have been limited in scope. For one, they focus almost exclusively on the lake's draining and the impact that had on the valley as a whole—they examine the lake's death, not its life. For another, they adopt one of two basic storylines: triumph or tragedy. The earliest literature shared the opinion of drainage proponents that the death of Sumas Lake was a triumph. As the first study concluded, the Sumas Reclamation Project took "an 8,000-acre area of mud and water"—an unproductive wasteland plagued by mosquitoes—and turned it into "as fine a stretch of farming country as one could wish to see." This view of Sumas Lake as a wasteland and the economic benefits brought by its dewatering prevailed in the following decades. It found expression in local histories up to the end of the last century.

Meanwhile, an opposing plot line has emerged, which refashions the story of the lake's early death as a tragedy. Authors of these works argue that the drainage project itself was poorly done, that its escalating costs outweighed the economic benefits and that the dream of an agricultural landscape of small family farms was never met. More pointedly, this literature has highlighted the negative effects of the lake's draining: the loss of a cherished natural feature; the environmental impact; and most importantly, the devastating damage it inflicted upon the Sema:th people, who depended on the lake for their livelihood.[2]

The tragedy for the Sema:th continues to this day and cannot be brushed aside, and this book does not try to diminish it. Yet to truly appreciate that tragedy, we must know what Sumas Lake was like before it was drained. This book sets out to tell the story of Sumas Lake's full life: beginning with its birth during the last great Ice Age, and ending with its premature death and lingering presence into the 21st century. The history of the lake is not limited to its death, nor can its storyline be confined to one theme, whether triumph or tragedy. The story is much too big for that. Through the thousands of years of its existence, Sumas Lake played a central, determining role in the natural and human history of the region, its influence reaching out to the rest of BC and beyond. The goal, then, is the true reclamation of Sumas Lake: from a past that has forgotten it, and a present that has physically erased it.

CHAPTER 1

GLACIERS TO WETLANDS

S umas Lake was born more than 8,000 years ago, a late child of the last Ice Age. The hard rock that formed two of its mountainous shores and its deep bedrock date back even further. To the northwest sits Sumas Mountain, its oblong bulk rising 3,000 feet above the former lake's surface. Directly across the Sumas Valley to the southeast, Vedder Mountain is equally imposing, its long ridge running parallel to its twin. The base of these mountains, some four miles apart, formed immovable natural boundaries for Sumas Lake's waters.

The Sumas and Vedder formations are distinct, their separate masses of rock forged from 65 million to 400 million years ago. Plunging steeply downward, the mountains' slopes meet somewhere far beneath the current valley floor. If the sedimentary layers of Sumas Valley were stripped away, we would be left with a sharp, V-shaped trough; and if this trough were filled with water, it would produce the classic mountain lake seen nearby at Cultus, Chilliwack and Harrison Lakes. But bedrock has never been reached at the centre of the valley, so we do not know exactly how deep this trough was. The deepest test hole dug by geologists plunged a full 864 feet, hitting only sedimentary soil and thick clay. Leading scientists estimate that the deepest bedrock is to be found at 1,100 feet below the surface.[3]

Lying atop the bedrock of the Sumas and Vedder formations are hundreds of feet of clay, sand and gravel deposited over the past two million years. This was the age of the great glaciers, when continental ice sheets advanced and retreated in more than a dozen epic cycles, with the last ending a mere 9,000 years ago. During this last glacial cycle, the restless ice advanced and retreated several times in rapid succession, shaping and moulding the landscape of Sumas Valley. The dramatic escarpment, some 150 feet high, that forms the valley's western limit marks the westernmost limit of Sumas's last ice sheet; it also served as the western shore of a young Sumas Lake.

As the Sumas ice withdrew, water rushed across the landscape, dredging channels and flowing into depressions. Much of this new water came from the melting glaciers themselves; the rest came from newly formed rivers and streams, which rushed down from watersheds that stretched into the surrounding mountains. The most important of these early rivers was not Fraser River—as scientists and writers have assumed for decades—but the Nooksack to the southwest. The Nooksack River and Valley were created prior to their Sumas counterparts, with the earlier retreat of glacial ice eastward into the Cascade Mountains. For most of the postglacial period, the full volume of the Nooksack travelled north into Sumas Valley, not due west as it does today.

As Nooksack water flowed north, it pooled atop Sumas Valley and deposited thick layers of sediment upon the existing floor of glacial and sea deposits. Like all river sedimentation, heavier material such as rocks and gravel was dropped first, while lighter, finer sediments were carried ever farther out. The process built up a fan or underwater delta that sloped downward from today's town of Everson to the middle of Sumas Valley. We can see this fan today in the contour of the land: a 15-mile-long ramp, gradual and unbroken, that descends from an elevation of 85 feet at Everson, crossing the border at 35 feet, then hitting the deepest part of the former Sumas Lake bed at under five feet.

Sto:lo oral history, handed down over countless generations, corroborates what scientists are saying now. In 1962, 80-year-old Chilliwack elder Bob Joe told an interviewer that, in olden times, "part of the Nooksack River came through Sumas, Sumas City here, emptied out on this Sumas River." Amy Cooper, another Chilliwack elder, passed along her people's account of the Nooksack: "It divided up somewhere in the States and came through Sumas Prairie, out to the lake, and the other…emptied out near Bellingham."[4]

Over time, though, the Nooksack River began to change course. A berm gradually built up at the high end of the Nooksack fan; as the berm grew, more and more of the river's water was deflected westward. At some critical point, the berm became high enough to deflect all of Nooksack River to the west. Yet still, during years of very high runoff, the Nooksack River jumps its banks and returns to its ancient flow northward into Sumas Valley. But even with its waters gone, the Nooksack has left its mark on Sumas Valley, depositing the better part of the soil that makes up the surface and subsurface of the valley's western half.

As the Nooksack fed Sumas Lake from the southwest, the lake's edge moved farther and farther to the northeast. When the last of the ice was gone, Sumas Lake lapped up against the Cascade Mountains, from Vedder

Crossing to the Cheam uplands. The floor here climbs from an elevation of five feet at the lowest point of Sumas Valley to 35 feet nearly 16 miles away at Rosedale, before rising dramatically to 100 feet at the Cheam uplands. In ancient times, with water levels considerably higher relative to the land, Sumas Lake sprawled over this gently sloping floor. At its fullest extent during the postglacial period, then, Sumas Lake stretched some 33 miles from its southwestern shore near Everson to its northeastern limit at the Cheam uplands in the northeast. With an average width of four miles, Sumas waters covered over 132 square miles (85,000 acres).

One final piece was left to add to Sumas Lake's expanse, for the delayed melting of the Sumas ice block released a wholly new source of water.

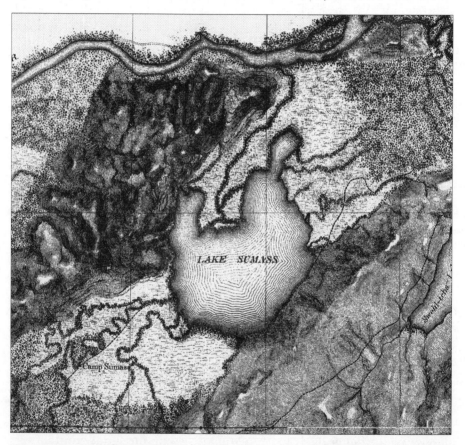

This map was one of the earliest made of Sumas Lake, prepared from exhaustive work on the ground by the Northwest Boundary Survey. It shows the main features and vegetation of Sumas Valley. To the northeast of the lake is lower Sumas Prairie and lower Sumas River, flowing into Fraser River; to the northwest, Sumas Mountain; to the southwest, upper Sumas Prairie and upper Sumas River; and to the southeast, Vedder Mountain. Portion of "The North West Boundary from Point Roberts to the Rocky Mountains" (1868) [nara, rg 76, cs66, map 7].

Up until then, the upper Chilliwack River had been held back by an ice dam at Vedder Crossing; when the dam weakened and finally broke, fresh water poured down into Sumas Lake. And as with the Nooksack to the southeast, the liberated Chilliwack River built up an underwater delta of sediment that survives today. Starting at an elevation of 100 feet at Vedder Crossing, the semicircular fan drops to 35 feet within a mile and a half in all directions. To the west, the elevation continues downward to the bottom of the old Sumas Lake bed. Due north it descends to 30 feet approaching Chilliwack city centre, while eastward it levels out at just below 35 feet.

Sumas Lake now was fed by two large watersheds: the Sumas and Chilliwack River systems. Taken together, the watersheds covered more than 615 square miles, at its widest stretching 50 miles from east to west, and 25 miles from south to north. The Sumas River basin encompassed 135 square miles, half of which lay south of the border. The upper Chilliwack River watershed drained 480 square miles in the towering Cascade Range, one-third of this in Washington State.

This picture of Greater Sumas Lake fundamentally changes our view of the history of Fraser and Sumas Valleys. Sumas Lake was not a fleeting feature of the valley's past—gone now for over a century—but a long-lived, dynamic force within the region. Nor was its impact confined to the shrunken dimensions encountered in the 19th century. For even with its reduced dimensions, Sumas Lake was a dominating presence in the valley. Most visible were the annual cycles of flooding, which expanded the lake's reach two to three times over. Twice every year, the lake swelled with the rise of flood waters in the Fraser, Chilliwack and Sumas Rivers. Each spring—from late May through mid-June—melting snow packs in the vast Chilliwack and Fraser watersheds fed those rivers.

Draining more than 90,000 square miles (one-quarter of the province's land mass), the Fraser River runs 855 miles down the spine of BC before entering the Pacific Ocean at the Gulf of Georgia. In a typical year, the Fraser can rise 10 feet at the mouth of the lower Sumas River; during the worst flood years, it can climb more than 20 feet. And because at the spring freshet the height of Fraser River topped that of Sumas Lake, the swollen waters reversed the flow of lower Sumas River and fed the rising lake waters. Meanwhile, the upper Chilliwack River was going through much the same flood cycle. Like the Fraser, the Chilliwack experienced a dramatic spring freshet, with three-quarters of its yearly runoff coming in May and June.

The Chilliwack River usually peaked a week or so earlier than the Fraser because its meltwater travelled much shorter distances. But the two rivers'

Sumas Lake as viewed from its rocky southeastern shore, which was exposed during low-water season. At high water, the shore was pushed up to where the photographer was standing, at the foot of Vedder Mountain. City of Vancouver Archives, LGN 1144, photographer British Columbia Electic Railway Company.

high waters did overlap, with their combined volumes swelling the size of Sumas Lake. During average years, the lake expanded from a low-water point of 14 square miles (9,000 acres) and a depth of nine feet, to 25 square miles (16,000 acres) and a depth more than twice that. Exceptional freshets brought exceptional flooding. In 1903, Sumas Lake reached a depth of 28 feet and spread out over 31 square miles (20,000 acres). During the half-century between the earliest flood records and the draining of Sumas Lake, the lake came within three feet of this mark nine times and surpassed it three times—in 1876, 1882 and 1894. The last year witnessed the greatest flood ever chronicled: the Fraser River peaked more than three feet above the 1903 line; Sumas Lake reached a depth of 31 feet and expanded to 47 square miles (30,000 acres).[5]

Sumas Lake also grew with a second high-water season. During late autumn and early winter, heavy rain and wet snow fell on Fraser Valley,

the Sumas River watershed and lower elevations of the Chilliwack River drainage area. Chilliwack River rose dramatically for a second time; in some years, the winter waters were as high as the spring freshet. The main waterways of the Sumas basin—Sumas River and Saar and Arnold Creeks—experienced just one freshet. Waters stayed low from June through September, but rose to their heights anywhere from late November through January.

Above-average rainfall routinely expanded the lake's shore to the southwest while causing localized flooding on upper Sumas Prairie. More extensive floods occurred when the Nooksack River overflowed its banks and breached the narrow divide between it and Sumas, returning to its ancient flow northward. The Nooksack River drained over 580 square miles of Washington State's Cascade Mountains; subject to the region's rainy season, it too peaked in late autumn and early winter. We do not have records prior to 1900, but in the first decades of the 20th century the Nooksack overflowed into Sumas a half-dozen times (in 1909, 1917, 1921, 1932, 1935 and 1937). The 1935 flood is the best documented of these: that year, water moving up from Nooksack River combined with runoff from the upper Sumas watershed; flood waters reached their peak in January, inundating 4½ square miles (3,000 acres) in Washington State and over 20 square miles (13,000 acres) north of the border.

The very traits that were considered fatal flaws of Sumas Lake—yearly flooding, symptoms of its aging, its shallowness—made it an exceptionally fertile place for plants and animals. Lake scientists tell us that an aging lake possesses a higher concentration of nutrients than a young one, because with time organic material has built up in it. And shallow water itself produces more of the plants, insects and microscopic animals that form the bottom of the food chain, as energy from the sun and wind reaches a higher portion of the lake. Moreover, a lake that grows and shrinks through yearly flooding is far more fertile than one that does not. The secret to this lies in what is known as the littoral zone, the area between the lake's low-water and high-water shores. The rise of flood waters brings in nutrients, soil and fresh oxygen; when the water retreats, these are left behind and the land is exposed to sun and air, creating a greenhouse effect.

The lush reeds, grasses and bush that surrounded Sumas Lake testified to its almost supernatural fertility. John Lord of the Northwest Boundary Survey described the aftermath of the life-giving spring flooding:

> In June the water again subsides; after this the growth of the various grasses and sedges (*Cyperaceoe*) is rapid beyond anything I have ever witnessed elsewhere. In two months the grass attains a height of [between] four and seven feet. As the water disappears, swarms of insects accumulate, as if by magic; birds of various species arrive to devour them, build their nests, and rear their young.[6]

What Lord witnessed here were the intricate connections between Sumas Lake, its yearly cycles and the natural environment surrounding it. Today, we have better tools to understand the ecosystem—a rich and complex web of plant and animal life—that stretched out from the lake's centre, beyond its edges to the farthest reaches of Sumas Valley.

Lord's contemporaries and those White immigrants who arrived later were largely blind to this web of life, and the lake's shape-shifting nature made many uncomfortable. But we live in the age of ecology, and we can literally see what they could not. The ecological perspective of the plant and animal life of Sumas Lake is a broader perspective, one that thinks in terms of transitions from one ecological zone to another, and also of the roles species played within those zones. Animals, plants, nutrients and energy were constantly moving across these zones, cycling between lake, wetland and land. We can, then, think of the ecology of Sumas Lake as a series of concentric zones moving outward from the lake's centre—like waves rippling out from a pebble dropped in water. Each of these zones was defined by the length of time it was covered by water and how deep this water was: covered all the time, every year for a number of weeks, or only during exceptionally high flooding (every five, 20, 50 or more years). The Sumas ecosystem thus consisted of the lake itself (at low water), the yearly flooded littoral zone and the drier land beyond this.

In historical times, the centre of the lake ranged from a depth of nine feet at low water, to double that during an average high water, to 30 feet at exceptionally high water. From here to the band of shallow water along its shores was open water, relatively free of plants on its surface or lake bed. Shallow lakes usually have bottom vegetation because sunlight can penetrate all the way to the lake bed. But the Sumas waters were murky: they were often muddy (due to the silty bottom), were constantly in motion or roiled (because of flooding and persistent winds) and were filled with micro-organisms such as plankton. Again because of the constant motion of its water, Sumas Lake was never colonized by surface plants such as water lilies, which can take over more stagnant bodies of shallow water.

Vegetation started to appear closer to the lake's shores. Some of these plants were fully submerged, but the more prolific were called emergent plants—rooted in the water, their long stems shooting upward, emerging above the surface. Nourished through their roots by the lake soils and water, their stalks and fronds fed off the sunlight and oxygen-rich air. They grew to such a height and so densely that it was difficult to move through them, which made them a perfect nesting ground for waterfowl. The Sema:th even mastered the skill of running atop their intertwined stalks to escape hostile invaders. Bulrush, cattail and horsetail were the dominant emergent plants.

Moving from the low-water shores to land that was yearly flooded, we come to the plants most associated with Sumas Lake and Valley: the rich indigenous grasses that stretched for miles. The grasslands on either side of Sumas Lake marked the extent of the yearly high waters. The fresh waters nourished the plants before withdrawing and letting the sun raise them. At the same time, seasonal flooding kept the fertile plains free of bush and trees, which otherwise would have quickly invaded the area and pushed out the meeker grass species. The lower Sumas grassland extended some two miles from the lake's northeast shore and four miles between Vedder Mountain and McGillivray Creek. Upper Sumas grasses reached up to 3½ miles from the southwest shore of the lake and four miles from Vedder to Sumas Mountain.

Common reed grass and brome grass straddled the zone between lake and wet prairie; the rest of the plains were taken over by thick growths of blue-joint grass that could reach five or six feet high. White boundary surveyors made note of the "long and coarse grass" that covered the Sumas prairies in the 1850s. One spring the following decade, Methodist missionary Ebenezer Robson described a trip across lower Sumas Prairie: "Walked through prairie to Miller's. Grass to my shoulders and so laden with dew that it rained down heavily when touched."[7]

Moving farther from the lake, toward land raised slightly above the yearly floods, clumps of bushes, shrubs and vines could be found among the grass. As the elevation increased, these bushes became thicker and more prevalent. This was land that might be flooded two or three times a decade. Some species thrived where the soil was sandy and drained well, others where the soil was thick with clay and so retained water. Berry bushes were much prized; indigenous blueberry, cranberry, saskatoon berry and others formed an important part of the Sema:th diet, as did root plants such as blue camas and wapato. Less loved, but still useful, were devil's club and stinging nettle; studded with razor-sharp thorns, their thick vine stalks grew with abandon wherever given the chance. Meanwhile, species of maple and willow trees gained a foothold as thick bushes, but were stopped from growing to full height by semi-regular flooding.

Finally we arrive at the upland areas, which were above the flood waters except during exceptionally high waters. Here trees characteristic of the larger region's coastal forest type could grow to their full heights. Douglas fir and western red cedar dominated, some reaching over 200 feet. Where the stands of fir and cedar thinned, cottonwood, willow and maple took hold. A thick undergrowth of brush and ferns covered the forest floor. This forestland extended beyond the grassland on either side of Sumas Lake: on lower Sumas Prairie, the two were equal in size; across the lake, the forest was more than twice the size of the grassland, stretching well into Washington State. The first Whites to travel through upper Sumas described "an immense plain or flat, thickly covered with timber." In places it was "so thick that a cannon ball would hardly penetrate."

Trees and brush also dominated the dozen or so ridges that rose above the grassland on upper Sumas Prairie. The sandy soil supported a mix of cottonwood, willow, broadleaf maple and the occasional Douglas fir; berry and vine bushes provided ground cover. The ridges peaked as high as 30 feet above the valley floor; composed of sandy silt and clay, they stretched out in oblong arcs that paralleled the southwest shore of Sumas Lake. Some of these ridges were created when prevailing winds from the northeast produced wave action in the lake, which in turn sculpted underwater dunes. These dunes were then left exposed as the lake retreated, rising first as islands, then as terrestrial ridges. Ridges also formed along the lake's receding shorelines; the two largest—Kennedy and Lakeshore or Telegraph—grew as spits jutting out from Sumas and Vedder Mountains, respectively. In historical times, these created large sandy beaches, much used by Natives and Whites alike. George Gardner, an American member of the Northwest Boundary Survey, was more accurate than he could know when he recorded his first view of upper Sumas: "The whole prairie has the appearance of having once been an immense lake with small islands scattered through it, that are now mounds or ridges over-grown with brush and few trees."[8]

On lower Sumas Prairie, a handful of broad swamps broke up the transition from grassland to forest. The biggest of these sat just north of upper Vedder River, 2½ miles east of the lake. The 800-acre "Great Swamp" was dominated by cranberry bushes and dead cedar. Immediately to its southwest sat a cedar swamp, half the size, which straddled Vedder River. Along the northern edge of lower Sumas Prairie, a 120-acre willow swamp straddled the transition between grassland and a forest of massive cottonwoods. The latter took up the stretch of land from the mouth of lower Sumas River to Chilliwack Mountain.

The rich plant life that thrived in and around Sumas Lake in turn supported a rich and diverse population of animals. As one scientist writes, shallow, aging lakes and their adjacent wetlands are "known as *nature's supermarket* for the role that they play in supporting food chains, both aquatic and terrestrial. Wetlands are where critters go to eat or be eaten." Shallow lake and wetland habitats also provide places to breed and offer many species protection from predators. Wetlands are the single most important environment for life on this planet, because of both the diversity and the abundance of species that live on them. Taking up less than one percent of the earth's land, wetlands provide habitat for an astonishing 80 percent of land-based species, including humans.

This abundance started at the bottom of the food chain. In the open section of Sumas Lake, sunlight pouring into the shallow, organically rich water created algae, which were eaten by micro-animals known as plankton.

Plankton were devoured by fish, which in turn were food for diving ducks and water mammals such as otters. Countless numbers of insects hatched in the shallow waters and plant stalks along the lake's edges, quickly maturing as they fed off the surrounding reeds and wetland grasses. The most notorious of these were mosquitoes, which plagued the Sto:lo and Whites alike.

Midges (usually called sandflies) also were prolific. Midges are the most common aquatic insect in the world; nearly all early sources identify the hordes of insects they saw around Sumas Lake as mosquitoes, but it is possible many of these were actually midges. In Sema:th oral history, mosquitoes and midges were created at the same time. When a cannibal creature (either Saskts or Cannibal Woman) is tricked by children and shoved into a fire to burn, the small sparks become mosquitoes, the large sparks sandflies. John Lord devoted most of his writing on Sumas Lake to mosquitoes; he gave only passing reference to the "tiny burning fly...or sand-fly," even though he admitted the midge was an equally bloodthirsty foe.[9]

Surface-skimming insects, underwater plankton and lake-bottom vegetation fed a resident and seasonal fish population. All five species of Pacific salmon spawned in Sumas Lake, along upper and lower Sumas Rivers and in smaller tributaries such as Saar, Arnold and Marshall Creeks. Every year, millions of salmon passed from Fraser River through the lake on their way to upper Chilliwack River, Chilliwack Lake and Cultus Lake; millions more of their fry passed back down the following year. A healthy population of sturgeon was even more dependent on Sumas Lake for spawning. The white sturgeon was an elusive leviathan that spent most of the year hugging the bottom of deep pools of water along the Fraser and Harrison Rivers, and in Harrison Lake. From May to July, large numbers sought out the shallow waters of lower Sumas River and Sumas Lake to spawn. As elder Rose Sparrow recalled, "the greatest place where sturgeon used to be was Sumas Lake...sturgeon lake that was." Various trout, stickleback and sucker species were abundant, as was a whitefish commonly called roundfish (more properly, menominee or mountain whitefish).

Birds represented the greatest diversity of animal life on and around Sumas Lake. Almost 200 species and subspecies depended on the lake and its wetlands for their habitat. These species were either year-long residents or seasonal migrants; they fell within three broad categories. The first were land-based songbirds, such as swallows, sparrows and wrens, which nested and bred in the valley's thick bushes, feeding off insects. The second group were raptors, such as eagles, osprey, hawks and owls, which feasted on fish and small mammals. They nested on limbs of trees that towered over the valley floor, providing both protection for their young and the perfect vantage point for hunting.

The third category—water-based birds—itself can be divided into subgroupings. Most ducks were dabblers, like the ubiquitous mallard, feeding from the lake surface or upending in shallow water to reach lake-bed plants. Others were divers, going after fish in open water or tearing up lake-bottom vegetation. Off the lake itself, three species of swans and six species of geese were voracious grazers of grass and reeds. For waterfowl, the dense band of reeds along the lake's shores provided protection for their nests, making Sumas Lake the ideal location for breeding. Every year, millions of migratory waterfowl stopped over at Sumas to feed, breed and moult. Indeed, Sumas Lake was an integral link in the Pacific Flyway that stretched from western Mexico north to Alaska.

The fish and waterfowl of Sumas Lake and Valley were the most sought-after animals by Native and White settlers. Mammals were fewer in number and not as significant a resource—but they were still important, to both the lake's ecosystem and its human residents. Elk were the largest mammal species to make use of the lake. The hulking herbivores came down from the mountain slopes to feed on the valley's grasslands. As Chief William Sepass recalled, "formerly elk were as numerous as cattle around Sumas Lake." White-tailed and black-tailed deer also enjoyed Sumas's fresh waters and rich grasses. Deer were a common sight at Fritz Stromberg's home at the foot of Vedder Mountain: "Sometimes they used to come right down. I've seen deer coming right across the lake here—swim the lake, or wade the water." The presence of large herbivores attracted predators such as wolves, Pacific cougars and black bears. More plentiful were smaller, aquatic mammals ideally suited to the lake and wetlands: beaver, Canadian river otter, Pacific muskrat and Pacific mink. Numerous species of voles, moles, mice and shrew made their homes in the valley's wet soil.

This broader view of Sumas Lake's ecosystem—that links the lake and surrounding wetlands into a functioning whole—reveals the crucial roles it played locally, regionally, even globally. For one, it supported plant and animal populations that were as diverse as they were abundant. The boundless array of species and sheer number of individual plants and animals were truly astonishing. This abundance and diversity benefited not just Sumas Lake and Valley, but the region as a whole. Deer, elk, cougars, wolves and bears came down from the surrounding mountains to feed on the rich valley floor. The sturgeon population along Fraser and Harrison Rivers came to Sumas Lake to spawn; salmon that lived most of their lives in the Pacific Ocean travelled to and through Sumas, also to spawn. And for countless waterfowl migrating along the Pacific Flyway, the lake was an oasis where they could rest, eat and breed. All these species depended on Sumas Lake and Valley to survive. Globally, Sumas's diversity helped the survival of species threatened in other parts of the world. If something happened to a Sumas species elsewhere—habitat loss, overhunting or some other destruction—it would not yet be extinct.

Sumas Lake and its wetlands also played a central role in the water system of Fraser Valley. Their ability to absorb and hold water moderated the impact of high- and low-water seasons. "The value of water storage by wetlands," a leading scientist writes, "is to reduce flooding in wet weather and to maintain the flow of streams and rivers during dry weather." This crucial role of flood mitigation was not understood by White residents and officials who successfully pushed through the lake's draining. The 1948 flood would demonstrate how important Sumas Lake was in controlling the region's high waters, although the lesson went unseen. With the lake gone and its largest natural spillway blocked, the Fraser River found somewhere else to go, causing more damage than the even greater flood of 1894.

Finally, the wetland nature of Sumas Lake would determine the way humans viewed and used it. The Sema:th and their neighbours had few problems accepting and working with the lake the way it was. They made the most of the resources available and adjusted their own seasonal rhythms to the seasonal rhythms of the lake. In their eyes, there was nothing wrong with the shallow, aging lake, nor the wet prairies that were not wholly land or water, but both. As one environmental historian notes, "Unlike Euro-American land use, Native use of birds and wetlands did not require the rigid division between water and land promoted under western private property regimes." The Sema:th view of the world itself was based on transitions and transformations, not the rigid distinctions of the White world. The space in between things—a littoral zone in the cosmos—was as real as the things on either end. The physical and spiritual, human and animal, land and water—all occupied this world together, continually moving from one form to another.

White newcomers would find it necessary to adapt their ways to the demands of this novel physical landscape. But they did so grudgingly, for they wanted to change Sumas Lake and Valley to support their own way of life. They introduced alien plants (potatoes, wheat, clover) and animals (cattle, horses, pigs), and struggled to establish their ideal of the family farm supported by intensive agriculture. From the start, they dreamed of ridding the land of its wetness, of draining the lake and dewatering the valley.

The wetness of the land stopped them from creating the life they so desired. It also was something that had no place in their grand view of the natural world, which was built on the distinction between two fixed elements—land and water. Lands that were not wholly dry, and water that was not sufficiently wet, were not understood or accepted on their own terms. Instead they were vilified, written off as "dismal" marshes, swamps and bogs. To scientists, officials and farmers, "wetlands were 'wastes': useless, worthless, bothersome places that blocked travel, bred mosquitoes, frustrated settlement, and generally threw up the most annoying and inconvenient barriers to human progress." Where and whenever possible, the thing to be done was drain them. Only later, through the second half of the 20th century, did scientists and the public redefine these in-between spaces as wetlands—an environmental third way. And only then was progress made in understanding how important they were. Unfortunately for Sumas Lake, it would be too late.[10]

CHAPTER 2

FIRST PEOPLES

We cannot be sure when and how people first appeared in Sumas Valley. Like all peoples the world over, the Sema:th and their Sto:lo neighbours have their own narratives of how this came about. Speaking with anthropologist Diamond Jenness eight decades ago, Katzie elder Old Pierre recounted his own people's "book of Genesis." Unlike the Christian tale of Adam and Eve, whom the Great First created "in your country far away," Pierre said, "here…the Lord Above worked on a different plan: for He created not one couple only, but groups of people in various places; and to each of these groups He assigned a special leader."

For the Sto:lo, the act of creation was performed not once but several times. In the far distant past, shortly after the world itself was created, chaos overtook the land and all things in it. To set matters right, the Great First sent the first humans—the tel swayel, or "sky-born people"—who fell to earth at various places "to become the original leaders of either individual settlements or entire tribal communities." Sometime after the era of the tel swayel, the world again became a fluid place, populated by "mythic, shape-shifting beings." More tribes were created, this time from ancestral animals, who, after finding a home in a particular area, were transformed into a tribe's First Man. Sturgeon for the Lakahamen, black bear for the Chilliwack, mountain goat and sandhill crane for the Pilalt, and beaver for the Matsqui: these were the founding fathers of their people.

The final age in early Sto:lo history was that of the Xexa:ls, three brothers and a sister who entered a world that was "not quite right." As the quartet travelled through the Sto:lo homeland, they transformed people, animals and landforms to make the world right again. Additional tribes were created as good individuals were transformed into First Men. By the time they finished, Old Pierre concluded, the Xexa:ls had "arranged earth as it is today."

Along the way, the brothers and sister left behind physical reminders of their visits, transformer rocks and sites that Sto:lo recognize to this day.

More subtle marks also were etched into the landscape, such as the footprints left at Devil's Run, an important Sema:th fishing site on Fraser River below lower Sumas River. Speaking to anthropologist Marian Smith in the summer of 1945, elder Fred Ewen described the Xexa:ls' visit to Sema:th territory and explained how these footprints came to be. After descending the Fraser River as bear cubs, the siblings returned upriver as humans. Travelling along the foot of Sumas Mountain, they stopped at Devil's Run, where a human giant was fishing with a dip net. After helping the man catch a salmon, the Xexa:ls ordered him to leave his "footprints on that rock...toes, heel, two footprints marked on the rock...to prove to people that he [the human giant] had been there."

Nearly a century earlier, a similar account was recorded by George Gibbs, a member of the Northwest Boundary Survey. In spring 1858, a small fleet of canoes operated by a Sema:th chief and crew carried the boundary survey team up Fraser River. Gibbs wrote in his journal that, as the party passed in the shadow of Sumas Mountain,

> on the south side of the river...the Indians pointed out a boulder lying on the shore, exhibiting a band of harder substance. This they stated was a S'Hui-yahm. He was catching sturgeon when S'Haalse [Xexa:ls] told him there were strange Indians coming. He replied that he was not afraid of them, but he lied, and S'Haalse turned him into stone.

Elsewhere in his journal, Gibbs transcribed transformer accounts for other locations along Fraser River; these are the earliest written records of the Xexa:ls, their travels and work.[11]

Even after the Xexa:ls exited westward toward the setting sun, the work of peopling—or rather repeopling—the Sto:lo homeland was not finished. Sometime after the departure, a great flood inundated the region, covering everything but the highest mountain peaks. Over the decades, Sto:lo elders have shared various accounts of this flood, which, while differing in some details, share the same plot line. As flood waters rose, drowning many in their villages, survivors from the various tribes took to their canoes. Riding up with the waters, they tied on to one of the region's mountain peaks. The canoes then broke free and were dispersed; once the waters receded, the craft came to ground at different places, which became the survivors' tribal homes.

Half a century ago, Chilliwack elder Dan Milo explained how the flood carried the Sema:th to their home along upper Sumas River. "A flood, years and years, thousands of years ago," covered the Fraser Valley, drowning all but a handful of people. The peak of Sumas Mountain stayed dry, and here the Sema:th canoes tied up. As the water receded, the Sema:th descended with it. They stopped midway along the southwest slope of the mountain and sought shelter in a cave, where they waited until the valley floor below dried out. Finally, they looked down upon Sumas Prairie "and grass began to green, you see. They began to think it must be getting pretty dry down there, so they dragged their canoes down to the old Sumas River....Well they were all saved, those that come down with their kids, they went to their home."

It is not surprising that the great flood has been a common, central feature in Sto:lo historical narratives. The home of the Sema:th and their neighbours was and is a watery landscape: transformed every year by seasonal flooding, inundated even further in exceptional years every decade or century. The greatest flood recorded since the arrival of White newcomers was that of 1894; scientists estimate that a flood that size occurs every 200 years. The Sto:lo have been here many times that long, so generations of their ancestors would have witnessed waters as high and higher than those of 1894. With the right conditions, the perfect flood would have covered nearly the entire floor of the lower Fraser Valley, leaving only the mountainsides above water. The great flood of Sto:lo oral histories was fashioned after these real, historical floods.

What the oral histories do not contain is also significant. The Sto:lo have no accounts of migration in or out of their homeland: the Sto:lo did not arrive from somewhere else, but were created here; and they were the first people to occupy this land. After meticulous and extensive fieldwork among the upper Sto:lo, pioneering anthropologist Wilson Duff reported that his "informants knew of no traditions of migrations or of earlier populations." Decades later, Sto:lo leaders released a political manifesto that declared, "We are not the 'first' immigrants of this territory, we have always been here."[12]

This conviction was put forcefully, yet with good humour, by Sarah James and other elders who, through the 1970s, worked to record and revive the Halkomelem and Nooksack languages. The elders dismissed both White religious and scientific theories of how the region was first populated:

> Q: Are there any legends of how the Nooksack came to exist, came to be?
>
> Sarah James: When God created us, He created you and He created us and He put us where He wanted us to be.

Philomena Solomon: And we didn't even come from China either. [laughter]

SJ: No, or Japan or Russia. What they say, well you come from Japan. No, God put us here. And that's why we're here. And Mr. White-Man was put on the other side, well, that's where he come from.

Whatever their content or form, Sto:lo accounts of their own people's past are histories of this land and this land only. White immigrants who began arriving a mere century and a half ago saw things differently. They believed that humans were created in one place: their Christian mythology looked to a Garden of Eden, thought to have existed somewhere in Mesopotamia; later, scientific accounts identified the Great Rift of eastern Africa as the birthplace of humanity. From these ancestral homes, humans pushed outward to occupy the rest of Africa, Eurasia and Australia, leaving the Americas as the last habitable continents to be populated.

Migration-based theories claim that people originally moved into the lower Fraser region as early as 7000 BC, in the wake of retreating glacial ice. The earliest ethnologists envisioned the first settlers as interior hunters who moved west from the mountains into the valley. Others have since argued that the first inhabitants came from ice-free territory in today's Washington State, moving north into the lower Fraser as the ice retreated. A more recent theory is gaining wider acceptance; it posits that the earliest peoples worked their way southward from Alaska by sea, leapfrogging from one ice-free coastal site to another. When they arrived at the mouth of the Fraser River, they moved east up the valley.[13]

Whatever the origin of the ancient settlers of the Sto:lo homeland—inland or coast, sky-born people or Xexa:ls transformations—the earliest physical traces of human occupation date back to the end of the glacial age. At either end of lower Fraser River, the remains of campsites have been radiocarbon-dated to between 7000 and 6000 BC. Midway along the Fraser, ancient remains were found seven miles downstream from lower Sumas River at Xa:ytem, and an equal distance upstream at Scowlitz.[14]

The Xa:ytem site rises above the north bank of Fraser River, west of Hatzic Lake. Here archaeologists found some 16,000 ancient tools and other artifacts, along with the remains of dwellings, the oldest of which was dated to 2800 BC. The most dramatic feature of the site was a man-sized transformer rock—Xa:ytem himself. For the Sto:lo, Xa:ytem came into being during the time of the Xexa:ls, when four local chiefs challenged the sibling transformers and were turned to stone. Before departing, the Xex-a:ls transformed a Sema:th boy—who at the time was training to become a warrior—into Thunderbird and gave him the responsibility to watch over Xa:ytem. Thunderbird dutifully kept watch from his cave on the western slope of Sumas Mountain, above Kilgard.

From 1000 BC on, the climate in lower Fraser Valley grew increasingly warm, the landscape more fertile. The population of Sto:lo increased, as did the number of larger, more permanent settlements. The Scowlitz site was one such settlement. Sprawled along a two-mile stretch on the west bank of Harrison River, Scowlitz was first utilized some 3,000 years ago and perma-nently settled by 500 BC. Residents here built a complex of plank houses and pit houses; they also constructed relic-laden burial mounds.

Down the Fraser a short distance from Scowlitz, we encounter the first remains of human activity in traditional Sema:th territory. Two sepa-rate sites—sitting atop narrow shelves squeezed between Sumas Mountain and Fraser River—date back as far as 400 BC and show signs of use into the 20th century. The first location is a three-mile stretch on either side of Wade's Creek, midway along Sumas Mountain. Archaeologists have identi-fied a half-dozen distinct clusters here; these have yielded stone tools, cere-monial objects and both circular and rectangular house depressions. There also is anecdotal evidence of ancient basketry, which is highly unusual given the wet conditions of the site.

A mile up Fraser River from Wade's Creek is Liyomxetel, a narrow shelf 200 yards long historically known as Devil's Run. Due to physical conditions, archaeologists have been unable to carry out systematic digs on the site. Yearly flooding, erosion from the Fraser and construction of the Canadian Northern Rail line have disturbed or destroyed much of the shelf. Nevertheless, surface surveys conducted from the 1950s on to recent years have unearthed hundreds of artifacts. Hunting and fishing tools in-cluded knives, scrapers, abraders and projectile points; woodworking im-plements consisted of mauls, adze blades, chisels and drills. The tools have been dated from 500 BC to 500 AD. Cultural remains such as a soapstone vessel (carved into the shape of a winged turtle) and a number of circular dwelling depressions have been found, while earthen burial mounds were discovered nearby. The site produced even perishable artifacts; the most significant are three "nearly complete woven baskets," which belong to a cultural style that flourished from 2,400 to 1,400 years ago.

Sema:th oral history corroborates the physical evidence that Liyomx-etel has been occupied and used extensively over the past two millenniums.

Kilgard elder Ray Silver recently confirmed, "Our Indian people used to go down there for thousands of years." Silver added that the site had been used well into the 20th century, including by himself: salmon were caught off the point and cured in a smokehouse built there.

Travelling farther upstream, little more than a mile from Devil's Run, we reach the confluence of the Sumas and Fraser Rivers. Here, on the southwest corner of the Sumas River mouth, an ancient settlement was founded; historically known as Sumas Bar, the village grew over the centuries into the

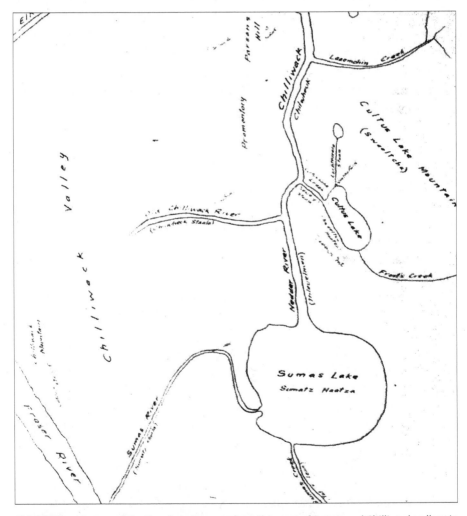

Chief William Sepass of the Skowkale Reserve drew this map of Sumas and Chilliwack valleys in 1918. Sumas Lake is linked to both the Fraser River and upper Chilliwack River systems, showing how important it was to the Sema:th, Chilliwack and Nooksack from ancient times to the last century. Chilliwack Museum and Archives, 2004. 052. 2870.

largest settlement of the lower Sema:th. The surface of the site has produced Stone Age artifacts, and basket fragments have been salvaged from its clay-rich beach. Most of these fragments were constructed in a style widely used between 350 BC and 600 AD. One sample was even older: the distinctive pattern of its weaving dates to a design used between 1300 and 300 BC.

From their location at the mouth of Sumas River, the ancient Sema:th could feed off the abundant runs of salmon, eulachon and sturgeon along Fraser River. They also could turn southward and follow the salmon and sturgeon up Sumas River into Sumas Lake, where a teeming supply of plants, fish, waterfowl and game awaited them. There is evidence that the Sema:th did just that as early as 400 BC. Decades ago, Canadian and American archaeologists unearthed the remains of a series of ancient sites southwest of Sumas Lake. The sites clustered along the three main streams that flowed into the western shore of the lake. In 1953, University of British Columbia archaeologist Walter Kenyon made contact with a local farmer who had plowed up a large cache of artifacts on the west bank of Sumas River, several hundred yards north of the border. This cache included stone mauls, adze blades, projectile points, abraders (whetstones) and food vessels. Farther east, a diverse collection of stone tools, spear points and carvings was discovered scattered along Saar Creek, on both sides of the border. No evidence of dwellings was found, suggesting that the various sites had been occupied on a seasonal basis: for hunting, fishing and plant gathering, as well as for manufacturing and maintaining tools.

A quarter century later, more sites farther up Sumas River were uncovered by an archaeological team from Western Washington University. Along a 500-yard stretch from the border southward, three separate locations were identified, two on the west bank of Sumas River, one on the east bank. These sites yielded a modest collection of stone tools (adzes, saws, chisels) and a handful of fire-cracked rocks, which pointed to sporadic, seasonal occupation. The one remarkable find was an inch-long micro-blade, which team leader Keith Montgomery "tentatively identified as a light brown obsidian." Obsidian—dark natural glass forged in volcanic furnaces—was highly prized by stone-tool makers because it could be rendered razor sharp by chipping; it was perfect for knives, arrowheads and spearheads. Obsidian fragments found at Xa:ytem came from Oregon, nearly 400 miles to the southeast. If the Sumas microblade was of the same material, then the Sema:th acquired it from the extensive trade network that ran the length of the Pacific Northwest.

Another, larger site was discovered less than a mile farther up Sumas River—a strip 200 yards deep, running 300 yards along the river bank. Nearly 100 stone tools were unearthed, along with a well-used fire hearth. Ten sculpted bowls also were found, with recessed tops and ornamental sides. Five of these bowls were shaped into zoomorphic (animal-shaped) figures, including a seven-inch owl and an eight-inch fish. The size of the site, the number of artifacts, the deeply blackened fire hearth and the animal bowls led Montgomery to conclude that the location was used more actively and extensively than sites downstream. He labelled this the first of two "semi-permanent seasonal resource procurement stations" found by his team.

The most significant finds on the ancient Sumas flood plain were unearthed along the third and smallest tributary southwest of Sumas Lake. For most of its course on both sides of the border, Arnold Creek meanders along the foot of Vedder Mountain; some 400 yards south of the international line, it meets up with Mud Slough. Starting at this junction, and stretching out 700 yards along the west bank of Mud Slough, three evenly spaced sites were discovered and systematically excavated. The first and third of these locations yielded nearly 50 lithic artifacts, along with fire-cracked rocks. The type of remains found suggests the locations were used seasonally, for short periods of time, to acquire and prepare food.

The largest of the three Mud Slough sites was discovered midway between the first two. Over 2,000 ancient artifacts were found in a densely distributed pattern, along with clear evidence of wood structures built around a pair of fire hearths. This was the second of two "semi-permanent" settlements on Mud Slough identified by Montgomery. The site yielded a full array of stone tools: from mauls, chisels and anvils to drills and awls. More than a dozen elegant adze blades lay alongside; ranging in size from two to six inches long, each tapered to a cutting edge that remained clean and sharp centuries after they were made.

The majority of artifacts—spear and arrow points, knives, blade fragments, scrapers—were directly related to the acquisition and preparation of food, clothing and other necessities. The settlement was ideally situated to take advantage of the area's rich food resources: the berries, fish, birds and small mammals that flourished in and around Sumas Lake; and the deer and other game that took refuge up the slopes of Vedder Mountain, only yards away. Vedder Mountain also provided these ancient Sema:th with the hard-rock material needed for their tools, as such ores could not be found in the soft sedimentary ground of the valley floor.

Lying among the trove of practical stone tools was a handful of ornamental objects: a slate disc bead, a teardrop pendant and a pair of intricately carved animal figures. One of these six-inch figurines was a bowl or ladle, with the head and wings of an owl. The other was an atlatl weight or handle, sculpted into a mammal of some sort (possibly a deer or mountain goat). An atlatl was a wooden extension used to throw spears; at that time, the use of stone weights was most common in the upper Fraser Valley area.

The atlatl weight and owl bowl were in the same style of the zoomorphic vessels found at other Sumas sites. As early as the 1950s, archaeologist Kenyon noted the "unusually high concentration" of such carved objects they and local farmers had unearthed on upper Sumas Prairie. A few of these artifacts made their way into local museums, but many more are thought to have disappeared under farmers' plows or into the living rooms of private residents. The magnificent animal carvings revealed that Sema:th culture was becoming increasingly sophisticated, with symbolic art and accomplished artisans. This development was part of a wider cultural awakening through the Sto:lo homeland during this time.

Two stone artifacts unearthed by archaeologists at the Mud Slough site in Sumas Valley just south of the border: an owl-shaped bowl and mammal-shaped object. Montgomery, "Prehistoric Settlements of Sumas Valley" (1979).

Along with this mass of lithic artifacts, the Mud Slough archaeology team also unearthed a number of fire hearths and postholes. The oval hearths were clay-lined and filled with fire-cracked rocks; the largest hearth was two feet by four feet and sat a short distance from a slightly smaller twin. A string of seven postholes arced in a ragged line 16 inches away from the edge of the hearths. The holes were three to six inches in diameter and over a foot deep. Montgomery argues that poles driven into these holes supported both temporary, lean-to habitations and fish-drying racks; the structures were purposely built around the firepits to best capture their heat. Montgomery concluded that these were not the remains of large plank houses; the number and pattern of postholes did not match those found at Scowlitz and other sites from this time. However, it is possible the ancient dwellings at Mud Slough were more permanent than Montgomery credits, given the size of the posts and how far they were driven into the ground. Add to this the abundance and variety of artifacts, and a picture emerges of Mud Slough as an established and important centre of settlement and activity, the first that we know of in Sumas Valley.

The Western Washington University team did not have the resources to obtain radiocarbon dating for the remains it uncovered. But based on comparisons with other dated findings along the coast and up the Fraser Valley, Montgomery places the Sumas River and Mud Slough artifacts between 400 BC and 400 AD. Projectile points unearthed at Mud Slough were close matches to ones previously found at Liyomxetel, which were decisively dated to this time. More recent digs at Devil's Run have uncovered adze blades identical to those from Mud Slough.

Thus, the archaeological record reveals that, sometime between 400 BC and 400 AD, the ancient Sema:th advanced from their settlements along Fraser River up Sumas River, crossed Sumas Lake and established themselves on upper Sumas Prairie. The lake extended much farther to the west and south at this time, which meant the Mud Slough sites were closer to, perhaps even on, its shore. Moreover, modern aerial photography has revealed the presence of "meander scrolls" along Mud Slough and Arnold Creek, which are signs that a considerably larger river once flowed here, which also would have given the Sema:th better access to resources and easier transportation.

The Sema:th settlements in Sumas Valley were linked to a wider Sto:lo world that was maturing culturally and materially. Travel, trade, intermarriage and shared cultural practices strengthened the ties between the various Sto:lo peoples. One of these shared customs was a sophisticated "burial complex" that spread across the region from 500 to 1200 AD. At sites throughout Fraser Valley, archaeologists have unearthed mortuary mounds: each the grave of a single individual, buried along with jewellery and other valuable items. The mounds reveal a culture that was amassing more material wealth, but also a culture with growing disparities in access to that wealth, increasingly stratified between high- and low-status families.

More than a century ago, amateur ethnologist Charles Hill-Tout stumbled upon a number of these mounds on either side of Sumas Lake,

along the lower slopes of Sumas and Vedder Mountains. Hill-Tout immediately recognized what he was looking at because he had recently excavated a number of similar "ghost heaps" around Hatzic Lake. Each of the
Hatzic mounds consisted of an outer earthen shell, 15 feet across and 11
feet high. Within was an inner cairn "built of jagged blocks of stone, of
varying weight and size, taken from the mountain side." Hill-Tout did not
excavate the Sumas mounds, but he noted that each would have interred a
single individual, along with his or her valuable possessions.

Unfortunately, in the decades since Hill-Tout stumbled across them,
no one has been able to locate the Sumas Lake burial mounds. Hill-Tout
himself did not say exactly where they could be found, and by now they
may be completely overgrown by trees and bush. It is possible avid ama-
teurs, even Hill-Tout himself, razed the mounds while "excavating" them,
or that they were destroyed by farmers or loggers clearing ground. The
closest we come to modern verification of the Sumas mausoleums is a recent archaeological inventory of Fraser Valley, which notes "a large number
of precontact earthen burial mounds on the lower northeastern hillside of
Sumas Mountain in the vicinity of Liyomxetel." It is not a stretch, though,
to view the burial mounds as successors to the older villages unearthed by
archaeologists at the base of Vedder and Sumas Mountains.[15]

We have brought the early history of human occupation on and
around Sumas Lake up to several centuries ago, relying on archaeological
evidence and Native oral histories to do so. We now turn to the more recent
past, when in addition to Sto:lo accounts we have access to the first written
records, produced by White newcomers. The picture of the Sema:th that
emerges from these sources is of a vibrant, populous society built around
a central geographic feature—Sumas Lake. The lower Sema:th occupied
the wetlands northeast of the lake, the upper Sema:th the prairie southeast
of it. Sumas Lake, though, did not divide the Sema:th as much as it unified
them: family ties knitted them together, they travelled easily across the lake
and they shared equally in the valley's abundant resources.

Well into the 1800s, the main village of the lower Sema:th was located
on the northern bank of the lower Sumas River mouth, on a sandy spit jutting out into the Fraser River, known as Sumas Bar. When the first Whites
began arriving in the region, the village was the Sema:th's most important
settlement. While eclipsed later by the upper Sema:th hamlet of Kilgard,
Sumas Bar remained in existence into the early 20th century. Yet the village
has been either ignored or misrepresented by the historical literature on the
Sema:th and Sto:lo.

A closer look at the primary material reveals both the existence and the importance of Sumas Bar. From the 1860s on, Sema:th and other Sto:lo sources spoke of a major settlement here, although they did not give a precise or commonly used name for it (in neither Halkomelem nor English). In the 1860s, the Sema:th themselves identified the settlement as "Sumas River," or simply "Sumas Village." Ketrelem was identified as its chief, but the settlement's Halkomelem name was not recorded. Nooksack elder George Swanaset was born here, as were his mother and uncle; he identified it as "the village on Sumas Bar," or simply "Sumas Bar," a name recognized by Dan Milo. More recently, drawing upon stories his elders passed on to him, Ray Silver explained that the Sema:th "stayed there too. They used to live there...right on the mouth of the [Sumas River]."

Non-Sto:lo sources have provided additional information on the Sumas Bar site. The American and British contingents of the Northwest Boundary Survey left vivid descriptions of a large, stockaded village. In late August 1857, after making his way northward from Nooksack River, across Sumas Lake to Fraser River, American George Gardner found himself at Sumas Bar:

> These Indians live principally at the mouth of Sumass River near the banks of Fraser River in quite a large stockade fort, evidently built in imitation of the Hudson Bay Company's forts, and so situated as to command the entrance to Sumass River.

When the British boundary commission arrived a year later, Sumas Bar impressed Lt. Charles Wilson as a prototype of the major settlements in the area:

> The villages are composed of several substantial wooden houses, and are sometimes, as at Sumass and other places on the Fraser River, enclosed by a stout palisading of young firs, some fifteen feet high, fixed firmly into the ground, with sufficient space between them to point a musket through.

Observations from other members of the Northwest Boundary Survey, along with the calculations of recent scholars, suggest the population of Sumas Bar stood at around 400 through the first half of the 1800s. The previous century, before disease decimated the Sema:th, this population would have been much greater, perhaps as high as 1,200.

During the second half of the 1800s, the settlement regularly appeared on maps produced by colonial and government officials. Royal Navy captain Richard Mayne's widely-used nautical map of the lower Fraser River located an "Indian village" on the sandy beaches at the mouth of the "River Smess." Royal Engineers tasked with laying out the first Native reserves were given a list of a half-dozen of the most important settlements to include, one of which was "a village at the mouth of the Sumass River." In 1864, the first official reserve map was drawn up; it showed a settlement of three large longhouses commanding the mouth of Sumas River, which was at the centre of a sprawling Lower Sumas reserve. Through the following decade, surveyors laying out roads and official township lines also show Sumas Bar as the main lower Sema:th settlement. Land surveyor William Ralph made meticulous sketches of Sumas Valley in his field books. At Sumas Bar, he drew four large, perfectly aligned Sema:th longhouses, and an additional one on an island guarding the river mouth. The chart made from Ralph's surveys identifies the village as an "Indian Reserve"; official township maps made in the following three decades refer to it as either a reserve or a village. From 1906 on, the settlement disappears.[16]

The Sumas Bar settlement has been discussed at length here, first to clear up confusion over its existence and location, and second because of its importance. The mouth of lower Sumas River was the passageway between Fraser River and the entire Sumas Lake watershed. The stockaded village at Sumas Bar guarded this passageway, giving the Sema:th control over Sumas Lake and Valley. Other tribes seeking access to the valley's rich resources needed permission from the Sema:th to do so. Sumas Bar also gave the Sema:th unquestioned access to the Fraser River, the Sto:lo's highway. From here they travelled the length of the lower Fraser, trading goods and maintaining social ties with other tribes. The Sema:th were renowned for their skill at navigating the Fraser's powerful currents and swirling eddies—so much so that when White traders, miners and surveyors arrived, the newcomers relied heavily on Sema:th canoes and crews for transport. And the Sema:th's presence on the Fraser River gave them a share of the mighty waterway's teeming runs of eulachon, salmon and deepwater sturgeon.

This presence on the Fraser was not confined to Sumas Bar alone. With the stockaded village as their capital, the lower Sema:th held sway over a five-mile stretch of the river, occupying satellite sites on its south and north banks. Westward along the base of Sumas Mountain, the Sema:th continued to use Wade's Creek and Liyomxetel as seasonal encampments. Through the 19th century, as White settlers and government officials restricted Sto:lo access to crucial resources, Liyomxetel became even more important to the Sema:th. Situated on a rock-strewn lowland over a mile west of Sumas Bar, Devil's Rock juts out into the Fraser, forming a pool of deep water close to the shoreline that was ideal for net fishing. Large numbers of Sema:th and other Sto:lo congregated here to harvest the yearly runs; permanent buildings were even erected to cure the salmon, sturgeon and eulachon they caught.

While the Sema:th and their Sto:lo neighbours have made use of Liyomxetel for countless generations, the more commonly used name—Devil's Run—came into being just over a century ago. Yet there is no agreement on how the site got this name, or what it means. Some say it comes from the abundance of steelhead (occasionally referred to as "devil fish") at this part of the river; others attribute it to the lethally swift stretch of water off its banks, which has claimed the lives of many Sto:lo fishermen; still others claim it was where whisky bootleggers unloaded their illicit cargo.

A more intriguing explanation is that the name's source lies in centuries-old oral tradition: most particularly, the transformer account that comes to us through elder Fred Ewen. As we have seen, Ewen described how, at the precise location of Liyomxetel, Xexa:ls encountered a giant perched on a boulder fishing for salmon. After helping the giant catch a salmon, Xexa:ls ordered him to leave imprints of both his feet in the rock, to prove that he had been there. The literal translation of Liyomxetel—"devil's foot place" or "devil's foot device"—and the elements of Ewen's transformer tale strongly suggest this was the source of the name Devil's Run. The presence of the giant, who in other Sto:lo accounts is a malevolent being, a Sasq'ets or devil; the footprints he leaves in the rock while using it to fish, as a foot device; and the location of the tale all point to a devil's foot place or device. Moreover, the fact that Xexa:ls helps the giant catch salmon at that location explains how the site came to be such a rich fishing spot.[17]

From their central settlement of Sumas Bar, the Sema:th also controlled the opposite bank of Fraser River, running along the south shore of Nicomen Island. Directly across from Sumas Bar sat Papekwatchin, which functioned as a sort of suburb or satellite. From here, the Sema:th had an unobstructed sightline westward, around the bulge of Sumas Mountain and down Fraser River. Sentinels posted here could keep a vigilant watch for enemy raiding parties coming upriver from the coast. The site also functioned as a seasonal meeting place for the Sema:th and their Sto:lo neighbours, a role denoted by the translation of the name Papekwatchin itself—"spreading out your tents."

To the east, the Sema:th historically held sway along the south bank of Fraser River, between Sumas Bar and Chilliwack Mountain. The main site here was Lackaway, at the mouth of Wilson Creek. From the mid-1800s to the early 1900s, Lackaway was recognized as Sema:th. Through the first half of the mid-20th century, the small village became tied more closely with the Chilliwack, and was identified by Sto:lo elders as Chilliwack. But even then, Lackaway remained a numbered Sumas reserve, and the Sema:th made regular use of it as a transit stop, a place to pull in and meet up with others while travelling from and to Sumas Bar, Sumas River and Sumas Lake.

Sumas Bar gave the Sema:th a share of the resources and travel corridor of Fraser River. Turning southward, the Sema:th exercised exclusive control over lower Sumas River and the peninsula that ran along it into Sumas Lake. Archaeologists have found evidence of human tools and dwellings at sites along this 4½-mile stretch. The Sema:th occupied and utilized the peninsula through the 19th century. They cultivated potato patches along the low, wet land; one early White official noted many of these spread out along half the length of the lower Sumas peninsula. The Sema:th also operated a 200-foot sturgeon weir "across the Sumass River where it left Sumas Lake." Here they established a settlement on either side of the river, which some sources identify as T'exqe:yl.

An older village known as Lochchamaquim was located on McGillivray Creek, a short distance east of lower Sumas River. Archaeological finds have been recorded here; a large number of artifacts were unearthed and carted away when McGillivray Creek was dredged as part of the Sumas Lake drainage project. Chief William Sepass described Lochchamaquim as a longhouse village that stood some 300 to 400 years ago. The Sema:th and Chilliwack appear to have shared another encampment farther up McGillivray Creek. Identified by Dan Milo as Tehm-eh-kwiy-ehl—"at mosquito time"—it was a place to which they fled to escape the seasonal plague of mosquitoes.[18]

The expansive wetland south of McGillivray Creek, to the foot of Vedder Mountain, also was traditional Sema:th territory. We do not know how far east this zone of influence extended prior to the arrival of Whites. One historian has speculated that it may have included the soggy terrain on either side of lower Chilliwack River. As the lower Chilliwack landscape dried with the westward retreat of Sumas Lake, and the Chilliwack people moved onto the valley floor, the area east of the lake—what William Sepass labelled the "Sumas swamp"—acted as a buffer between the Sema:th and their new neighbours. This allowed the Sema:th to maintain control of the eastern shore of Sumas Lake and of the handful of large creeks that flowed into it. A network of trails east of Sumas Lake helped the Sema:th keep control of the area; the network linked up one pathway westward to upper Sumas Prairie and another that scaled over Vedder Mountain to Cultus Lake.[19]

Discussion of the lower Sema:th presence on Sumas Lake brings us to Snanith, the Fraser Valley's own Atlantis. Local historian Oliver Wells asserted that Snanith was "a village on the upper end of Sumas Lake, which moved out into houses built over the lake's surface during the summer, to get away from mosquitoes." Wells located the land-based village near the mouth of Vedder River, at the foot of Vedder Mountain; he sited

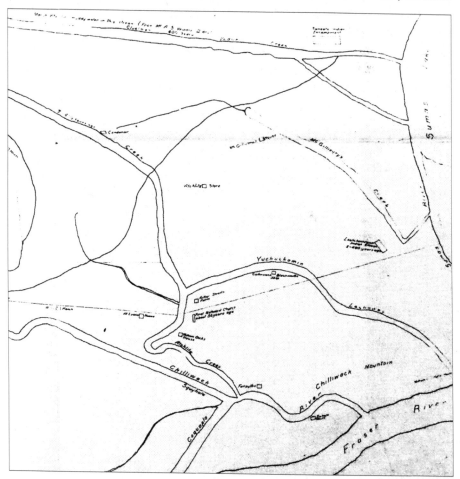

A map of Chilliwack Valley and lower Sumas Prairie drawn by Chief William Sepass, showing the various waterways and historic Indigenous sites. Chilliwack Museum and Archives 2004.052.2871.

the lake settlement—a cluster of four square residences—due west, some distance from the lakeshore. While recent scholars have accepted Wells's claims, Sto:lo oral histories provide no support for them. When asked directly, elders Bob Joe, Dan Milo, Cornelius Kelleher and Ray Silver all said they had never heard of any stilt village on the lake.

We do know that the Sema:th made seasonal use of raised platform dwellings on Sumas Lake. In July 1859, Lt. Charles Wilson of the Northwest Boundary Survey spent a hot summer night in "an Indian hut built in the middle of the lake upon piles." Later, he and his crew sailed across Sumas Lake "much to the astonishment of the Indians on the lake, between whose houses we passed with a slashing breeze." Naturalist John Lord visited the lake dwellings "very frequently" and gave a more detailed account of them. Each of the large platforms was "fastened to stout poles driven like piles into the mud at the bottom of the lake." Lord did not provide any numbers, but he did note that the platforms were "scattered over the lake, each with its little colony of Indians." From what we can tell, Lord and Wilson's route onto and across Sumas Lake was well to the north of the supposed site of Snanith, closer to the lake's midpoint. And the platform huts they saw there were not confined to one spot or village; they were more widely used than scholars have recognized. The migration to lake huts was not confined to a single village or site, but was one tactic used by Sema:th from all around Sumas Lake to escape the yearly plague of mosquitoes.

The Snanith myth itself originated in Methodist missionary Thomas Crosby's ignorance of the upriver Halkomelem language. In January 1868, Crosby arrived in Sumas Valley and grandly announced, "I am off to Nah-nates, fourteen miles away, at the head of Sumas Lake, to preach to the Indians." Further reading of Crosby's account, of the more detailed diaries of his successor Charles Tate and of other sources from the time makes it clear that the upper Sema:th village he visited was Kilgard and that the "head of Sumas Lake" referred to the mouth of upper Sumas River. As confident in his linguistic skills as he was in his spiritual righteousness, Crosby had misunderstood the directions given him, confusing the literal meaning of Snanith—"on the other side of the lake"—with the village he wished to visit.

The evidence we have from Sto:lo sources reveals that Snanith did exist, but during a much earlier period. A 1918 map of Sumas Valley by William Sepass showed a large "Indian Encampment" identified as "Saneats" near the mouth of Vedder River. Sepass did not specify when this settlement existed, but it appears to have been of the same vintage as Lochchamaquim to the south: that is, 300 to 400 years old. Recent archaeological work in the area has yielded numerous artifacts, including a ground stone maul and fragments from lithic tools. Moreover, elder Dan Milo's accounts of the devastating epidemic that struck the Sema:th specifically located a major village near the mouth of Vedder River: "At Yarrow, that's [where] the group of Indians lived you see. On the sand of the Sumas Lake."[20]

Across Sumas Lake, a series of upper Sema:th settlements stretched out west of the lake. In recent times, the most important of these was the village of Kilgard, which was recognized as the "main tribal home" of the upper Sema:th. However, Sto:lo elders such as William Sepass and Bob Joe have testified that this was not always so—that the Sema:th had moved to Kilgard relatively recently, a move triggered by changes in the physical environment.

Elder Lotte Tom provided the most detailed account of this migration. Tom was Sema:th by birth, but after marrying she moved to her husband's Nooksack village. She explained how, in the aftermath of a great flood many generations earlier, her ancestors "started to repeople the Valley." They built a settlement of pit houses at the junction of Johnson Creek and Sumas River; named Temixwtem, it was populated by both Sema:th and Nooksack families. Here, the two peoples learned each other's language and intermarried, forming a bilingual, bicultural village. Sometime later, during her great-grandfather's young manhood, another flood forced the people out of their pit houses and into a massive, planked longhouse. Again, Sema:th and Nooksack lived together, each family occupying its own partitioned section. A decade after that, Temixwtem itself was abandoned and the people split up. Families with closer ties to the Nooksack moved south toward Goshen, while the rest formed a new Sema:th village just north of the border at "Whatcom." After yet another flood, the Sema:th moved north again, to the rising ground at the foot of Sumas Mountain, where they built Kilgard.

Tom's account of the northward migration of the Sema:th is corroborated by both physical evidence and testimony from other elders. Temixwtem sat at the same location—the confluence of Sumas River and Johnson Creek—as the large site excavated by Keith Montgomery's team. And Nooksack elders such as Frank Reid recalled seeing abandoned "pithouses at təmíxʷtən on Sumas Prairie" that had been occupied before the coming of White immigrants.

The successor to Temixwtem likewise was documented in the material and oral record. Remains of the Whatcom settlement—over a mile north of the border, wedged between upper Sumas River and Whatcom Road—survived into the 20th century. In 1953, long-time resident W.D. Porter reported that local farmers had been plowing up artifacts for decades. Porter also recalled a cluster of four or five abandoned plank houses "arranged in a line along the east bank" of Sumas River that used to stand on a neighbour's property. A short distance off were a handful of depressions Porter called "sweat-baths," which may have been the remains of pit houses.

The Whatcom settlement reached its peak in the mid-19th century. At just this moment, it played a central part in averting war between the Sema:th and the Chilliwack. When a dispute between the two peoples threatened to escalate, a high-status Whatcom man married a descendant of the legendary Chilliwack warrior T'xwelatse, who had been transformed into stone. The marriage defused the situation and cemented a new alliance. As was custom, the woman moved to her husband's home, bringing with her the three-foot-high incarnation of T'xwelatse. Soon after, most of Whatcom village moved north to Kilgard, but several prominent families remained. The Commodores, Wealicks and Sams stayed on until 1884, when the lynching of Sema:th teenager Louie Sam by an American vigilante mob just south of the settlement convinced them it was time to move. T'xwelatse was left behind during this rushed exodus, to be unearthed later by a local farmer.

Sometime earlier, the main body of upper Sema:th had sought refuge from the annual threat of high water farther northward at Kilgard. Known as Kwekwei:qw in Halkomelem, the village acquired the name Kilgard after a clay-brick plant was constructed nearby. A wide array of artifacts unearthed in the vicinity—including carving tools and fishing gear—documents the earliest human occupation here. Most notable are finds made on the raised ground between Marshall Creek and Sumas Mountain, on the prairie below near the confluence of Sumas River and Saar Creek, and along Kennedy Ridge farther east. The village followed the pattern laid out at the Whatcom settlement: a line of four or five large plank houses stood along the north bank of Marshall Creek, at its confluence with upper Sumas River. Each plank house was 60 feet long and housed numerous families. By the 1890s, Kilgard's population had decreased greatly and the houses were largely abandoned.[21]

Reflecting their importance, Kilgard and Sumas Mountain play central roles in Sto:lo oral histories. In versions of a catastrophe account—of disease and drought—a Kilgard boy and Snanith girl are the sole survivors of their people. They marry, settle at Kilgard and begin to repopulate

Sumas Valley. Various flood narratives tell of how the upper Sema:th and other Sto:lo take to canoes and tie up atop Sumas Mountain. The two Halkomelem names for Sumas Mountain originated in the flood accounts: Teq'qeyex, referring to the gap left when the mountaintop broke off, dislodging the canoes moored to it; and Kwekwei:qw, literally "sticking up," due to Sumas Mountain remaining above water during the flood.

While Kwekwei:qw refers to Sumas Mountain proper, the name was used regularly by the Sema:th and their neighbours for the Kilgard settlement. Ethnologists from Franz Boas in the 1890s to Oliver Wells nearly a century later identified the village by its Halkomelem name. Kwekwei:qw took on added meaning after the draining of Sumas Lake. In the 1970s, Sema:th and Nooksack elders taking part in language workshops translated the word as "fish heads sticking up." Linguist Brent Galloway attributed the updated meaning to the fact that "for several years after [the lake's draining], the heads of trapped sturgeon were left exposed."[22]

Two points need to be noted as we close our discussion of the early history of the upper Sema:th. First, the archaeological record suggests that the establishment of Temixwtem and the subsequent migration north to Kilgard—sometime from the late 1700s to the early 1800s—was not the first occupation of the area around Kilgard. Most likely, in the wake of epidemics that struck them during this time, the upper Sema:th withdrew from here to Temixwtem, where they linked up with surviving Nooksack. Second, the northward migration to Kilgard makes sense from an environmental perspective. Sumas Lake was shrinking over these centuries, filling in with sediment brought down from its watershed. We know the Sema:th occupied the area along the current international border between 400 BC and 400 AD—as the lakeshore receded to the northeast, the Sema:th moved onto the newly exposed prairie, initially making seasonal use of it, then establishing more permanent settlements.

CHAPTER 3

SEMA:TH XO:TSA

Ｎone of the historical records available to us provide an original Halkomelem name for Sumas Lake. Sto:lo oral histories identified Sema:th as the name of the people who lived on either side of the lake, but they did not apply it to any geographical feature. The earliest written accounts from White newcomers used numerous variations of Sema:th. Hudson's Bay Company men started out with Maes, Mace and Smaize, before settling on Smess. The Northwest Boundary Survey briefly used Soomass, then more consistently Sumass, applying it to the lake and people. Shortly after, British authorities adopted Sumas as the official name for the lake. Then, through the second half of the 1800s, White sources attached the name Sumas to the key geographical points of the area: thus Sumas River (upper and lower), Sumas Mountain, Sumas Prairie (upper and lower) and the newcomers' settlement of Sumas. Translating back into Halkomelem, Sumas Lake itself became Sema:th Xo:tsa, xo:tsa being the word for lake.[23]

Of course, the lack of a recorded Sema:th word for Sumas Lake was not an oversight, nor did the Sema:th think so little of the lake they did not name it. Just as the Sto:lo referred to Fraser River simply as "the river," so Sumas Lake was known as "the lake"—so central was it to the Sema:th's existence and identity. This was how the Sema:th referred to Sumas Lake when pointing out the valley's geographic features to the Northwest Boundary Survey. Going back further in time, Sumas Lake was at the centre of the stories the Sema:th told about themselves. Trickster tales of Raven, Mink and Skunk took place on and around the lake, as did harrowing accounts of drought and flood, disease and famine.

The Sema:th's reliance on Sumas Lake started at the most basic level, for it provided the material resources that made their way of life possible. Its resources fed them, clothed them, sheltered them and transported them. This abundant supply started from the ground up, with the yearly renewed stands of grasses and rushes. Sema:th women collected cattails

Just like this Cowichan woman, Sema:th women collected long reeds that grew alongside waterways and fashioned them into flexible, waterproof mats (1912). Royal BC Museum and Archives, D-08941.

and bulrushes that flourished in shallow water along the fringes of the lake. The stalks were sun-dried, then sewn together; needles were carved from hard wood, and thick thread made from twisting smaller rushes. Naturalist John Lord observed that "mats thus made are perfectly rain proof." The work was laborious: a rug measuring three feet square required over 100 individual stalks. The flexible mats were carried by the dozen to resource sites, where they were fashioned into seasonal dwellings. Women also wove intricate baskets from the sharp-edged grass harvested along the lakeshore, and scrubbed pots and dishes with the rigid, raspy stalks of scouring rush, giant horsetail and common horsetail. These last three were used by craftsmen as a form of sandpaper for cedar canoes and other wood products.

Humble root vegetables constituted an important part of the Sema:th diet. The flat expanse southwest of Sumas Lake, Lotte Tom recalled, was "a very fertile prairie which was plush with wild vegetables." Wapato, blue camas and the less common wild carrot were the most sought after. Wapato (called "Indian swamp potato" or "Indian potato" by Whites) was the major source of starch for the Sema:th, while the sugars in blue camas provided much-needed calories. The two species grew in the wetlands on the edges of Sumas Lake and along low-lying banks of its tributaries. "The roots were the size of asparagus roots, the skin was tender and white," explained elder Agnes James. "You eat them raw and they taste like parsnips. They grew in big patches and everyone staked out where they were going to dig."

An even greater variety of bush berries awaited Sema:th harvesters a step farther from the lakeshore. Through late spring and early summer, numerous species ripened within easy reach on the valley floor; toward the end of summer and early fall, Sema:th ascended the slopes of Sumas and Vedder Mountains in search of later-blooming fruit. Among the more favoured species, salmonberries were the first to ripen, followed by thimbleberries, wild strawberries, Canada and bog blueberries, and blackcaps; saskatoons, blackberries and salal were picked later in the year. Leaves of the bushes were used for tea, often with medicinal effects; ripe berries were eaten fresh, added to other foods as sweeteners or dried into cakes to trade or eat later. Yearly flooding kept the valley floor clear of trees, allowing the berries to thrive.

Low bushes and other leafy plants were also important food sources. Western dock (or wild rhubarb) flourished along creeks on upper Sumas Prairie; the stems were boiled and made into a bitter jam, which sometimes was sweetened by other berries. Various ferns—from the towering bracken to the modest licorice fern and swordfern—were harvested for food and medicine. Even the noxious stinging nettle had uses: its leaves were boiled and eaten, hence the name "Indian spinach"; dry leaves were steeped to make "Indian tea," which provided vitamins A and C; and fibre from dried stalks was twisted into thread and twine. A second form of Indian tea was made from the Labrador tea plant. Also known as "swamp tea," the plant's aromatic leaves could be picked any time of the year; the steeped leaves produced a tasty and highly popular drink. Labrador tea was so commonly used that a section of upper Sumas Prairie was named after it. Lexwmo:qwem— meaning "always swamp tea"—lay between Sumas River and Saar Creek, southwest of the old Whatcom settlement.

Moving farther away from Sumas Lake, grasses and bushes gave way to thick stands of trees. Clutches of wild crabapple grew on the banks of Vedder River. Its fruit was eaten when ripe; its bark was used as medicine after childbirth and as a form of birth control. The fast-growing broadleaf maple was known as the "canoe paddle tree," its strong, flexible wood utilized for that purpose; meanwhile, longer canoe poles were fashioned from Douglas fir.

No tree was as important to the Sema:th as the western red cedar, known as "the mother tree of the forest." Its wood was pliable yet easily split; its fibres were ideal for weaving and twining; and both wood and fibres were waterproof. The Sema:th enjoyed access to significant stands of cedar on either side of Sumas Lake. To the northeast, a cedar forest stretched northward from the Sumas cranberry bog, along the edge of lower Sumas Prairie's grasslands. To the southwest, a strategic stand surrounded the old settlement at Whatcom, which was set aside as a reserve in the 1800s but then taken away in the early 1900s.

The large plank houses erected at Temixwtem, Whatcom, Kilgard and Sumas were constructed wholly from cedar: sturdy posts and beams for the frame, long straight planks for the walls and roof. Overseeing construction of a storehouse for the Northwest Boundary Survey, George Gardner marvelled at the craftsmanship of local carpenters. He wrote in his journal: "The cedar planks we purchased from the Indians, who split them out with great skill for building their winter quarters. I have seen one they made that was 20 feet long, 2 to 3 wide, 2 inches thick." The Sema:th also relied on cedar for transportation and clothes. Both the multi-purpose half-log canoe and smaller shovel-nose canoe were hewn from cedar logs. The former craft transported the Sema:th up and down Fraser River, and across the open waters of Sumas Lake; the latter, flat-bottomed boat was ideal for the shallow fringes and sluggish tributaries of the lake. Woven cedar bark was the standard material for clothing: the short apron was everyday wear for men and women; the cape, versatile blanket and rain hat were worn when needed. Cedar supplied material for countless other uses, from ropes to tools to ceremonial masks; and the intricate baskets for which the Sto:lo are renowned were reinforced with stripped cedar roots and saplings.[24]

Along with a rich supply of plants, Sumas Lake provided the Sema:th with abundant fish, birds and game. This set the Sema:th apart: no other people along the lower Fraser had access to such a diverse population of animals that lived in, on and around the lake. "We used to get our meat, ducks and fish out in this lake and on the prairie," Chief Selesmlton explained in 1915. "We go out on the mountains on each side of this lake and get all the meat we want....These ducks used to be so thick around here that we could kill all we wanted."

For countless generations, fish was the mainstay of the Sema:th and Sto:lo diet. The Sema:th's presence along the Fraser gave them a share of the river's runs of salmon, sturgeon and eulachon. They also controlled the array of species that thrived in Sumas Lake, and in the rivers, streams and sloughs that flowed into it. "Sumas Lake used to have sturgeon," Edward Kelly from Kilgard recalled, "and various types of salmon, and trout, a lot of trout." Of the five species of Pacific salmon known to Sumas Lake through pre-contact times, the spring was the main food species, followed closely by the sockeye; pink, chum and coho were taken, but they were much less prized and generally not cured or preserved. John Lord of the Northwest Boundary Survey witnessed Sema:th and Chilliwack fishers taking salmon "in large numbers...in the Sumass, Chilukweyuk, and Sweltza rivers, and indeed, in all inland lakes that are accessible to fish from the sea." The Sema:th used spears, harpoons, dip nets and seines to catch their prey. Lord witnessed another technique at the mouth of lower Sumas River, where the Sema:th employed "a very ingenious kind of net worked between two canoes, with which large numbers of salmon" were taken. The previous spring, while bivouacked on an island across from this very spot, an American survey member was taken by surprise: "The entire tribe of Sumass Indians came this morning to this point, in order to establish a camp for the salmon fishery."[25]

Salmon spawned by the millions in and around Sumas Lake, but usually they were caught elsewhere. The lake itself was best known for its sturgeon. Every spring, white sturgeon travelled to the shallow waters of Sumas Lake to spawn. The Sema:th took them with hooked lines, harpoons and sturdy, billowing nets. The Sema:th also constructed a large sturgeon weir across lower Sumas River, at the point it left the lake. Interviewed in the 1930s, William Sepass vividly recalled: "At Sumas Lake, the Indians had a long weir. They walked along this, raking the bottom with a hook on the end of a pole. When they hooked a sturgeon, the hook became loose from the pole, but remained attached to a long line." A generation later, Bob Joe provided a more detailed description:

> At this point [of the weir] the river was about 200' wide and up to 20' deep, with a hard clay bottom and a slow but steady current. The main supports were large poles as much as 8" in diameter. Pairs of these were driven into the bed of the river, their tops crossing, and across the crutches so formed long cross-poles were bound. Five of these 40' to 50' cross-pieces were required to cross the river. The fence consisted of a series of poles 4" or 5" apart, their lower ends driven into the bottom, their upper ends resting on the cross-pieces. Along the top of the weir was a walk three poles wide.
>
> In the mornings, when the water was fairly clear, one could see sturgeon resting against the weir, held by the current. Carefully a noose was slipped over the head of the fish, then it was harpooned, quickly dragged away from the others, and landed in shallow water. When enough sturgeon had been caught, the weir was opened.

The construction, maintenance and use of the weir was shared by the upper and lower Sema:th.

Sturgeon was a secondary fish for most Sto:lo, lagging well behind salmon. It was much more important for the Sema:th, as the latter's oral histories show. The irrepressible John Lord wrote that the Sema:th "are exceedingly fond of sturgeon-flesh, and usually demand a high price for it." Moreover, sturgeon roe—caviar—was considered a delicacy, as it is today. "The Indians," Lord continued, "dry these eggs in the sun and devour them with oil, as we eat currants and cream. It would surely pay to prepare caviare on the Russian plan, even to send it to the English market."

Sturgeon was the source of another precious commodity for the Sema:th: a powerful fish glue known as isinglass. Isinglass was a paper-like membrane made from the air bladders of fish, located in the backbone and abdomen. After extraction, the sturgeon bladders were dried and rolled into bundles for storage. When soaked in water, the isinglass bundles turned into a liquid paste, forming the strongest animal glue known. Ideal for binding

In deep waters, Sema:th and other Sto:lo fished for sturgeon with long harpoons—some over 50' long. Each pole was tipped with a barbed spearhead, which was attached to a long rope. After piercing the thick scales of a bottom-feeding sturgeon, the spearhead detached from the pole and the fisherman used the role line to gradually reel the fish in. *Sturgeon Spearing on the Fraser.* Reprinted from John Keast Lord, *The Naturalist in Vancouver Island and British Columbia*, Richard Bentley (London, 1866).

organic materials and for waterproofing, isinglass glue was used extensively by the Sema:th. While too numerous to list here, the glue's uses included stiffening and strengthening bows by adhering animal sinew to them, and waterproofing and binding cedar-bark baskets, canoe bailers and the like. The Sema:th were still manufacturing sturgeon isinglass through the mid-1900s, when anthropologist Wilson Duff observed that "from the 'purse' along the backbone was obtained the valuable sturgeon-glue (mɛt)." In the 1970s, Nooksack and Sema:th elders identified mɛt as the "flat organ in sturgeon which was skinned off and boiled down for glue."

Historians have failed to grasp the significance of isinglass to the Sema:th and its connection to the schools of sturgeon found in Sumas Lake. Production, use and widespread trade of the "sturgeon-glue" reveal how sophisticated the Sema:th use of resources truly was. Historians also have failed to note that isinglass became an important trade item between the Sema:th and the Hudson's Bay Company. The company, though, wanted isinglass for other purposes: it was used by Europeans as a gelatin to preserve food, and as a clarifying agent for beer, wine and cider. Even after the company lost interest in isinglass, the Sema:th continued to produce and trade the coveted product. Cornelius Kelleher recalled the "sturgeon mats [mɛts]" sold by the Sto:lo at the Wade's Landing store. "Old man Wade used to buy a lot of that—every Indian that caught a sturgeon saved that and dried it and took it to him. He bought it for so much a piece or so much a pound."[26]

The numbers and diversity of Sumas Lake's fish presented an embarrassment of riches for the Sema:th. Steelhead trout were highly prized as food, second only to salmon. The choicest spot to catch steelhead was off the mouth of Vedder River, as it flowed into Sumas Lake, where gillnets were used. Various species of sculpin and stickleback were caught and eaten, as were the freshwater Salish sucker and migrating largescale sucker. Bob Joe recalled how suckers would "come in schools…up on the Sumas River."

Another valued fish—a slender, silvery species first identified as round-fish—has long since disappeared from Sumas Lake. John Lord left a memorable account of a round-fish harvest on the lake:

> From the edge of the pine-forest, where the little streams came out from the dark shadow into the sunshine, up to the lake, the prairie was like a fair. Indians, old and young; chiefs, braves, [women], children, and slaves; were alike busy in capturing the round-fish, that were swarming up the streams in thousands: so thick were they that baits and traps were thrown aside, and hands, baskets, little nets, and wooden bowls did the work; it was only requisite to stand in the stream and bail out the fish. Thousands were drying, thousands had been eaten, and as many more were wasting and decomposing on the bank.

The teeming schools of fish, which had ascended Fraser River into Sumas Lake, were split and sun-dried, much as salmon was.

Unfortunately, Lord did not properly classify the fish, and ever since there has been confusion over exactly what species it was. Some Sto:lo sources have identified it as a grayling or largescale sucker. A closer examination of both the historical sources and the physical attributes, habits and nomenclature of various possible species leads to the conclusion that it was either the menominee whitefish or the mountain whitefish. Both menominee whitefish (also known as round whitefish) and mountain whitefish match Lord's physical description. And both species gather in great numbers to spawn in shallow lakes, streams and rivers throughout the province.[27]

Thus, through the middle of the 1800s, Sumas Lake provided the Sema:th with an abundant supply of whitefish, something their neighbours did not have. Whitefish provided a different mix of nutrients than other fish, which broadened and enriched the Sema:th diet. A half-century later, this supply was gone, partly a casualty of the province-wide decline in whitefish species, but also the victim of more local factors, such as encroaching White agriculture and overfishing.

The diverse bird life of Sumas Lake also gave the Sema:th direct access to another resource their neighbours lacked. Waterfowl were nutritious and delicious, and the Sema:th avidly hunted them. Edward Kelly recalled that "ducks were out there by the millions, way out, and the geese." Lotte Tom was equally awestruck: "In one night's hunting you [could] fill your canoe with ducks." Canvasback, pintail, wood ducks and teal were common fare, and the ubiquitous mallard was so familiar that the Halkomelem word for it—teleqsel—was used for ducks in general. The Sema:th also hunted and ate the lake's three species of geese: Canada, Hutchins's (or brant) and white-fronted.

The Sema:th used various ingenious methods for hunting fowl. Small bags were woven from stalks of grass or cedar bark; armed only with these, Sema:th hunters would wade through the high, thick grass along the lakeshore. The ducks had a hard time flying through the grass, so they could not escape when the hunters grabbed them by the necks and stowed them in bags. Larger nets were fashioned from twisted bulrushes and used on the lake itself. "Hunters set a net flat on the water, and placed dead salmon underneath it," William Sepass explained. "The ducks dived to get the salmon, and came up under the net, so that their heads were caught." In another daytime tactic, poles 15 to 20 feet long were erected in two canoes, a fine-meshed bulrush net strung between them. Camouflaged with thatches of grass and reeds, the canoes drifted slowly across the lake toward a flock of ducks. When close, hunters dropped the net on the lake surface; most ducks were immediately trapped, and those that dove were "ensnared by the neck when they came up for air."

The most sophisticated means for taking waterfowl involved teamwork and a structure the length of a football field. A century and a half ago, Charles Wilson wrote:

> Across the entrance of small streams, or slues, to which wild
> fowl resort long poles are erected at certain intervals, between
> which nets are spread; at night, fires are lighted at the foot of

the poles, which frightens the wild fowl, who flying towards the light, come into contact with the nets and fall down to the ground, where they fall an easy prey to the expectant Indian.

The Nooksack to the south and Katzie to the west also built the large suspended-net traps. The Nooksack device was situated at the mouth of Bertrand Creek: two slender cedar poles 40 feet high were planted several hundred feet apart; a massive net was attached to the poles with rings of cedar bough; and the net was raised by ropes running through pulleys at the top of the poles, and was quickly dropped when a flock of geese or ducks flew into it.

Sema:th hunters commonly used fire at night to lure ducks and geese. The most popular technique was to set out onto the lake in camouflaged canoes, carrying lit torches; when fowl flew toward the light, they were shot or netted. Also at night, campfires were lit on small, sandy islands in the lake. Geese and ducks "by the hundreds—perhaps by the thousands" were drawn to the fires, Sema:th elder Francis Kelly explained, flying just over the heads of awaiting hunters. The birds "were then shot and gathered by boat in the fire's glow. There was no trouble getting geese or ducks by this method." On upper and lower Sumas Prairie, hunters constructed blinds covered with grass and rushes, from which they shot geese attracted by pitch fires suspended overhead.

Along with ducks and geese, sandhill cranes, trumpeter and whistling swans, bald eagles and various kinds of grebes also were taken. Pigeons and gulls were sometimes eaten, but only when other species were scarce. Land-based birds were less common fare than waterfowl; raven, crows, owls and woodpeckers were not eaten, or rarely so. The only land fowl regularly hunted were the two indigenous species of grouse: Oregon ruffed grouse and sooty (or blue) grouse. In spring, when large numbers of grouse nested in the Sumas grasslands, they could be tracked by their thumping call. Hunters snuck up on them through the thick grass and bush, dispatching them with slingshot, arrow or (more recently) buckshot.[28]

Mammals were less important than fish and waterfowl as food, although their importance increased in late winter and early spring when caches of dried fish ran low and hunting remained good. Mammal by-products—hides, bones, antlers, sinew and fat—found many more uses than those from fish and birds. Of the predator species, only the black bear was hunted for its meat.

Wolves, which were numerous in the lower Fraser Valley before Whites arrived, were viewed as a special species. Bob Joe recalled a commandment he had been taught as a child: "Never kill wolves!" Amy Cooper added that, unlike Whites, Sto:lo did not view the wolf as an enemy; he was "highly respected. Even if he stole from you, [you] wouldn't harm him." One possible explanation for the wolf's special place in the Sto:lo world comes from an oral history recounted by Katzie shaman Old Pierre eight decades ago. Pierre spoke of a Sema:th hunter named Skelum who travelled up Vedder Mountain in search of game. Having no luck, he descended to the foot of the mountain, where he stumbled upon a camp of wolves; Skelum rushed the wolves, but he was quickly captured. Instead of killing him, the wolves gave the hunter a potent, charcoal-tipped arrow, which he later used to kill numerous bears. "We wolves were once human beings like you," the wolf chief said, "and we will help you." More recently, elder Joe Louie recalled a similar tale of his father's, a renowned hunter who others "figured had this wild wolf for his gathering, for whatever he's hunting for bear, deer, or elk."[29]

Meanwhile, the Sema:th regularly hunted deer and elk for meat, leather and by-products. Through the 1800s, both black-tailed and white-tailed deer were plentiful around Sumas Lake, and venison was considered excellent eating. Deer were hunted on the valley floor during cooler months of the year, and up Sumas and Vedder Mountains during summer. The Sema:th trapped deer in deadfalls, or stalked and shot them with bow and arrow, and later, muskets. Hunters also took cover in thick brush and imitated the cry of a doe by whistling through a hollow reed; once lured close enough, the buck could be taken by arrow or gunshot. The Sema:th used deer hide for clothing, winter moccasins, rope and drums; its antlers for tools; its bones for awls and needles; and its fat for soap. American elk were another highly prized species. Several times larger than their deer cousins, elk were much harder to bring down, but they provided that much more meat, hides, antlers, bones and fat. Deer remained an important resource for the Sema:th well into the 20th century, but the American elk did not. Once "as numerous as cattle around Sumas Lake," elk had all but disappeared from the valley by the early 1900s, a loss keenly felt by the Sema:th.

Smaller mammals found the wetlands and prairies flanking Sumas Lake an ideal habitat. Muskrat, beaver, racoon, rabbit—even the quirky, misnamed mountain beaver—were hunted and trapped by the Sema:th for meat and pelts. The pelts were used for clothing and as valuable trade items, particularly after the arrival of the Hudson's Bay Company.

The Sema:th gratefully partook of the rich plant and animal life offered up by Sumas Lake. But the swarms of insects that rose from the spring flood waters were less welcome. The Sema:th understood that scores of bird and fish species feasted on the seemingly endless supply of mosquitoes, crane flies and sandflies. For themselves, the insects were something to be fought against or avoided. People covered up as best they could, binding their legs in strips of cedar or cloth. Exposed skin was smudged with soot or vermilion to frustrate the insects' keen sense of smell. And mosquitoes were driven from houses with smoke, produced by throwing bracken ferns onto wood fires.

The most effective defence was simply to get away. As mosquitoes did not travel far across open water, the Sema:th struck out onto Sumas Lake to escape them. Some camped on sandbars jutting into the lake; others took refuge in huts built on stilts farther out from shore. John Lord found these refuges scattered across Sumas Lake, each with its "little colony" of inhabitants and "fleets of canoes" moored alongside. The huts' floors consisted of large platforms "fastened to stout poles driven like piles into the mud at the bottom of the lake.... The little fleet of canoes are moored to the poles, and the platform reached by a ladder made of twisted cedar-bark." The Sema:th built their platform huts in other locations as well. In June 1858, an American prospector travelling up Fraser River came across "a large ranch of Indians camped on a low island or sandbar" just past the mouth of Sumas River. "The whole camp was on a platform erected near the middle of [Fraser] river, about ten or twelve feet in height, where they lounged and slept, to get above the immense swarms of mosquitoes."

The Sema:th and their neighbours often travelled farther to escape the swarms. Through the peak months of June and July, early White surveyors and officials routinely came across villages "vacated on account of the mosquitoes." They too found clusters of Sto:lo camped "on sandbanks and small islands in the Fraser until the nuisance abated." Conveniently, the peak mosquito period coincided with salmon runs up Fraser Canyon; every spring, Sto:lo left in large numbers for Yale, where the fish were plentiful and the mosquitoes scarce.

The mosquito was such a persistent presence in Sema:th life that it acquired its own mythology as one of the most vicious and relentless of creatures. Warriors might seek to possess the mosquito's powers by adopting it as a spirit helper on the eve of battle. A legendary warrior of the lower Sema:th even took the insect's name. Qwa:l—mosquito in Halkomelem—embodied the spirit power of his patron helper. His exploits were heroic and bloody; just as with the mosquito, Qwa:l's tenacity and strength were honoured and his destructive ferocity feared. Transformer accounts of how mosquitoes came to be stressed the dark side over the light. In one tale, a group of young people playing on the sands of Sumas Lake are captured by Sasq'ets, a giant, who takes them back to his camp to eat. But the children best the giant and throw him on his own fire, and the sparks that fly up become mosquitoes. In other versions the giant is replaced by Th'owxiya, a cannibal woman; in still others, the Xexa:ls themselves cast the creature into the fire, and its scattered ashes become mosquitoes. Common to most tales, mosquitoes acquired their taste for blood from the cannibal creatures that begat them, and they continued to plague humans as a reminder of the malevolent beings that once walked the earth.[30]

The Sema:th, of course, were not the only ones to make use of Sumas Lake and its resources. They exercised control over the lake, its surrounding prairies and mountain slopes; but neighbouring peoples could gain access, through family ties and a shared past. The Nooksack were the most closely linked to the Sema:th, and they were permitted the greatest access to Sumas Valley. This might surprise us, for the Nooksack were not Sto:lo and had no direct presence on Fraser River, the physical cord that bound together the Sto:lo world. And while most Nooksack spoke it, Halkomelem was not their mother tongue. Yet the Sema:th and Nooksack had a closely shared history, dating back centuries. In the wake of floods and disease epidemics, survivors of the two peoples came together to build Temixwtem, where they cohabited until they had recovered. The first White visitors noticed these close ties. George Gardner of the Northwest Boundary Survey wrote that the Nooksack men guiding their party were "related by marriage to the Su-mass tribe." Because of this, the party received permission to travel into Sema:th territory, moving north from Nooksack River to upper Sumas River and into Sumas Lake.

More than a century later, anthropologists working among the Nooksack were told that the Nooksack had been intermarrying with the Sema:th and other Sto:lo for centuries. A large percentage of the Nooksack elders who worked with these anthropologists had close family ties with the Sema:th, or were Sema:th themselves. George Swanaset was one of these: born at Sumas Bar, he and his Sema:th mother moved south of the border when he was a child, and his mother married a Nooksack man. Lotte Tom also was Sema:th; after marrying a Nooksack man, she spent the remainder of her life among her husband's people. Tom explained that "due to frequent intermarriage," many Nooksack could speak the Sema:th dialect of Halkomelem, and the Sema:th in turn "understood and could speak Nooksack."

Intermarriage and a common history paid off for both the Nooksack and the Sema:th—together, the two peoples shared access to nearly all of the Sumas River watershed. The Nooksack camped and fished along upper Sumas River and Saar Creek, north of the border; they also approached the southern shore of Sumas Lake via a stream known as Qwelstem, which formerly ran along the base of Vedder Mountain. And most importantly, the Nooksack were allowed onto Sumas Lake itself. Joe Louie and other elders noted that Nooksack yearly journeyed to Sumas Lake "to fish for steelhead and sturgeon, to hunt ducks, and dig roots." Some families travelled across the lake to fishing sites along Fraser River, which gave them a share of the salmon run. The Fraser and Sumas runs included the versatile sockeye salmon, which, along with white sturgeon, were not found in the Nooksack River watershed. Meanwhile, the rich berry bushes and beds of root vegetables on upper Sumas Prairie were open to the Nooksack. Travel between the Sema:th and Nooksack was commonplace, and the trails linking their territories were so well established that White newcomers would build their own roads atop them.

In return, the Sema:th were permitted to fish in Nooksack territory, including nearby tributaries such as Fishtrap Creek, and as far inland as the North Fork of Nooksack River, where chum salmon and steelhead trout were taken. They also had first crack at the most coveted of Nooksack commodities: the fine hair taken from mountain goats, which the Nooksack hunted in the Cascade Mountains south of the border. Sto:lo up and down the Fraser wove the hair into warm and durable blankets. The supply of goat hair was always limited, and so weavers had to mix in dog hair and other material—the more goat there was in the blanket, the more precious the blanket was.

Due north of the Nooksack, and northwest of the Sema:th, sat the territory of the Matsqui. The Matsqui intermarried with both the Sema:th and the Nooksack, and most spoke both Nooksack and Halkomelem. The westernmost ridge of Vedder Mountain stood between Matsqui territory and Sumas Lake; a well-worn trail ran along the mountain's descending slope, connecting the Matsqui village of Skah-na (at the southeast edge of Matsqui Prairie) to Sumas Valley. Matsqui families used the trail to travel to Sumas Prairie to pick berries, or to the lake to fish. Sto:lo on the north side of Fraser River also routinely visited Sema:th territory. The Lakahamen of Nicomen Island and Chehalis of Harrison Bay participated in Sumas Lake's valuable sturgeon fishery. As Ray Silver recalled, "all they had to do was cross the river, Fraser River, and they were in the lake....They came here hunting and fishing sturgeon." The Chehalis also hunted waterfowl on Sumas Lake and deer on Sumas Mountain. In the early 1800s, Hudson's Bay Company traders recognized these close ties, listing the Chehalis as "relations" of the Sema:th.[31]

The Chilliwack, the newest of the Sema:th's neighbours, also were described as relations. Chief William Sepass of the Skowkale band of Chilliwack, spent many of his youthful days hunting and fishing on Sumas Lake, when it "was filled with ducks, geese, sturgeon and salmon." Rose and Ed Sparrow spoke of regularly travelling to the lake, once again to hunt and fish. The Chilliwack's access to Sumas Lake was not as well established as that of the Nooksack and other Sema:th neighbours. The Chilliwack were recent arrivals to the valley floor, and so had less time to establish family ties and a shared history. From their original headquarters among the towering mountains near Chilliwack Lake, the Chilliwack gradually moved down upper Chilliwack River. By 1800 or so, they were securely entrenched just above Vedder Crossing. Two developments opened the way for their descent onto the valley floor itself: first, lethal epidemics created a population vacuum in the area; and second, the retreat of Sumas Lake westward opened up new land, now drained by lower Chilliwack River. Even after this, the territory between lower Chilliwack River and Sumas Lake was dominated by swamp, marsh and bog, creating a no man's land between the Sema:th and the Chilliwack.

The migration of the Chilliwack caused friction in the valley. As they moved down from Vedder Crossing, the Chilliwack clashed with the Pilalt to the north and east, and with the Sema:th to the west. According to Chilliwack elder Albert Louie, the Sema:th war leader Xeyteleq was determined to get rid of the newcomers, and he descended on them with his army; in the ensuing battle, the Chilliwack killed the famed Sema:th warrior and emerged victorious. Louie's depiction of the Sema:th as the aggressors has been accepted by recent writers; one goes so far as to charge Xeyteleq with attempting a "military takeover" of the Chilliwack. Of course, Louie was Chilliwack and understandably saw the conflict from the perspective of his people. From the Sema:th perspective, it was the Chilliwack who were expanding beyond their traditional territory; and in Sema:th accounts, Xeyteleq was a truly heroic figure. Upon hearing of an impending attack, Xeyteleq ordered his people up Sumas Mountain; he then descended to the sandy shore of Sumas Lake to make his stand. Xeyteleq died on the beach, his body riddled with arrows, but only after he successfully pushed back the attackers and saved his people. In the end, further hostilities were averted

The Sumas Band identified this woman as Toot-seem-ia, the daughter of Sumas Band warrior Xeyteleq. The Reach, P165.

by the high-status marriage between a Chilliwack woman and a Sema:th man, and the relocation of the transformer-stone warrior T'xwelatse to the husband's village on upper Sumas Prairie.

After this, relations between the Sema:th and their neighbours were generally free of conflict. The intricate web of family ties and reciprocal resource rights was strengthened by frequent travel, trade and social interaction. Sumas Lake and its tributaries were at the centre of much of this travel. Whether as host or guest, the Sema:th played a prominent role in the ongoing circle of gatherings that marked important events: potlatches, weddings, funerals, longhouse openings and dances. In October 1858, the Scowlitz, Pilalt, Chilliwack and Sema:th hosted a potlatch near the mouth of lower Chilliwack River. Hundreds of Sto:lo attended, from Hope downriver; dancing and feasting were followed by the exchange of gifts. The biggest giver was Set-hwam, chief of the upper Sema:th, who doled out 100 blankets. Along with their generosity, the Sema:th were renowned for their carpentry skills and for the swiftness of their young men in foot races. At intertribal gatherings, their arrival was eagerly awaited: they brought packets of dried sockeye salmon and white sturgeon, and distributed one to each adult; they also provided "Indian ice cream," made from whipped soapberry foam.[32]

While the Sema:th got along well with their neighbours, serious threats came from outside the lower Fraser, most notably from the Cowichan of southern Vancouver Island and the Lekwiltok of the island's northeastern coast. These "saltwater Indians" made regular raids up Fraser River and into its tributaries, including Sumas Lake. The raiding parties killed local warriors, abducted women and children for slaves, and carried away food and other precious resources. For generations, the threat posed by hostile islanders struck fear among lower Fraser Sto:lo. Simon Fraser made note of it in 1808; a half-century later, naturalist Caleb Kennerly witnessed a panicked stampede when the Sema:th and neighbouring Sto:lo heard that a small band of Cowichan was approaching. "The Cowichan are a very powerful tribe living on Vancouver Island," Kennerly wrote, "and these Indians are very much afraid of them."

The journal keeper at Fort Langley made note of a number of these raids. In October 1827, two parties—each consisting of Cowichan and Musqueam warriors—struck up Fraser River toward the Sema:th. The first, consisting of 86 men, returned empty-handed, but the second killed two Sema:th, captured "several women and children" as slaves and carried away large quantities of food, basketry and mats. The Sema:th were more fortunate the following spring, when a party of 150 Cowichan warriors passed them by on its way to attack the Pilalt, with devastating results. Two years later, in May 1830, the Sema:th were attacked by a much smaller force of Squamish fighters. Archibald McDonald, head of Fort Langley, wrote that "the Smaize tis Said Stood Feight [tight], & the assailants did not choose to advance."

To fend off attacks, the Sema:th employed a number of defensive tactics. The lower Sema:th maintained an imposing stockade at Sumas Bar, along with lookout points at Papekwatchin and up Sumas Mountain. Elsewhere, women and children took refuge in caves and camouflaged pits when under attack, or barricaded themselves in pit houses. Elder Hugh Kelly described one tactic that brilliantly exploited the wetlands of Sumas Lake. The upper Sema:th were also known as the Pepa:thxetel, for their wide, bear-like feet; they could run atop the interwoven surface of grass and reeds that grew along the edges of Sumas Lake, knowing that if they stopped, they would sink. When attacking canoes entered Sumas Lake and pulled up to Kilgard, the defenders were ready:

> They ran away from the village out onto the swamp grass—
> they were pretending to run away. The Coastal Indians chased
> them there. Then the Kilgard men suddenly dropped onto
> their stomachs; they spread their arms and legs out to support
> their weight. The Coastal warriors thought the Kilgard men
> had disappeared because they couldn't see them through the
> tall grass. The Coastal Indians stopped and looked around.
> Once they stopped running their feet broke through the tan-
> gled grass roots. They sunk! Then the Kilgard men jumped
> up and ran back at them with their war clubs. They clubbed
> them to death. That's how our Kilgard people used the land
> to defend themselves.

As with most societies, the Sema:th memorialized great warriors; their names and deeds were passed down from generation to generation. The most legendary of these were the giant-men Xeyteleq and Qwa:l. They too had mastered the technique of running along the thatched grass on the edge of Sumas Lake, luring their enemies into the watery trap. As we have seem, Xeyteleq gave his life in defence of his people.[33]

Meanwhile, Qwa:l was both honoured and feared. Filled with the power and ferocity of his spirit-helper mosquito, Qwa:l defended the Sema:th against coastal attackers. But he was best known for leading blood-drenched reprisal attacks on Cowichan and Lekwiltok villages, slaying men by the score and bringing back slaves and booty. The Sema:th's attitude toward Qwa:l mirrored the ambivalence most societies feel toward their warriors: respect for the fighter's willingness to put himself at risk and his ability to use violence in protection of his people; yet fear that that violence could break the fragile bonds of peace and social order, unleashing war and strife without end.

CHAPTER 4:

FIRST ENCOUNTERS

For countless generations, the Sto:lo of the Fraser Valley had their homeland much to themselves. The only outsiders to intrude were the lethal "saltwater Indians" from Vancouver Island. Even after Europeans and Americans started visiting the region's coastal waters in the late 1700s, none ventured up Fraser River, for they did not know it was there. This changed in spring 1808, when fur trader Simon Fraser led a party of two dozen North West Company men through Fraser Canyon and down the lower Fraser River. Fraser was seeking a transportation route by which the company could move furs from its newly built posts in northern BC to the coast—in particular to the mouth of Columbia River, as yet the only major river known on the coast. Fraser hoped and believed that Fraser River (which of course was not named Fraser River yet) was a tributary or branch of Columbia River and that descending it would lead him to his goal.

Through June, Fraser's party pushed its way down the upper reaches of Fraser River. On June 29, he passed the future site of Hope and continued rapidly downstream, encountering large Sto:lo villages along the way. On the 30th, Fraser made note in his journal of "a large river coming in from the left, and a round Mountain a head which the natives call *shemotch*." Some histories of the Fraser and Sumas Valleys mistakenly identify shemotch as Fraser's phonetic rendition of Sumas or Sema:th. But the Halkomelem words for what we now call Sumas Mountain did not sound anything like shemotch. The northeast half of the mountain was known as T'exqe:yl, the southwest half as Kw'wek'e'i:qw. Sema:th was properly used to identify the people, not a geographic feature. It was attached to the mountain only later, by British officials who fell into using the name Sumas to describe the various parts of the valley.[34]

Two days later, on July 2, the North West men reached the first saltwater well up from the mouth of Fraser River, where Fraser took a quick latitude reading. Disappointed that he was well north of the Columbia

River mouth, Fraser ordered a hasty retreat back upriver. Travelling day and night, the party was harassed by increasingly hostile Sto:lo, who saw no benefit in helping the dirty, tired crew of strangers.

For nearly two decades, no effort was made to follow up on Simon Fraser's expedition. During that time, the Hudson's Bay Company (HBC) absorbed the upstart North West Company and inherited the latter's interests west of the Rocky Mountains. In 1827, the HBC established Fort Langley on the southern bank of Fraser River, some 30 miles upstream from the mighty river's mouth. Largely ignorant about the Fraser Valley, the company was determined to explore and exploit the resources of these new lands and waters. Accordingly, in November 1828, it dispatched Francis Annance and eight men to examine the Fraser River as far up as Harrison River, where they encountered several hundred Sto:lo gathered for the fall salmon fishery. A month later, Annance led another party upriver, carrying a dozen beaver traps, one week's provisions and instructions to hunt down whatever beaver or elk it could. The party found very little beaver or elk, but it did make a surprise discovery. Upon his return to Fort Langley, Annance reported to his boss, Archibald McDonald, who wrote:

> About 25 miles up they turned into a small creek to the right which in a few hours brought them to a lake of 10 miles long and 6 wide at the extreme end of which there is a Considerable extent of low clear Country—intersected with numerous ponds and little Channels well adapted for wild fowl—here they Spent the best part of two days and killed 4 Swans 3 Cranes 10 Geese & 40 ducks.

This was the first time Sumas Lake had been seen by White visitors. The ever-practical McDonald gave little thought to the moment's place in history; he was more impressed with the number of geese, ducks and cranes Annance brought back. The rich haul confirmed reports from local Sto:lo that "a great quantity of wild fowl" congregated at the lake during their seasonal migrations. In April 1829, another small party spent three days there, taking a half-dozen "fine fat Cranes" and 60 geese. Company men revisited "Goose Lake"—as they then called it—the following spring, but came back empty-handed for "they arrived at the Lake too late."

In the following decades, the abundance of waterfowl from Sumas Lake, Pitt Lake and the Fraser River delta was a boon to the Fort Langley men, for the rich meat supplemented their monotonous diet of dried salmon and boiled potatoes. But the HBC was in the fur business; it did all it could

This is the earliest known photograph of Fort Langley, taken in 1862. The fort is on a low bluff overlooking Fraser River. Sto:lo would land at the foot of the bluff, and trading would take place where the sole man is standing. The Kwantlen controlled much of the trade from their village located directly across the river. Royal BC Museum and Archives, A-04313.

to persuade the Sto:lo to trap and trade ever more beaver, marten and mink pelts. Compared to other Sto:lo such as the Kwantlen, the Sema:th were infrequent partners in the fur trade, as Fort Langley's records show. On May 9, 1829, Archibald McDonald was taken by surprise when "a few of the Mace [Sumas] Indians Came down today with 10 or 12 Skins." A decade later, a census of the Fraser Valley undertaken by the company found that the Sema:th had traded no furs at Fort Langley that year, while the neighbouring Chilliwack had brought in only a score of pelts.

Through its early years, Fort Langley did not live up to the expectations of its founders. Under relentless pressure from the HBC's upper management to produce more furs, McDonald decided to go on the offensive. Early in 1830, he hatched a plan "to fix a small trading house in the back country" south of Sumas Lake, in Nooksack territory, using the lake itself as a transit route. The area was believed to be rich in fur-bearing animals, and the hope was the Nooksack could be persuaded to direct their trade north to Fort Langley rather than south to American traders and their Skagit partners. Once again, Francis Annance led a party up the Fraser to Sumas Lake; the group crossed the lake, ascended upper Sumas River and reached Nooksack River after a short portage.

Annance and his men found only empty villages, as the Nooksack had scattered to escape Skagit raids. McDonald's plan to forge a Sumas Lake fur trade route came to nothing; he realized all the company could do was encourage the Nooksack to trade northward through the Kwantlen, Fort Langley's established middlemen. Frustrated in the short term, this latter policy bore fruit over the following decades. In 1857, the American commissioner for Indian Affairs reported that the Nooksack made regular use of a trail to Fort Langley, "where they carry all their furs and get all their articles of trade from the Hudson Bay Company." A century later, Nooksack elder Josephine George still remembered olden days when Kwantlen traders, seeking beaver and muskrat pelts, were regular visitors to their villages.[35]

Fort Langley never became the fur trade centre it was intended to be. Certainly, the wetlands along the lower Fraser were ideal habitats for the water-loving mammals so coveted by the company. But the Sto:lo could not be coaxed, cajoled or bribed into changing their fundamental way of life, with its reliance on fish and waterfowl. There was little to gain in devoting more time and effort to hunting and trapping little furry mammals, and much to lose. This was a blessing for Sumas Lake, which was spared the fate of other regions where the fur trade depleted the population of beaver and other wetland mammals. Beaver in particular played a crucial role in maintaining these wetlands. Their obsessive dam building created and preserved countless ponds and small swamps. When beavers were hunted out of an area, their dams fell apart, draining these ponds and swamps—themselves home to rich plant and animal life.

Instead of a fur trade mecca, Fort Langley grew into an important provision post, producing food and exportable commodities other than pelts. The most important of these commodities was fish, notably salmon. In spring 1829, Archibald McDonald got a taste of things to come when a small number of Sema:th appeared at his door with a dozen pelts and "four fresh salmon, best tasted and richest I have ever seen in this country." Through the 1830s, Fort Langley directed more and more of its efforts to acquiring and processing salmon—caught by Sto:lo, salted in barrels and exported. The following decade, salmon surpassed furs as the post's most valuable commodity, feeding hungry customers along the coast from Columbia River to Alaska, and westward to Hawaii.

To meet this growing demand, the company established a series of fishing stations along the lower Fraser, closer to Sto:lo fishing grounds, where the salmon were salted and packed. During the heyday of the 1840s, the company operated semi-permanent establishments near the mouths of the Chilliwack, Harrison and Coquihalla Rivers; less substantial stations were built at other strategic spots. There is evidence that one of these smaller stations was located at the mouth of lower Sumas River. Late in the summer of 1857, in preparation for his first trip up the Fraser, George Gibbs talked with HBC officials at Fort Langley about what lay ahead upriver. One important spot, he noted, was "S'mass, at the Company's fishery, on north side of the river, opposite the lake." More than a year later, just days after BC was officially proclaimed a colony, company officials presented the new governor with a list of sites they considered HBC property. Along the lower Fraser, this list included Forts Langley, Hope and Yale, land at the mouth of Harrison River, and the "Point at the Forks of Smess River."[36]

Salmon was not the only species of fish from which the HBC wrung a profit. The company also acquired large quantities of sturgeon meat and isinglass, both of which were exported. As we have seen, Sumas Lake was renowned for the abundance of sturgeon that spawned there, and the Sema:th had perfected the process of rendering isinglass from the fish's air bladders. The isinglass trade started slowly, but by the mid-1840s the company was exporting nearly 500 pounds of the substance each year. These were truly remarkable amounts, considering the commodity was cured, saved and traded in lightweight dried bundles. While the Sema:th made use of reconstituted isinglass as a powerful glue, the HBC sold it as a clarifying agent for beer, wine and cider. By the later 1850s, though, the company had abandoned the isinglass trade, unable to compete with other suppliers who had discovered ways to render the commodity from cheaper, more readily obtained species such as cod.

For three full decades, the small contingent of HBC men at Fort Langley represented the only non-Native presence in the Fraser Valley. Through this time, the company's direct engagement with—and impact upon—the area's physical and human landscape remained modest. Its single-minded purpose was to secure as many marketable furs and fish for export as it could. This goal alone determined how much or how little effort the HBC put into exploration of the region, and how much or how little it engaged with the Sema:th and other Sto:lo. Company men visited and came to know Sumas Lake and its inhabitants, but they left us only a handful of journal entries by which to piece together their activities.

In spring 1857, the Northwest Boundary Survey broke the HBC's monopoly of the area; fortunately for us, it left behind a wealth of historical material. A decade earlier, the US and Britain signed the Oregon Treaty, which set the 49th parallel as the official border between their possessions west of the Rocky Mountains. But nobody knew where the 49th parallel was; after letting the matter lie, the two governments decided that an official survey needed to be done to determine, map and mark the new line.

The Northwest Boundary Survey consisted of two separate commissions, one American the other British. Each commission consisted of a team of trailblazers, surveyors and astronomers, along with map-makers, artists, scientists and ethnologists. The American commission was led by Archibald Campbell, an engineer from the War Department; his second-in-command was Lt. John Parke of the Army Corps of Engineers, who oversaw operations in the field. The rest of the party were civilians, carefully chosen because of their training and past experience in boundary work. The British commission was dominated by military men: most were Royal Engineer officers, including the man in charge, Col. John Hawkins; an army artillery captain, a navy surgeon and two civilian doctors completed the team.[37]

The Americans took to the field 12 months before their British counterparts, and stayed a full year ahead throughout. In July 1857, Archibald Campbell ordered Lieutenant Parke to establish an operating base at Semiahmoo, just north of the 49th parallel on the coast of the Fraser Valley. Through August, Parke despatched two reconnaissance parties to Sumas Lake. The first canoed up Fraser River, ascended lower Sumas River and entered the lake. The second, led by George Gardner, travelled up Nooksack River, portaged to upper Sumas River and then moved downstream to Sumas Lake. Gardner wrote:

> The Sumass Lake is not very deep but covers an area of seven or eight thousand acres which is greatly extended at high water. It is situated between mountain ridges trending northeast and southwest, in a large prairie covered with a luxuriant growth of grass.

Several weeks later, upon his return with a much larger contingent, Gardner established Camp Sumass on one of these ridges—later known as York Ridge—three miles southwest of Sumas Lake and half that distance north of the 49th parallel. Rising from the south bank of upper Sumas River, York Ridge elevated the camp above the lake's yearly high waters. The camp soon grew from its original pair of tents to a dozen. The delicate astronomical instruments were set up some distance away from the men's quarters, so the vibration of walking feet would not throw off their readings. To provide a steady foundation, the instruments were mounted atop pilings driven into the sandy prairie soil. From fall 1857 through spring 1858, Camp Sumass was the American commission's base of operations in Fraser Valley and the second astronomical station after Camp Semiahmoo. Astronomical readings from it and Semiahmoo were used to determine the location of the 49th parallel along the entire 45-mile stretch that separated the two camps. The Sumas station was also the reference point for running the line eastward over Vedder Mountain.

Meanwhile, survey crews were dispatched from Camp Sumass in all directions, and they meticulously charted the region's waterways, prairies and mountains. The entire length of the line between the meridian of Camp Sumass and Semiahmoo was painstakingly traversed, geographic readings taken and notes made of landscape features. Swiss-born Henry Custer scaled Sumas and Vedder Mountains, tracked from upper Sumas Prairie westward, and undertook a two-stage circumambulation of the shores of Sumas Lake, plotting its contours for the first time.

To ease the difficult task of provisioning Camp Sumass, the American commission established a depot at the mouth of lower Sumas River, across from Sumas Bar. The site was used to store supplies and as an overnight campsite for parties heading to Camp Sumass or travelling farther up Fraser River. Here, crews bound for Camp Sumass could transfer from the large canoes, whaling boats or—after the Fraser gold rush—steamboats used to ascend Fraser River, to smaller canoes capable of navigating the shallow waters of Sumas Lake and its tributaries.

By early summer 1858, the American commission had completed its astronomical and surveying work at Camp Sumass. In July, it moved east to establish a depot near the mouth of lower Chilliwack River, erecting a substantial log storehouse finished with cedar-plank floorboards provided by local Sto:lo craftsmen. From the new site, the Americans pushed inland; they set up a series of temporary astronomical stations and camps in the towering mountains south of upper Chilliwack River and farther east on Chilliwack Lake.

That same month, the much-delayed British party arrived in Victoria. Informed of the Americans' progress, Colonel Hawkins decided his first step would be to dispatch a reconnaissance party of his own "to the American Station at Sumass." After further delay, a crew commanded by Capts. Robert Haig and Charles Darrah travelled up Fraser River, into and across Sumas Lake, and ascended upper Sumas River; the British party arrived at the site of the former American camp on August 30. When Lt. Charles Wilson showed up two months later he found his comrades "very comfortable up there, the tents having been pitched for some weeks and the floor littered with dry fern."

Using Camp Sumass as their base of operations, the British focussed their efforts on verifying the American commission's latitudinal readings.

Controversy soon erupted when Haig claimed that the Americans had erred by several hundred yards in setting the line. At first, each side dug in, insisting their results were correct; but the issue was resolved after some heated correspondence between the commissions' commanders. Taking a closer look at the numbers, Haig and the British conceded they had miscalculated. They now accepted as valid the calculations done by the Americans along the whole length of the line from Camp Semiahmoo to Vedder Mountain. As a result, Hawkins decided in October 1858 to relocate Haig's astronomical team from Camp Sumass to a new station at the south end of Cultus Lake.

The dispute over latitude readings revealed a problem that would bedevil the boundary survey—the disparity in personnel and equipment between the commissions, and the stubborn resistance of the commission heads to the idea of working together. Put simply, the Americans were better trained, more experienced, and they possessed superior instruments. At the time, latitude was calculated by observing the positions of known stars.

Captains Haig and Darrah pose at an observation tent. Their Zenith telescope is pointed skyward, ready to make the nighttime readings they would use to calculate their latitude. Miscellaneous Items in High Demand, PPOC, Library of Congress/Public Domain.

The more nighttime readings you could do, in as little time as possible, the more accurate your calculations would be. The American instruments could make 20 to 30 readings before midnight, with little time between each. The British could manage only two or three all night, six to eight hours apart; stars moved great distances during this time, magnifying any error that might creep in. The notoriously cloudy weather of the region added further to their difficulties.

To his credit, Captain Haig learned from his early mistake and quickly came to appreciate the Americans' skills and resources. Late in 1858, he travelled from Cultus Lake to the American astronomical station at Camp Sumass to ask if the Americans would be willing to lend him any of their instruments. Haig got the help requested, but his visit caught the Americans by surprise. Writing in his journal, surgeon and naturalist Joseph Harris praised Haig for putting ego aside, but the American could not rein in his own pride and prejudice:

> Our instruments did all the English boundary work. This sur-
> render ended our fear that the English knew more about their
> business than we did. We gave them everything we had in the
> way of tables, rules and formulae, which they were only too
> glad to accept. It was a fine manly thing for Haig [to do]...
> and was not typical of the English bull-headedness.[38]

In 1859, and periodically through the following years, the British com-
mission returned to Camp Sumass, using it as a base for crews hewing a line through forestland along the border. To provision it and the Cultus Lake camps, the British established a depot at the mouth of lower Sumas River. In the spring of 1859, they built a log storehouse there, raised up on stilts to keep it above high water, along with sheds to accommodate pack mules and horses. A trail was constructed along the north and west sides of Sumas Lake to connect the depot with Camp Sumass, complete with bridges spanning the numerous streams along the way. Later, a similar trail was blazed east of Sumas Lake, to link the Sumas River depot and Cultus Lake camp. But the distance between these sites was too great to travel in a day, so an "intermediate station" was established on lower Sumas Prairie—somewhere between Lewis Creek and Vedder River—to serve as an overnight stop for mule trains.

Colonel Hawkins noted that these trails were good for only part of the year, until they were "altogether cut off by the periodical rising of the waters which covered the prairies surrounding the Lake to the depth of several feet." During this time, the survey had to take to canoes manned by Sema:th paddlers. In July 1859, the British commission erected a new depot at the mouth of lower Chilliwack River, immediately across from the American depot. It also built a headquarters camp two miles due south, where its officers and men stayed. British surveying efforts now were directed inland, first at Cultus Lake, then up Chilliwack River to Chilliwack Lake.

The Northwest Boundary Survey wrapped up its surveying work west of the Cascade Mountains in late fall 1859. The British commission had advanced as far as Chilliwack Lake, while the Americans had pushed well beyond, reaching the Osoyoos Valley. The following spring, the two commissions moved their headquarters to Fort Colville, Washington Territory, to carry out surveying the line east to the Rocky Mountains. The British would leave a large party behind, to physically mark the border across the Fraser Valley.

Through all this work, the British and American commissions consisted of more than just the officers, surveyors and scientists who led them. Each commission had its contingent of enlisted men and hired civilians to provide protection and undertake the manual labour. But these men lacked the local knowledge required to serve as guides and were too busy with other tasks to take on the arduous job of transporting survey parties and supplies. The commissions thus had to turn elsewhere for guides and transport.

The British followed in the footsteps of the Americans throughout, so they had little need for local guides. They relied on large numbers of horses and mules for transportation, which they drove north from Oregon. They also brought in ranch hands from California—whom they identified as "Mexicans"—to look after the animals and to work as packers. Meanwhile, from the very start the American commission employed local Nooksack and Sto:lo for these jobs. During their first overland trip to Sumas Lake in August 1857, the Americans were transported by a Nooksack crew, which took them up Nooksack River, across to upper Sumas River and downstream to the lakeshore. Here, expedition leader George Gardner hired canoes, paddlers and guides from Sema:th villages across the lake to take them farther. Because the Americans were accompanied by their closest neighbours, the Nooksack, the lower Sema:th chief Skaakle welcomed the newcomers into his people's territory—but only if they switched to Sema:th crews.

In the following months, the American commission came to rely on the Sema:th as its source of labour and local knowledge. With Sema:th leading the way, the Americans criss-crossed Sumas Lake's physical landscape, measuring and recording its contours. Later that year, a Sema:th crew led by Skaakle carried the Americans on their first voyage up lower Chilliwack River to Cultus Lake. The following spring, Skaakle and upper Sema:th chief Setwahm led a large American party up Fraser River, as far as the mouth of Harrison River. Along with their geographic knowledge, access to canoes and expertise, Skaakle and Setwahm drew on cultural and political ties in providing diplomatic protection to their wards, ensuring the latter were accepted by Sto:lo along the lower Fraser. Skaakle also became a regular visitor to the main American camp at Semiahmoo. He played a crucial role as messenger and labour contractor, travelling to Nooksack and Sto:lo villages to secure men for crews. These crews were essential, since the Americans relied solely on human packers and canoes through their first year of operations, not having access to pack mules.

As they moved up Chilliwack River to Chilliwack Lake, the Americans relied less on the Sema:th and more on Chilliwack packers and Thompson guides, such as the remarkable Thiusoloc and his father. But members of the American commission were keenly aware that they would have been unable to carry out their mission without the aid of the Sema:th and their neighbours. Reporting on the first season of surveying, when the Americans depended on Sema:th help, Gardner wrote: "These trips have all been performed without the employment of a single animal. The supplies and camp equipage being transported in canoes when streams were available; and when not, Indians served as packing." For his part, Parke praised the Sto:lo's "honesty and fidelity," and master surveyor Henry Custer expressed admiration at their "most minute topographical knowledge."

The close working relationship between the American commission and local Natives was helped along by personal connections made between their members and the Sto:lo. Russell Peabody was one of the first White settlers to arrive on Bellingham Bay. Sometime in the 1850s, he entered into a "country marriage" with a Sema:th woman, and they had three children. When the American commission arrived, Peabody was hired as its chief provisioner, bringing in bountiful supplies of local fish, waterfowl and potatoes. He also used his family connections to arrange Nooksack and Sema:th guides and crews for the Americans, and to obtain permission for the latter to travel through the former's territory. Back at Camp Semiahmoo, Caleb Kennerly also took a country wife, if only briefly. In late 1857, Kennerly wed the young daughter of the chief of a nearby Semiahmoo village, cementing the ties between the Americans and Semiahmoo. But Kennerly abandoned his bride when the American commission moved its operations eastward; some months later, she gave birth to their son, George. Kennerly died at sea in 1860; his son outlived him by nearly a century.[39]

While differing in the extent to which they relied on the knowledge and resources of the Sema:th and their neighbours, both the British and American commissions had been instructed to observe and report on the region's Native peoples. In part this was a necessity: the small number of survey men could not risk antagonizing a local population that vastly outnumbered them, so they had to make some effort to understand it. In part this was a Trojan Horse, for early knowledge of Native peoples would help the British and American officials who would soon arrive to better rule over that population. And in part this emerged from the spirit of the times: the thirst for knowledge about new lands and exotic peoples that went hand in hand with the expansion of empire and nation.

During their time with the Northwest Boundary Survey, George Gibbs, Caleb Kennerly, John Lord and Charles Wilson all recorded their impressions of Native life on and around Sumas Lake. Gibbs and Wilson compiled the first lists of upriver Halkomelem words and terminology. In 1866, Wilson published a 177-word vocabulary of "Sumass-Chilukweyuk" words he collected in 1859, rendered phonetically according to the British Admiralty's manual on ethnology. The list comprised numbers, verbs, family relations, body parts, household objects, natural features and animals. A list of 18 proper names of men and women followed, including Sema:th chief "Skaa-kil."

George Gibbs brought greater experience and expertise to the task. A graduate of Harvard Law School, Gibbs served on two previous surveys of the American west, compiling vocabularies of the Native peoples in territory newly acquired by the US. Gibbs's Halkomelem vocabulary leaned heavily on Sema:th words for different species of fish, birds and mammals. Recognizing its central importance in Sto:lo lives, Gibbs identified no fewer than six Sema:th names for salmon: one for each of the five species of the Fraser River, plus the steelhead trout. To this he added additional words differentiating between young and mature fish and the like. Gibbs also provided a brief list of Sema:th people he met: for men, Skeh-ukl (Skaakle) and Set-hwam (Setwahm); for women, Mal-to-natt, See-al-ta-nath, Sal-eh-how-yel and Home-hom-ten.

The most significant ethnographic legacy of the Northwest Boundary Survey, though, was its recording of Sto:lo and Nooksack place names. Sadly, this legacy remained hidden in American government archives for over a century. Most of the British commission field records were destroyed at the order of Colonel Hawkins, so we cannot know what ethnographic material was lost. Given the British focus on physically marking where British sovereignty began, and their ensuing haste to anglicize the surrounding landscape, it would be surprising if any of their officers kept systematic records of existing Native toponyms.

By contrast, from the time they took to the field, American surveyors conscientiously recorded Sto:lo place names. The reliance on Nooksack and Sto:lo men to guide, transport and supply its parties provided the American commission with ample opportunity and motive to master local toponyms. The earliest maps produced by the commission featured Halkomelem names: including Soo-mass along lower Sumas River, Stahta-low or Tatala'oo for upper Sumas River, and Ske-menn for Marshall Creek. Significantly, this was the first recorded use of a variation of Sto:lo. Sto:telo—here Stah-ta-low or Tatala'oo—means "little river" or "creek"; it is a diminutive of sto:lo, which means "river." The fact the Sema:th applied it to upper Sumas River shows they considered it the major waterway in their territory, just as the application of Sto:lo to Fraser River demonstrates the latter's primacy for the Sto:lo peoples.

Henry Custer—the Americans' most gifted surveyor—acknowledged the debt he owed the Natives who worked with him: "We gained most of our first knowledge of the country, as also many of the names of its mountains, smaller streams, and lakes" from Indigenous guides. As he travelled the region's waterways, valleys and mountains, Custer diligently recorded these names, rejecting the routine practice of replacing them with new anglicized labels. Custer made full use of his Native guides. Trekking east along upper Chilliwack River, he asked Thompson chief Thiusoloc to map out the forbidding mountainous terrain. Thiusoloc and his father produced a pair of maps: bounded on the north by Fraser River and on the south by Nooksack River, on the west by lower Chilliwack River and on the east by Skagit River, the charts showed the locations of streams and rivers, prominent peaks and alpine lakes, along with the Indigenous names for these.

The work of George Gibbs was equally impressive. During a three-week expedition up Fraser River in spring 1858, Gibbs amassed an "Indian Nomenclature" that recorded the Halkomelem name and description of 131 villages and geographic features from Fort Langley to Hope. Given the fact that the American party travelled with Sema:th guides and crews, it is not surprising that Sumas Lake and Valley received much attention. Sumas-area toponyms included Sluch-kehn (Sumas Mountain), Mam-ook-wum (lower Sumas Prairie) and Keh-ka-la-hun (Vedder Mountain). Gibbs

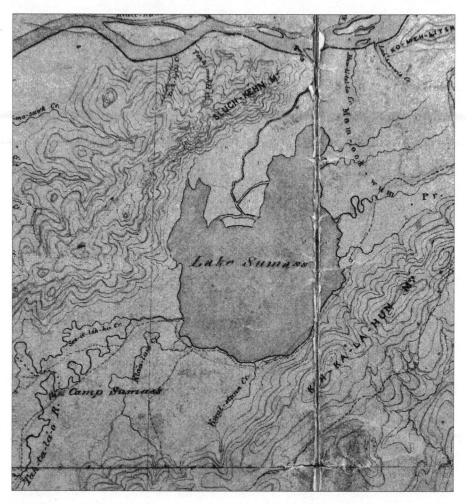

The Sumas section of a sweeping map prepared by the Northwest Boundary Survey, which identifies the Halkomelem names for the region's geographic features. Native Place Names [c 1860] [nara, rg76, cs68, map 1].

also compiled and transcribed a list of place names first recorded by Custer during the latter's early surveys of Sumas Lake and Fraser River. Among the sites identified were Tah-ta-la-o (upper Sumas River), Klaa-lum (Saar Creek) and Shahs-ma-koom ("the swamp" on the western edge of upper Sumas Prairie).[40]

The culmination of the American commission's ethnographic work was a sweeping map that stretched from the mouth of Fraser River to Fort Hope along the north, from Puget Sound to Chilliwack Lake on the south. Geographic features and topography were inked in meticulous detail by John Parke, the chief cartographer. To these were applied the Halkomelem names collected by Custer and Gibbs from Sto:lo sources. Only a handful of the chart's sites and features sported English names, while 244 Sto:lo place names identified the rest: waterways, lakes, prairies, swampland, mountains and villages. Most detailed sections were those the Americans had spent the greatest time surveying, including the prairies to the southwest and northeast of Sumas Lake, and the mountains to its southeast and northwest.

This map of Sto:lo place names was the most astonishing document produced by the Northwest Boundary Survey. Even greater than its scope and accuracy was the ability of its creators to see people and places other Whites could not see—a Native landscape that was invisible or extinct to the newcomers, but present and alive for the Sto:lo whose home it was. In recent years, scholars working to reattach Sto:lo and Nooksack names to their rightful places have leaned heavily on the ethnographic material collected by Gibbs, Custer and their colleagues. These scholars have labelled the American commission material "by far the most useful" of all written records, and the quality of its linguistic work "very high for its day." The most important sources for Sto:lo place names, of course, have been Sto:lo elders themselves. A comparison between their names and those provided by Gibbs and Custer reveals that the Americans got as close to the real thing as a non-Halkomelem speaker of the mid-1800s could get.[41]

The Northwest Boundary Survey's mandate also included study of the region's physical landscape: its topography, flora and fauna. Along with surveyors, astronomers and map-makers, the survey included men trained in botany and zoology. Caleb Kennerly doubled as surgeon and natural scientist for the Americans, but his death in 1860 scuppered plans for an official report on the region's flora and fauna. Royal Navy surgeon and botanist David Lyall carried out methodical surveys of the Sumas and Chilliwack Valleys through the summers of 1858 and 1859. He recorded and catalogued nearly 100 plant species commonly found there, and he published his findings in England's most prestigious botanical journal. John Lord's work reached a wider audience. His two-volume opus *The Naturalist in Vancouver Island and British Columbia* identified and recorded hundreds of species of mammals, birds, fish, reptiles and insects Lord had found at Sumas and Chilliwack. *The Naturalist* was published in 1866, and it immediately became essential reading for those seeking first-hand information on the physical landscape of the middle Fraser Valley.

The Northwest Boundary Survey parties also were instructed to make visual images of the lands they surveyed. This met the general desire for advancing scientific knowledge of the region's landscape. It also met a more practical need: through sketches and pictures of prominent geographic features—most often mountain ridges and peaks—surveyors not only oriented themselves on the ground, but they enabled those who followed them to do the same. Having experimented with photography during the Crimean War, the British government outfitted its commission with camera equipment and a photographer. But upon arriving at Victoria, its trained photographer promptly deserted for the Fraser River goldfields. Nobody else in the British commission knew how to operate the clumsy, temperamental instruments; Charles Wilson was an amateur painter and he gave the camera a try, without success, and no photographs west of the Cascade Mountains survived.

The Americans relied on more traditional techniques. Artist Francis Herbst accompanied the earliest survey parties into the field, and painter James Alden followed at a more comfortable distance. Alden produced the first visual image of Sumas Valley to be seen by the outside world—a sweeping portrait of the landscape west of Sumas Lake. A detailed rendering of Camp Sumass is the painting's focus, with lower Sumas Prairie spreading out in the mid-ground. Sumas Lake is concealed by a tree-lined ridge; behind that, a panorama of mountain peaks forms a jagged horizon. Alden's portrait of Camp Sumass is well-known, one of a series of paintings that established his reputation as one of the foremost landscape artists of the American West in the 19th century. Yet it is possible Alden never set foot there. We do know that Alden travelled up Fraser River, sometime in 1858 or 1859; he painted a number of scenes from Fort Langley to Fort Hope, all of these from vantage points on Fraser River. But there is no record of Alden leaving Fraser River for the more arduous trek across Sumas Lake to Camp Sumass.

More likely, Alden's *Camp Sumass* was based on the work of his colleague, Francis Herbst, who began surveying and drawing Sumas Valley in late summer 1857. Over the following weeks and months, he produced a series of elegant landscape sketches and panoramas. One of the first of these was an ink drawing of Camp Sumass, which was nearly identical to Alden's later portrait: the same tents amid the same trees and brush. If anything, Herbst's sketch was the more lifelike; here he succeeded, where so many other artists have failed, in capturing the stately trees and rich underbrush of the Fraser Valley floor. Herbst's drawing did not include the middle ground and back ground that appeared in Alden's painting. The latter could have taken these from other landscape drawings and mountain panoramas Herbst completed at the time; the similarities between the works strongly suggest this was so.

James Alden of the American Boundary Commission produced this colour painting of the wide expanse of Sumas Prairie and Camp Sumas, looking east to Mount Cheam. Sumas Lake is hidden behind the line of trees and bushes in the middle ground. "Camp Sumass. Sumass Prairie looking north." James Madison Alden/Public Domain.

Herbst's other work from this time included a half-dozen panoramas of surrounding mountain peaks and ridges, taken from different vantage points: Camp Sumass, the mouth of lower Sumas River, and Sumas Lake. To ensure accuracy, Herbst used a *camera obscura*, a simple box with a lens mounted on one side and an angled mirror on the other. The lens projected an image onto the mirror, which reflected the image up to glass on the top of the box; the artist placed a piece of paper on the glass and simply traced the image.

Herbst also produced a series of more detailed, in-field sketches, which added a middle ground of trees, bush and grass to background profiles of mountains. Both upper and lower Sumas Prairie were portrayed; and for the first time, Sumas Lake itself appeared, as seen looking eastward from the mouth of upper Sumas River. The lake bends behind a copse of trees and flows into "Sumas River thru gap" behind Sumas Mountain; across the lake, an unbroken line of trees marks the lakeshore, the foot of Chilliwack Mountain rising from it. A closer look reveals four canoes—scarcely visible at first—beached on the banks of upper Sumas River, with two men watching over them. The boats have the distinctive lines of Sto:lo river canoes and most likely came from nearby Sema:th villages.[42]

The ethnographic, scientific and artistic contributions of the Northwest Boundary Survey were truly significant. For the first time, the vibrant human and physical landscape of Sumas Lake was being revealed to outsiders. But the main reason the British and American commissions were there was to survey and map the region. Of all its work, the maps produced by the survey—from preliminary field charts to the official documents drafted and signed in Washington and London—had the most direct impact on the history of Sumas Lake. And nearly all the original survey and cartographical work was carried out by the American commission.

Through late summer and fall 1857, the Americans methodically surveyed Sumas Lake and Valley, plotting their features in leather-bound field books. These field books were then returned to the commission's headquarters at Camp Semiahmoo, where they were worked up into more formal maps. The man responsible for this task was chief surveyor and astronomer John Parke, a lieutenant in the US Army Topographical Engineers. At West Point, Parke received formal training in applied engineering and topographical sketching. In 1851, while serving on the US–Mexican Boundary Survey, he completed the first accurate map of the newly acquired American Southwest. Within weeks of the Americans' initial expeditions on the Northwest Boundary, Parke completed the first tentative sketches of Sumas Lake. These accurately portrayed the lake's north and west shores, where his teams had travelled, but the shape of its south and east rim was left to speculation. As more field books and reports came in, Sumas Lake and Valley gained greater and greater detail. Sumas Lake took on its distinctive almond shape, and the serpentine courses of its tributaries were carefully followed.

Late in 1857, Parke gathered together all the fieldwork from that first year and produced an elegant *Progress Sketch—North Western Boundary Survey*. The map's western edge ran from the mouth of Fraser River southward to Puget Sound, its eastern limit from the mouth of lower Chilliwack River southward to Cultus Lake. Parke gave particular attention to Sumas Valley here, reflecting the focus of the commission's work. Sumas Lake was rendered to scale and accurately located, as were surrounding features: the contours of Sumas, Vedder and Chilliwack Mountains; the paths of lower and upper Sumas River; the site of Camp Sumass; and the trail from there to Bellingham Bay, along Nooksack River. Also, a bold line along the 49th parallel bisected the chart into north and south halves—the first time the border had been rendered with any precision. The line's location had been determined by the readings taken by the Americans at the Semiahmoo and Sumas astronomical stations.

Late in 1858, Parke drafted another all-encompassing map, which incorporated survey work done through a second year. The modestly titled *Preliminary Sketch of Reconnaissances and Surveys* charted the American commission's rapid progress eastward, up to Chilliwack Lake as far as the upper reaches of Skagit River. It also filled in the gaps south and west of Sumas Lake, with greater detail given to the surrounding waterways, mountains and trails. Vegetation and contours of the landscape also were depicted: mountain slopes surrounding the lake by concentric lines of elevation; the lush grassland of Sumas Prairie by bunched short pen strokes; a large marsh immediately west by broken tufts.

After the close of 1859, when the boundary survey relocated east of the Cascades, Parke oversaw completion of a final master map that covered the same territory as his 1857 *Progress Sketch*. The ink line drawing achieved the highest level of precision and detail to date, from the meandering courses of the smallest creeks to the elevation contours of the highest mountains. The shape and size given to Sumas Lake itself would stay the same on maps through the rest of the century (with the exception of an exaggeration of the width of the lower Sumas River peninsula). Likewise for the lake's tributaries: upper Sumas River to the west, along with Marshall, Saar and Arnold Creeks; Vedder River to the east, along with Mud and Lewis Creeks. Parke's line sketch was used as a template for other maps, including the masterful chart of Sto:lo place names completed by George Gibbs. It also formed the basis for the survey's official maps, completed some years later in Washington, DC.[43]

Meanwhile, the British contributed little to the mapping of the border and its landscape west of the Cascades. This failure was due in part to shoddy government planning: the British commission was a year late in arriving; and when it took to the field, it lacked the modern astronomical instruments needed to do the job. The latitude readings from Cultus Lake were the only ones the British completed independent of the Americans, and these were later thrown out because of human error and the inferior instruments used.

An equally large part of the failure was due to Commissioner John Hawkins, who stubbornly clung to the conviction that the core task of the boundary survey—accurately computing and mapping the 49th parallel— was less important than physically marking the line on the ground. When he learned in summer 1858 how much surveying the Americans had already done, Hawkins expressed relief that his team would not have to undertake the same onerous task. Two years later—after the official survey work west of the Cascades was over—the colonel confessed to his superiors in the Foreign Office that his men had done "little or nothing…towards extending topographical researches."

Hawkins was convinced that the greatest task in front of him was ensuring that the region stayed within the British Empire. He viewed the influx of thousands of American gold miners with fear and loathing, and he was convinced that the American commission was secretly working to wrench the Northwest Coast from British hands. Hawkins believed that the best way to turn aside these threats was to clearly and physically mark the boundary line on the ground, and to do it quickly. To that end, starting in spring 1859, he devoted one of his two surveyors—Capt. Charles Darrah—and the bulk of his men to clearing a 40-foot swath through the thick forest and bush from Vedder Mountain east to Semiahmoo. The task was daunting: along the border near upper Sumas Prairie, axemen attacked firs 30 feet around and up to 250 feet high. Hawkins admitted that the line cutting was only "a near approximation to the Boundary," but the result was dramatic. Charles Wilson visited Darrah along the line that summer and described the scene: "We looked down on the long dark line of the parallel running east and west through the trees until the view was shut by the Schweltya hills in the distance." With the line cleared, the British then erected a string of iron pillars to mark the border itself. Forty-two obelisks—each three feet high and inscribed with the date of the Oregon Treaty—were planted at intervals along the line, from Point Roberts to the southeastern slope of Vedder Mountain.

Clear-cutting the line and erecting border monuments were the main British contributions to the boundary survey west of the Cascades. There was no British equivalent to the treasure trove of material—field books, sketches, draft maps—produced by the American commission. On its own, this would have been a serious failure for British authorities, as they were in dire need of dependable maps of the distant land they had just made a colony. Another party of Royal Engineers—based in New Westminster under the command of Col. Richard Moody—was given the task of providing these maps. Moody did not commit any of his limited resources to surveying the land south of Fraser River, from Langley up to the foot of the Cascades, believing the boundary survey had done so. The Royal Engineers' first maps, drafted in 1859, showed the lack of first-hand knowledge of the area. Two years later, a more detailed map filled in some of the blanks. For the first time, Sumas Lake and Valley were drawn to scale and with accuracy, as was the upper Chilliwack River valley as far as Chilliwack Lake. The map's drafters attributed this section—from Sumas to Chilliwack Lake—to information "furnished by Lieut. Co. Hawkins, R.E., H.M. Boundary Commission."

The work credited to Hawkins was done not by the British commission, but by the Americans. Hawkins had simply lifted the material from the American commission and passed it along to his British colleagues. The colonel's sleight of hand occurred at the first meeting of the two commissions, held at Camp Semiahmoo in July 1858. Hawkins and Captain Haig attended for the British; Archibald Campbell was not there, leaving Lieutenant Parke to represent the Americans. Hawkins and Haig listened with rapt attention as Parke described the extensive work already carried out by the Americans. Parke illustrated his talk with an early draft of his monumental *Preliminary Sketch*, which he let the British officers peruse. Whether Parke intended for Hawkins to leave with the map is not clear, but the British commissioner did just that. Hawkins was delighted with his new acquisition. As he wrote London, it saved the British commission the trouble and expense of undertaking "a similar and tedious survey, the country being of a very difficult and impenetrable nature for such work."

Hawkins gave copies of the map to both Colonel Moody and the Foreign Office. Moody incorporated the information into the Royal Engineers' 1861 chart, and then into their definitive map produced two years later. Another copy of Parke's sketch was seen in the possession of Joseph Trutch, the future colonial and provincial lands minister. At the time, Trutch was a private surveyor based in Victoria; he had just inked a government contract to carry out the first official land surveys of the lower Fraser River. The survey map produced by Trutch, and officially registered by Moody, was a near-perfect copy of Parke's chart, right down to the exaggerated width of the lower Sumas River peninsula. For decades to come, all early maps of Sumas Lake and Valley used by British authorities were based on the work of the American boundary commission.[44]

After completing its fieldwork among the peaks of the Rocky Mountains, the Northwest Boundary Survey relocated to Washington, DC, with its field books, sketches and maps. There, between 1863 and 1866, survey members meticulously charted the new borderline; three years later, the final maps were signed by Colonel Hawkins and Archibald Campbell, then published by their respective governments. The British maps divided the boundary line into six panels, each revealing a five-mile swath along the 49th parallel. On the Fraser Valley sheet, only the southernmost shore of Sumas Lake was captured, along with its main tributaries and upper Sumas Prairie. The Americans published a series of 10 panels, covering a much wider swath on either side of the border. These panels were the crowning achievement of the American commission map-makers—in rich detail and with true artistry, they illustrated the geographic features, topography and vegetation of the boundary region. The westernmost panel stretched from the mouth of Fraser River to the upper Chilliwack River valley. To the northwest and southeast of Sumas Lake, the relief of Sumas and Vedder Mountains was rendered through hachures, giving the illusion of three dimensions, as if their rugged ridges were rising out of the map's surface. The grasslands of upper and lower Sumas Prairies extended outward from the lake's southwest and northeast shores, giving way to a mixture of bush and tree, itself interspersed with swampland. The banks of tributary streams were lined with trees, as were the ridges along the lake's southern shore (see map in Chapter 1).[45]

The overall impression of the map was photographic; it said to the viewer that this was precisely what Sumas Lake and its surrounding landscape looked like. The perspective of the whole panorama was from well above above the earth's surface, but viewers could project themselves to any point on the valley floor and imagine the view they would meet—lake, stream or mountain, grass, forest or marsh.

The photographic quality of the map made it a powerful tool. This and other charts produced through this time extended knowledge of Sumas Lake to those who had never been there. They told prospective immigrants how to get there, directed surveyors in laying out new property lines and guided government authorities setting aside Native reserves. But these maps were not simple reflections of a real-life Sumas Lake. They excluded elements they did not wish to see and remade the reality they claimed to capture. On official government maps, Indigenous place names were erased, replaced by English names or crudely anglicized versions of the original Halkomelem. Sumas Lake itself was drawn in permanent lines, fixed in place. On one side of these lines lay water; on the other, land. Yet we know Sumas Lake was not like that at all; its size and shape changed seasonally and from year to year, and its fertile wetlands defied any either-or labels. This blindness—to the presence of the lake's first peoples, to the shape-shifting of the lake's landscape—would afflict White newcomers and determine their interaction with Sumas Lake for decades to come.

The symbolic and physical marking of the 49th parallel brought about a diplomatic division of the Northwest Coast between two of the world's most powerful, expansionist nations. It thereby averted the risk that the region would become the cause of tension or war. Of course, international boundaries are human constructions; they are clean and sharp only when drawn on maps. On the ground, boundary lines divide elements of the physical and human landscape that previously were connected. The 49th parallel lay just south of Sumas Lake, cutting across the latter's main tributaries from the south: the upper Sumas River, Saar Creek and Arnold Creek. One-half of this southern watershed lies on the American side of the border; this political division would complicate subsequent efforts to control the rise and fall of the lake; indeed, it complicates such efforts to this day. The international boundary also crosses an important transportation line that joined the Nooksack River valley to the upper Sumas Valley. The route was used extensively by the Sto:lo and Nooksack peoples, by the American boundary commission and—as we shall see—by thousands of gold miners coming north from Bellingham Bay.

Finally, the border imposed an alien barrier between Native communities that—for centuries, even millennia—had been closely linked, through marriage, social interaction and resource sharing. It ran across a large portion of the Sumas Valley, which the Sema:th traditionally shared with the Nooksack. With each subsequent generation, it became more and more difficult for the Sema:th and other Sto:lo to travel south, and for the Nooksack to travel north to Sumas Lake and Fraser River.

CHAPTER 5

HUNGRY NEWCOMERS

Prior to 1858, the shores and waters of Sumas Lake saw few non-Native newcomers, and the lands of the Sema:th were little disturbed. The Hudson's Bay Company traders and Northwest Boundary Survey commissions numbered a few hundred and they left only a modest imprint on the region. Then, almost overnight, this world was overturned. Beginning in March 1858, and rapidly gaining momentum through the spring, a rush of humanity invaded British Columbia in search of one precious commodity—gold.

News of this new El Dorado quickly spread southward along the Pacific coast, eastward across the continent and westward across the Pacific Ocean—and men came, first by the hundreds, then by the thousands. In the second half of May alone, some 10,000 men travelled up the lower Fraser River toward Hope and beyond. The onrush continued through the summer, abating with the approach of fall. By the end of 1858, more than 30,000 men—Americans, Chinese, British, Canadians, Europeans—had descended upon the sandbars and banks of the Fraser River and streams flowing into it. The Fraser rush slackened in following years, only to be revived in 1862 with the discovery of gold farther north in the Cariboo region.

The Fraser gold rush has long captured the imaginations of historians, for it possesses all the components of an epic, romantic past: the promise of riches untold for the few, the heartbreak of failure for the many, and enough hardship for everyone. Yet these writers have told this story from a specific point of view. For them, centre stage was the Fraser River, and the leading actors were the thousands of miners who travelled along the all-British route from Victoria to the goldfields. Their perspective is that of the steamboat-bound prospectors, colonial officials and newspapermen of the time, who sailed up the lower Fraser with minds fixed upstream, their view of Sumas Lake and Valley blocked by the towering bulk of Sumas Mountain.

At the same time, historians have been of two minds regarding the legacy of the dramatic events. The Fraser gold rush is rightfully seen as a watershed moment, for it opened the region to the world, enticed an unprecedented wave of immigrants and led to the birth of British Columbia as a colony. Yet this manic quest is faulted for its failure both to attract more permanent White settlers and to build a reliable economic foundation for the new colony. The gold rush era is set apart from the settlement era, dealt with in separate chapters.

The story of Sumas Lake and Valley during the gold rush did not follow the established script. The lake played a central role in the heady years following the discovery of Fraser gold, and the rush for spoils left a lasting imprint on the valley itself. The gold rush brought thousands of men through Sumas Valley and across Sumas Lake, travelling on a route—the Whatcom Trail—that rivalled the all-British line. Far from being a comet-like event that burned bright but left little behind, the gold rush produced a durable legacy. It led directly to the establishment of a permanent immigrant population in Sumas Valley and inaugurated an industry that would be the mainstay of the local economy for decades to come: the raising of livestock for transportation, meat and dairy. In the history of Sumas Lake, we cannot separate the era of the prospector from that of the pastoralist and new settler—each of these fed into the others.

The first stirrings of gold fever south of Fraser River started well before March 1858. In spring 1857, news emerged of possible finds along the Fraser just north of Fort Hope. Open war between Washington Territory forces and Native Americans had made older routes east of the Cascades dangerous. So three enterprising prospectors decided to test a new route, one they hoped would be safer, cheaper and shorter. Striking out from Bellingham Bay, the party travelled up Fraser River to Fort Hope and on through Fraser Canyon. William Yates, the Hudson's Bay Company trader at Hope, met the prospectors on their way up the canyon and saw them return, their packs now laden with some $2,000 of gold dust and nuggets.

It is not clear how these men reached the Fraser from Bellingham Bay: whether by boat northward and up the mouth of Fraser River; or overland, northeastward through Sumas Valley by what would be called the Whatcom Trail. The trail had existed as a footpath for countless generations, regularly used by the Nooksack and Sema:th. White immigrants on Bellingham Bay learned of it soon after their arrival in 1852, when Whatcom was founded as a town. As they pushed up Nooksack River through the mid-1850s, they worked to improve the trail. It is thus possible, even probable, that American prospectors travelled across Sumas Prairie and Lake on their way to Fraser River prior to the rush of 1858. Indeed, local lore has it that one of the first White settlers, Volkert Vedder, journeyed from Whatcom to Sumas Valley as early as 1856.[46]

Any miners who may have used Whatcom Trail before 1858 could not foresee the wave that followed in their footsteps. The stampede of gold seekers began the first week of March 1858. On March 3, Lieutenant Parke noted the news of gold finds north of the 49th parallel had sparked "much excitement" in Washington Territory. Two days later, the *Olympia Pioneer* reported "the alleged discovery of rich gold deposits to the northward in the British possessions." Reports of gold soon reached newspapers in Victoria, San Francisco and beyond. Fact and rumour swirled about as cries of "Eureka!" competed with snorts of "Humbug!" on the front pages of newspapers.

Sumas Lake itself was the subject of heated speculation as rumours spread that gold could be found there. The *Olympia Pioneer* claimed in mid-March that the American boundary commission "had discovered gold near Sumas Lake, on the American side." Rumours of "Sumas gold" were repeated through the spring and persisted well into summer. The *San Francisco Herald* reported in August that a Nooksack man had arrived at Whatcom with $13 in gold, including two large pieces, which he had "received from one of his tribe, who dug it at Sumas."

While drawing miners to Sumas Valley, news of gold there turned out to be humbug. The lowest point on the Fraser to produce paying quantities of gold was Fargo's Bar, several miles upriver from the mouth of lower Sumas River (the bar was quickly abandoned for richer finds up the Fraser). The Fraser River downstream from Sumas held none of the precious metal, and the Whatcom Trail through Sumas Valley delivered miners well below any paying bars. American newspapers eagerly promoted the American route. The *Puget Sound Herald* and the *Olympia Pioneer* confidently asserted that the miner needed neither map nor bushwhacker, for the route was "plainly marked by a well beaten Indian foot trail." Moreover, they argued, the Whatcom Trail bypassed Victoria and British colonial officials, with their fees and levies; it was shorter and safer (scores of men drowned crossing Georgia Strait); and money spent kitting up at Whatcom or Olympia stayed in American hands.

May, June and July brought more miners than ever through Sumas Valley. Prospectors poured "into Sumass prairie over the track from Whatcom towards the mining region of Frazer's River," noted Joseph Harris of

the boundary survey. Sumas Prairie was "now covered with the tents of em-
igrants," another Survey member wrote, with "a great number" of miners
camped on Sumas Lake's western shore.

Prospectors travelling through Sumas Valley left vivid descriptions of
the journey. With little regard for grammar, one report made note of "a
large number of canoes returning down Fraser River to the mouth of the
Sumas, which they navigate up to the head of Lake Sumas, and abandon
them [canoes] for the Whatcom Trail." These trips were far from smooth.
On the third day out from Whatcom, a hapless miner wrote:

> We entered a valley five miles long which was overflowed
> from a lake. The trail ran through the valley, and we were
> obliged to take to the water. When we started to take to the
> water we did not consider it would be above our knees, until
> we could reach where the Indians could take us in their ca-
> noes, but before we got half a mile were up to our waists. We
> made about four miles, and then the Indians brought us the
> balance of the way in their canoes.

Unknown to them, such American prospectors were encountering Sumas
Valley's perennial spring high waters; only the skill of local Sema:th canoe-
ists got them through it.

The difficulties of the Sumas leg of the Whatcom Trail led some to
consider alternate routes. In August, Bellingham Bay businessmen hired
Capt. John Delacey to find a way around Sumas Valley. But the route he
blazed followed the upper Chilliwack River into the forbidding Cascade
Mountains, and he returned convinced that Sumas Valley was still the better option. With the enthusiasm of a convert, he proposed using Sumas
Lake as a hub for an upgraded line. A new road would be built from Whatcom to a depot on the lakeshore; supplies and men would then be transported across the lake, up Fraser River to Harrison Lake and northward,
with Sumas Prairie providing ample feed for cattle and pack animals.

Delacey's plan for a new and improved Sumas Valley trail never mate-
rialized, as the Fraser River route became more established with the regular
running of steamboats from Victoria to Yale. But even when the Fraser gold
excitement began to wane with the approach of fall, thousands of miners
remained in BC and Washington Territory. George Gibbs reported in early
September that 3,000 expectant prospectors were encamped at Bellingham Bay; between 3,000 and 5,000 men spent the winter on mainland BC,
mostly between New Westminster and Yale.[47]

Through 1858, the Sema:th and their neighbours did not passively watch as thousands of outsiders descended upon their land. The Sto:lo christened the newcomers Xwelitem, meaning "hungry to the point of starving," or simply "the starving ones": starving literally (in need of food), and starving figuratively (hungering after ever more riches). The Sema:th took full advantage of the opportunities presented by these hungry new-comers. The difficult terrain and their general unpreparedness left the min-ers dependent on local Natives for transportation and food. One American correspondent described his early June trip:

> At Sumas village, which is at the mouth of the [lower Sumas] river, and connects with the lake of the same name, I found about thirty men, who had come through by the trail from Bellingham Bay. They were there without canoes, or any means of getting away—had been three days in reaching the spot....The Indians were almost all away, and those who were there, charged them roundly for passage to Port Hope in their canoes. They informed me, that there were a great number at the Lake, who were unable to get any further, there being no canoes there.

The plaintive letter of another miner showed this experience was not unique:

> [Sumas] lake is seven miles long and three or four miles wide. You have to procure a canoe to cross it; and when you get there, no canoe is to be found. There you are, in the midst of a thousand Indians, who are very ready to steal everything most have, unable to proceed. As for letting you have a canoe, they will not, except upon the most unreasonable terms.... The Indians play all sorts of tricks on the whites. They agreed to take one party of four across the lake and to Fraser River for $5 per day; but landed them on an island, where they left them to get away as best they could. They had to pay other Indians to take them off, when they returned to Bellingham Bay in disgust.

The Sema:th also used their renowned piloting skills and knowledge of Fra-ser River to canoe mining parties up from Sumas Bar—where prospectors congregated in numbers—to Hope and Yale.

As the demand for transportation and food rose, so did the Sema:th's prices. George Gardner noted that local Sto:lo and Nooksack quickly learned of the inflated prices charged at Whatcom, Fort Langley and Victoria, and "in imitation charged exorbitantly for salmon and sturgeon, as well as for their services." Even small salmon could fetch one dollar (the daily wage paid to Native workers by the American boundary commission), and were scarce at that. Joseph Harris reported that the Sema:th and Nooksack "were both driving such a good trade with the miners...[who] were willing to pay almost any price" for supplies and transportation. At the height of the gold rush, individuals could make three to four dollars a day transporting prospectors, while canoes with two or more crew fetched higher rates.[48]

The Sema:th and their neighbours were able to profit from the needs of White miners, just as they had seized the opportunities presented by the Hudson's Bay Company and Northwest Boundary Survey. But unlike the latter two, the hungry newcomers of the gold rush unleashed forces that forever altered the Sema:th's lives and homeland. As Whites arrived in large numbers, they brought along the animals they relied upon in their home countries: horses and mules for transportation, cattle and pigs for food. These animals needed to be fed, and local sources of edible grass needed to be found. BC was and remains a land of forest and mountain; grassland makes up less than one percent of its total land mass.

The "luxuriant grasses" of Sumas Prairie were a key part of Captain Delacey's plan for a new Whatcom Trail with Sumas Lake as its hub. Delacey wrote: "These grasses are of the most nutritional kind, and of several varieties, upon which thousands of cattle might pasture without visibly diminishing the supply." Henry DeGroot—a San Francisco journalist whose articles were republished in one of the first mining handbooks—described his journeys from Whatcom to the goldfields. "On the Smess prairies," DeGroot reported, "are many thousand acres covered with wild timothy and other nourishing grasses, from which hay of excellent quality could be made with greatest facility, the growth being very thick and standing four or five feet high." Along the edges of Sumas Lake, "swamp grass of different kinds, some being fine and nutritious, others almost coarse as tules," abounded.[49]

A number of astute miners were quick to seize this opportunity presented by Sumas Valley's grasslands. In early summer 1858, the first herds of mules, horses and cattle were driven along Whatcom Trail by miners. By fall, there were as many as 1,000 head grazing around Sumas Lake. Meanwhile, the American boundary commission received a much smaller

A portrait of John Lord taken in the field. Notice the riding crop, Scottish highland footwear and tam. Miscellaneous Items in High Demand, PPOC, Library of Congress/Public Domain.

number of pack animals, which it housed in a newly built corral near Camp Sumass. The commission drove its stock south to Oregon that winter. But the early miner-graziers decided to stand pat, convinced that Sumas Valley's natural grasses would see their animals through what they believed would be a mild winter. As temperatures dropped, hundreds of mules, horses and cattle huddled together in crude sheds that had been hastily erected. When heavy snow covered the prairie grass, the desperate stock sought out horsetail rushes growing on the marshy shores of Sumas Lake and surrounding riverbeds. The animals' digestive systems reacted violently to the alien fodder. "The most violent purging came on," John Lord wrote, "accompanied with cramps, rigors, utter prostration, and speedy death." More than 500 head perished in less than a month.

Lord was a veterinary surgeon who was responsible for the British boundary commission's animals. By autumn 1859, the British had some 100 mules and horses in the valley, along with an unspecified number of beef cattle. Determined that the disaster of the previous winter would not be repeated with his animals, Lord made preparations for the upcoming months. He ordered the indigenous blue-joint grass mowed and the fields reseeded with imported forage grass; this was then harvested in the fall and put up as hay for winter. He also brought in a supply of barley, moving it by canoe up the Fraser and Sumas Rivers to Sumas Prairie, where it was stored in a log shed. Lord did not appreciate the larger significance of his actions: by introducing new species of plants and animals, he was helping start the biological remaking of Sumas Valley.

The calamitous winter of 1858–59 and ebbing of the Fraser River gold rush did not discourage the early miner-graziers of Sumas. Thousands of miners remained in the colony, and new companies entered the field as mining became more organized and industrialized. In 1862, fresh finds in the Cariboo region sparked a second rush for gold. Through much of that decade, the successive mining booms fuelled the demand for food and transport, keeping prices high: meat sold for 40 cents per pound, flour for 30 cents; freighting rates to the Cariboo ranged from 15 to 18 cents per pound. Between 1861 and 1864, astonishing numbers of livestock were driven overland from Washington into BC: more than 7,000 cattle, 5,000 horses, 1,000 mules and 1,000 sheep. In 1862 alone, horse and beef cattle sales generated more than $500,000 in revenue. The majority of this stock travelled north along interior routes, but a considerable minority came via Whatcom Trail. At the same time, herds already in BC were driven from the interior to Sumas Valley for winter grazing, and moved back the following spring. A growing number of stock owners came to depend on Sumas Valley: from the colonial government itself, to private express companies, to butcher shops in New Westminster, Hope and Yale.[50]

Most of these stock owners made only seasonal use of Sumas Valley and did not lay claim to land there. Others established a more lasting presence, doing business in the valley and obtaining land through the pre-emption system. Pre-emption enabled male British subjects to acquire up to 160 acres (a quarter section) of open Crown land without paying for it. To gain ownership, the pre-emptor had to officially register his claim, then over the next few years build a house, erect outbuildings and put a part of the land into cultivation. The aspiring landowner was limited to one pre-emption, although he could transfer the claim from one property to another. He also was allowed to purchase additional land outright.

One of the earliest pastoral pre-emptors in Sumas Valley was Edwin Dodge, a San Francisco merchant who came to BC in 1860. In BC, Dodge started out as a trader and freighter out of Port Douglas (at the northern tip of Harrison Lake); he also worked for Ballou's Express, in charge of steamboat runs up and down lower Fraser River. In 1861, he formed E.T. Dodge & Co. to transport goods, gold and people overland from Port Douglas and Lillooet to the interior and back. Within two years, the firm was one of the largest in the colony; it also diversified, acquiring the steamer *Hope* and barge *Speedwell*. During this time, Dodge made regular use of Sumas Valley for grazing. Sometime before 1864, he recorded a claim to a large stretch of grassland running along the eastern bank of lower Sumas River. Dodge's Flats—as it soon became known—were a crucial part of Dodge's expanding empire. He pastured his own stock here and engaged hands to harvest the wild grasses for feed, while the *Hope* and *Speedwell* shuttled animals and silage in and out of Sumas Landing. By 1866, BC's gold-fuelled boom had ebbed, and Dodge decided it was time to move on. He folded his company, sold its assets and moved south to the lowlands outside La Conner, Washington, where he settled for the more regular life of mixed farming.

A second pastoral pre-emptor sank deeper roots into the Sumas Valley. We do not know where Peter Anderson came from, nor the date of his arrival in BC. We do know that he took advantage of the Fraser and Cariboo gold rushes to build a thriving business in New Westminster as a butcher and cattle dealer, catering to retail and wholesale customers. The need to secure pasture land for his ever-increasing herds brought Anderson to the northern edge of upper Sumas Prairie. On August 18, 1863, he recorded a pre-emption for 160 acres situated on a slough that ran "from the high lands into Sumass Lake." The slough soon took on Anderson's name (in following decades it came to be known as Lonzo Creek, then finally Marshall Creek). Here—in the shadow of Sumas Mountain, with the Sema:th as neighbours—Anderson grazed his stock and leased pasturage to other ranchers, including Edwin Dodge. Anderson pre-empted two more lots in 1871, one on either side of his first claim, expanding his Sumas holdings to 360 acres. While Anderson's primary residence remained in New Westminster, he lived at least part-time at upper Sumas, constructing a house and outbuildings there. He was listed as a resident of upper Sumas in directories from 1871 to 1890.

With the success of Dodge and Anderson, Sumas Valley soon became known as a stockman's paradise. In 1863, the *British Columbian* touted it as "well suited for stock-raising, which is the chief thing to be done in farming in this area." A few years later, the paper singled out the operations of Anderson and Dodge as proof that Sumas's climate and grasses were ideal for grazing stock. And there was ample space for more: "We are told that there is room for many thousands of cattle on the Sumass and other prairies on the Lower Fraser." By the end of the 1860s, Sumas graziers and dairymen had gained the reputation of supplying the fattest cattle and the best butter. The Sumas settlement, concluded the *British Columbian*, presented a picture of prosperity and tranquility: "The sweeping miles of rich prairie grass are now dotted over with cattle, fat and sleek."[51]

The early contributions of Dodge and Anderson have been overlooked by historians. Better known are a trio of men whose names have become synonymous with the founding of White settlement in Sumas and Chilliwack. Volkert Vedder, Thomas York and Jonathan Reece were among the first wave of prospectors to travel up Whatcom Trail in search of gold on Fraser River. Vedder arrived in San Francisco from New York in 1850, working as a freighter to the California gold mines for a number of years before heading north. York was part of a group of English coal miners hired by the Hudson's Bay Company in 1854 to work the company's coal interests on Vancouver Island (the group also included future robber baron Robert Dunsmuir). The Ontario-born Reece was last to arrive, drawn first to California in the 1850s, then north to BC in early 1858.

From what we can tell, the three initially crossed paths in Whatcom. York had moved there in 1856 to oversee the opening of a coal mine owned by American interests. It appears Vedder also made his way to Whatcom that year; local lore claims he travelled as far north as Sumas Valley, which would make him the area's first White visitor (apart from HBC traders).

Volkert Vedder was one of the first White immigrants to enter Sumas Valley. He arrived with the gold rush and remained the rest of his life, helping establish the valley's pastoral economy (1865). Chilliwack Museum and Archives, PP500066.

In spring 1858, Vedder, York and Reece set out on the Whatcom Trail for Fraser River. Over the following months, Reece panned bars between Hope and Yale. Fortune smiled on him and he immediately reinvested his profits; in early 1859, with financial aid from York, he opened butcher shops at Hope, then Yale.

Like Reece, York and Vedder saw the shrewdness of investing in businesses that promised more reliable sources of revenue than the will-o'-the-wisp of gold mining. Unlike Reece, the pair—a full generation older—possessed capital of their own, acquired from previous business ventures. In May 1858, York and his wife, Maria, opened one of the earliest inns at Yale. Leaving Maria to run the hotel and restaurant, York moved to Spuzzum, where he purchased and operated a ferry across Fraser River. The completion of Alexandra Bridge in 1862, several miles upriver, killed York's ferry operation; he returned to Yale, where he spent the next few years tending to his hotel. Volkert Vedder met with similar success at Yale. After panning alongside Reece, Vedder put his capital, experience and family—namely sons Adam and Albert—behind his own freighting company. Vedder & Co. transported goods up and down Fraser Canyon, and eventually into the Cariboo, employing more than a dozen teams of oxen at its peak.

Even as their business ventures in Hope and Yale took root and grew, Vedder, York and Reece moved to exploit the rich grasslands of Sumas Valley, through which they had passed on their way north. In 1859, Reece—again with financial backing from Thomas York—purchased 200 head of cattle in Oregon and drove them north to Whatcom, then over the Whatcom Trail through Sumas Prairie. Reece left the herd to graze at Chilliwack and Sumas, in the care of a hired hand, calling up small batches when he needed fresh meat for his Yale butchery. Volkert Vedder and his sons also wintered their stock in the Sumas Valley that year. In spring 1860, the Vedders returned to Yale, beginning a seasonal pattern they followed for the next decade: late fall and winter on Sumas Prairie, foraging their animals; then spring and summer at Yale, freighting to the Cariboo.[52]

The early graziers of Sumas and Chilliwack faced daunting challenges. Their businesses relied on being able to move their stock between Sumas, Hope and Yale on a regular basis. Steamboats were too expensive, and the few trails that existed were bad at the best of times; during high-water and rainy seasons they were impassable. One government inspector wrote in May 1861 that the trail was "very wet and muddy, caused by the passage of a number of mule trains from Sumas to Hope during the recent heavy rains." Winters—although much milder than east of the Cascades— were another challenge. From what we can tell through the written records, 19th-century winters were much harsher than those today. Frigid temperatures that froze Sumas Lake and Fraser River, along with massive snowfalls, were not uncommon.

Winter 1861–62 was one such season: heavy snow through November made overland travel impossible; temperatures plunged in the following weeks, reaching minus 15 degrees Fahrenheit at New Westminster and freezing Fraser River there to a depth of 9½ inches. The snow, cold and ice were even worse farther upriver. On Sumas Prairie, outflow winds coming from the mountains turned the situation lethal. The *British Columbian* reported in January that "great numbers" of horses, mules and cattle were dying at Sumas. The paper added, "Several men, the Indians say, have perished in a storm, and one more now lies at Chilowhack, half dead." Reece and Vedder were among those hit hard. In summer 1861, Reece had brought 300 cattle from Oregon up through Whatcom Trail. At Vedder's urging, he left them to winter on Sumas Prairie, under his partner's care. As winter took hold, several feet of snow blanketed the valley, covering the stock's forage. Reece had stored hay at Chilliwack, but the cattle could not reach it. By the time spring brought relief, some 200 head had perished.

Undeterred by the deadly winter of 1861–62, Reece continued to import cattle, and his butcher shop at Yale continued to turn a profit. By 1866, he had rebuilt his herd to 340 head, raising them alongside 220 hogs, 250 chickens and 20 horses. Meanwhile, Vedder and sons expanded their freighting business and started raising their own work oxen, then sold them as teams. One of their ads placed in the *British Columbian* offered for sale "14 yokes of work oxen and one new wagon, with yokes and chains complete for five yokes. The above cattle are in fine condition."[53]

Meanwhile, these men built up their land holdings in Sumas Valley. Beginning with his first recorded pre-emption in 1861, Reece concentrated his properties on land that would become the city of Chilliwack; but he still made liberal use of the Sumas grasslands for forage. In May 1862, Vedder pre-empted 160 acres along the southern edge of lower Sumas Prairie a short distance from Sumas Lake, in the shadow of Vedder Mountain. "The present trail passes through it and is indicated by four posts marked," Vedder wrote in his claim. "There is at present a house on it known as the 'Home.'" Further purchases over the following decade added 480 acres to his empire. The Vedder sons also were busy: each acquired a quarter section neighbouring on his father's property, Adam to the west, Albert to the south.

Like his business partner Reece, Thomas York continued to live in Yale through the first half of the 1860s. Then, seeking a less clamorous place to raise his children, York moved with his family from Yale to Sumas Prairie. In March 1866, he recorded his first pre-emption: a quarter section on the northern edge of lower Sumas Prairie, at the western foot of Chilliwack Mountain. A month later, York dropped this claim and took up another on the other side of the lake, "situated on the south west of the Sumass Prairie near the Whatcom trail." Over the next half-decade, he devoted his considerable energy and shrewdness to expanding his holdings, amassing a block of 470 acres that straddled upper Sumas River.

York's property soon became the centre of activity on upper Sumas Prairie. It was ideally situated for a grazing operation; seasonal flooding rejuvenated the yearly growth of grasses, while a long ridge raised his house, outbuildings and cattle pens above the high-water mark. York's herd of cattle grew accordingly, and he diversified into dairy, hogs, even chickens. By 1872, the *Mainland Guardian* described him as "the largest cattle owner and land occupier on the lower Fraser." York sat astride the Whatcom Trail, and his place soon became a stopping point for travellers, mule trains and cattle drives. In 1871, he built a 14-room house to accommodate paying guests, bringing the lumber for it across Sumas Lake by barge; he also operated a store "chiefly of liquid goods according to those who knew him."

The experiences of Sumas's early graziers clearly demonstrate how important Sumas Lake and Prairie had become to BC. Fraser River was BC's major highway, but Sumas Valley also was an indispensable transportation corridor. The *British Columbian* recognized this as early as 1862; it reported that "animals in large numbers are landed at Bellingham Bay, and driven thence up to Hope, simply in order to avoid the inconvenience and expense of the river transit." In short, steamboats alone could not transport the thousands of large animals required. Some years later, the paper urgently noted the danger of neglecting the land route to Yale: "Some hundreds of work animals have yet to come down to their winter pasture-ground on the Sumass and Chilliwack." Even into the 1870s, the *Mainland Guardian* could report from Yale that "large droves have been taken from here to the beautiful prairies of Sumas, where pasture is abundant." A government-sponsored survey from 1873 estimated that 3,000 "horned cattle" were being raised between New Westminster and Hope; of these, 1,300 were at Sumas and another 700 at Chilliwack.[54]

As shown in the lives of these White newcomers to Sumas—from Edwin Dodge to Volkert Vedder—the age of the prospector gave birth to that of the pastoralist and pre-emptor. Not long after their appearance, immigrants began to arrive who pinned their hopes of success on agriculture rather than the fickle promise of gold. In summer 1862, an unusual party of five arrived at Sumas: David Miller, with his young wife, Laura, and baby daughter, Lizzie, in tow; along with Laura's younger brothers, Chester and James Chadsey. The Millers and Chadseys had left Ontario the previous fall, wintered in Victoria, then crossed to New Westminster shortly after Lizzie's birth in March. The Chadsey brothers continued upriver to the Cariboo goldfields, but soon returned disappointed. At New Westminster, they obtained work from Edwin Dodge to harvest a supply of wild hay on Dodge's Flats. Arriving on lower Sumas Prairie in August, they were awestruck by the dense cover of bluegrass; here was the agricultural opportunity they were seeking, and they sent for the Millers to join them.

That October, after completing their haying contract, Chester and James recorded their first pre-emptions: 160 acres each on upper Sumas Prairie, encroaching on what would become Kilgard reserve. There is no evidence the Chadseys ever lived on the properties; by January 1864, they had moved their claims back across Sumas Lake to the land on lower Sumas Prairie they had first encountered as hired hands. At the same time, David Miller lodged his initial claim, the Chadseys his neighbours on the west, a man named John Langull on the east. Over the next seven years, Chester and James made a half-dozen new purchases, increasing their holdings to 640 acres each. By then, Miller had ceded his original claim to another Chadsey brother, George, and relocated to the banks of Fraser River. A second acquisition a few years later increased his holdings to 210 acres.

From the start, Miller and the original Chadsey brothers pooled their resources. The trio's claims bordered each other, forming a single, large holding; they even shared an informal "commons" located at the junction

George Chadsey with his growing family outside their wood-frame home on lower Sumas Prairie. One daughter has harnessed the family dog to a wagon, ready to take another daughter for a ride. Royal BC Museum and Archives, B-08437.

of their lots, which was recorded on land surveys of the time. They entered into a partnership—Miller & Co., named after the eldest member—to provide feed and pasturage for livestock. During their inaugural Sumas winter, Miller travelled to Oregon to purchase the company's first cattle, seed and farm implements, which arrived the following spring. In fall 1863, they began renting out their land as winter pasturage for other graziers, even taking charge of the latter's stock. They also started grazing cattle on islands in Fraser River, opposite Sumas; with water levels low through the winter months, cattle could easily swim to the fertile islands. Later, when changes in colonial laws permitted it, they took out pastoral leases for the islands.

Miller and the Chadseys shrewdly turned the natural resources of their new properties—nutrient-rich grasses coveted by stock owners—into an immediate source of income. The trio then used this income to set up their own agricultural operations. Drawing on the experience of mixed farming in Ontario, they planted non-indigenous crops intended for human consumption: potatoes, beets, oats and wheat. They also established the first dairy operation in Sumas Valley. In March 1865, the *British Columbian* reported, "Miller and Co are going into dairying on a big scale this coming summer, and will be able to supply the lower country with butter and cheese." That July, the company began selling "fresh butter from Sumass

Prairie" in New Westminster stores, and the product quickly became a fixture there.[55]

The emerging White settlement at Sumas stood out from the pattern in the rest of BC. While the latter was dominated by resource-extraction industries, there was a strong agricultural orientation at Sumas. This was so because the valley had something rare in BC: naturally arable land that could sustain at least some of the plants and animals favoured by the newcomers. The Sumas settlement also stood apart thanks to the early presence of women, children and families. As was the case for nearly all resource-based, frontier societies, BC's non-Native population was predominantly adult and male. In 1870, men outnumbered women three to one, a ratio that changed little over the next four decades. But at Sumas, women and children were present even among

In 1862, Laura Miller arrived on lower Sumas Prairie with her husband, David, newborn daughter, Elizabeth, and brothers Chester and James Chadsey. She successfully met the challenges of her new frontier life. (c 1865), Chilliwack Museum and Archives, PP500063.

the first wave of immigrants. Laura Miller, Jane Evans and Maria York, along with their children, accompanied their husbands to the far west. Other early spouses included Hannah Chadsey, wife of Chester Chadsey; Mary Lewis, wife of Thomas Lewis and sister of Charles Morgan Richards; Anne Hall, married to former Royal Engineer William Hall; and Harriet Hall, wife of former sapper Matthew Hall and sister of William Hall.

The stories of these women are as fascinating as any from this time. Twenty-six-year-old Laura Miller was three months pregnant when she left her Ontario home in fall 1861 for the long, arduous trek to Victoria. She moved to New Westminster within weeks of daughter Lizzie's birth; five months later, she arrived at lower Sumas Prairie and set about carving out a home on the lush grassland, seeing to the needs of her husband, brothers and infant daughter. A photograph of her from this time suggests why she was up to the task: small but not frail, determined and intelligent.[56]

Widowed at 35, Jane Evans raised a large family and operated one of Sumas Valley's biggest farms. Chilliwack Museum and Archives, PP500430.

Jane Evans was an equally remarkable woman. In 1863, Jane Wells set out from Ontario with her sister-in-law Sarah, joining Jane's younger brother and Sarah's husband Allen, in Yale. At Yale, the Wellses met Charles Evans, who hired Allen to manage his expansive properties on the eastern edge of lower Sumas Prairie. Soon after, on March 9, 1866, Jane married Charles at Yale Methodist Church. The couple's first son, John, was a honeymoon baby; Charles Jr. arrived the following year, and a year after that, daughter Sarah. Upon Charles's death in 1871, Jane became sole owner of the Evanses' Sumas properties and immediately moved the family there.

A widow at the age of 35, with three children under the age of five and responsible for hundreds of acres of fertile prairie and farmland, Jane set about making a new home. With determination and shrewdness, she succeeded in building one of the largest agricultural operations in the Fraser Valley. And she was wise enough to ask for help: nephews David and John Wells joined her after she sent word back to Ontario; she leased a large portion of her property to Chinese tenant farmers (soon the property was known as China Ranch); and she employed Sto:lo men on her land and Sto:lo women in her house. The result was not only material success, but a household that was exceptionally tolerant and liberal-minded for the time—or for any time. Years later, Charles Jr. would recall with emotion the loving Sto:lo women who nursed him and his siblings, and the industrious Sto:lo men who worked the family's land.

Along with the Miller and Evans clans, the Yorks also settled in Sumas as a family. Leaving England in 1854, Maria York, her husband Thomas, and daughter Phoebe, lived in Nanaimo, Whatcom and Yale before settling on upper Sumas Prairie in 1865. By then Maria and Phoebe York were well experienced with the rigours of pioneer life. The following year, 16-year-old

Phoebe left home to marry Charles Delaney, a former sapper who stayed in BC after the Royal Engineers departed. Delaney met Phoebe in Yale, where he was working as a blacksmith and wagon maker, and the two were married by an Anglican priest on September 3, 1866. The newlyweds settled in Yale, but tragedy soon struck. One Saturday evening in May 1867, Charles was returning home by steamer from business downriver; a few miles short of Hope, he "fell overboard and was no more seen." A widow at 17, Phoebe returned to her parents' home to grieve. Life brightened some months later when a Scots-Irishman named William Campbell moved onto the sparsely populated prairie. Phoebe knew little about 32-year-old Campbell's previous life when, on September 24, 1868, the pair were married in the Sumas Methodist Church.

Campbell was aware that his bride had previously married and had been widowed; he also knew enough to keep quiet about his own marital history. Shortly after 1862, when he recorded his first pre-emption at Maple Ridge (across the Fraser from Fort Langley), he had entered into a country marriage with 13-year-old Matilda Allard. Matilda was the niece of Cowichan Confederacy chief T'Soshia and daughter of HBC trader Ovid Allard. The couple produced two daughters—Mary Agnes and Jennie—before Campbell decided to move on. Abandoning Matilda to fend for herself and their daughters, he resettled on a ridge immediately southeast of the Yorks. To all appearances, William Campbell was a vigorous, rough-hewn bachelor in Thomas York's own image, and the Yorks were no doubt relieved when Phoebe and he got together.

The new Mr. and Mrs. Campbell moved with speed and cunning to increase their own land holdings. One month after their marriage, Phoebe applied for the military grant she was entitled to as the widow of a former Royal Engineer, signing her application papers "formerly Phoebe Delaney." The land she claimed was the same Maple Ridge lot her new husband had pre-empted in 1862, which he strategically abandoned. With this sleight of hand, the couple retained possession of a property William had worked on for years, while also freeing him up to pre-empt anew, this time on upper Sumas Prairie. By 1871, further purchases had expanded Campbell's holdings to 420 acres, second only to his father-in-law among upper Sumas landowners. Meanwhile, the couple were busily building a large family, producing seven children over two decades.[57]

By our standards, William Campbell's treatment of his first family was cold-hearted and cruel. Of course, he was not the only White newcomer to discard a Native wife and family when they became inconvenient: Hudson's

Bay Company governor George Simpson himself had done the same thing. Yet abandonment was not the norm. HBC factor and colonial governor James Douglas was loving and loyal to his Metis wife and children, as were numerous other company men. At Sumas, men such as Mortimer Kelleher and Richard Killig were likewise, manfully shouldering the responsibility of caring for their blended families. Kelleher was an Irishman who arrived in BC during the Fraser gold rush. Sometime before summer 1863, he settled on Sumas Prairie close to Peter Anderson, recording a claim to the land some months later. Kelleher ranched there for a few years but grew increasingly frustrated with the yearly flooding; he moved across the Fraser to Mission, where he started a family with Madeline Job, a Nooksack woman. Their son Cornelius would later play a large role in retaining and recording the stories passed on by his mother and her Nooksack and Sto:lo relatives.

German-born Richard Killig had a similar story. The gold rush brought him to Yale, where he ran an informal inn for a number of years. Sometime around 1863, he settled along a bend of upper Sumas River, between Kelleher's property and the shores of Sumas Lake. The following February, he recorded his claim to the 160 acres of wet prairie "adjoining the land owned by Che-Midstkie, the chief of the Sumass Indians" (the latter was the future site of Kilgard reserve). "Honest Dick," as he was affectionately known to locals, married into the Kilgard Sema:th, and the anglicized version of his name—Kelly—has remained prominent in the community ever since.

Overall, mixed relationships were uncommon in Sumas Valley because a large number of immigrant men arrived with wives and children. Also, White men who came as bachelors often found a spouse among their neighbours' households. There were three cases of this in 1868 alone: James Chadsey married Harriet Hall, the 24-year-old daughter of former Royal Engineer corporal William Hall; Harriet's older sister, Susan, wed Donald McGillivray; and of course, William Campbell found his bride Phoebe next door, under the roof of Thomas York. The fact that early White families tended to have a lot of children also contributed to the settlement's stability and gender balance. Rural living encouraged large families; more children meant more helping hands around the farm, with daughters assisting their mother in the farmhouse and yard, sons their father in the barns and fields. The four Chadsey marriages produced a total of 27 children: William and Jane, 12; James and Harriet, 7; George and Eliza, 6; and Chester and Hannah, 2. Phoebe Campbell gave birth to seven children, and Donald McGillivray's wife Susan had six children.[58]

Tragically, Susan died shortly after the birth of her son Donald in June 1880. Maternal and child deaths were a fact of life in Victorian times, but at Sumas they were rare. Of the 40 babies born to the Chadseys, Campbells and McGillivrays, only one died in childhood: James Alonzo Chadsey, the third son of William and Jane, who passed away at nine months old. It is difficult to say why Sumas families were healthier than those elsewhere; after all, the settlement was sparsely populated and isolated, lacking access to medical care. One factor may have been the ready supply of nutritious food that was available: fresh meat, vegetables and of course milk, which was so essential for mothers and infants alike. The valley also had plenty of Sto:lo and White women experienced in childbirth who served as midwives for their neighbours. And White women could and did rely on local Sto:lo women—as helpmates in raising children, or as experts on homespun medicines and remedies made from Sumas Lake's rich plant life.

The presence of women and children was essential to the success of early White settlement on both sides of Sumas Lake. For one, it made that population more stable. Sumas farm families were literally rooted to their new homes, and all their efforts and resources were invested there. For another, wives and daughters contributed directly to the material success of their families and the local economy. The family farm was a single economic unit, with no clear separation between the workplace and home and with all family members doing their part. And while farmers might appear land rich, the agricultural economy of Sumas was cash poor. Modest amounts of money came in for market products such as butter, but most of the family's needs had to be met close to home, through barter or by making things themselves.

The abilities and hard work of farm wives and daughters were as important to a family's success as those of their husbands and sons. They kept their crude log dwellings clean and healthy; they made and mended the family's clothes; they planted and tended to large home gardens; they saw to farmyard animals such as chickens and ducks; and they turned all this into food, through the plump seasons of summer and early autumn as well as the lean months of late autumn and winter.

CHAPTER 6

A SECOND EDEN

Within 15 years of their first arrival, White immigrants had acquired roughly one-half of the land on either side of Sumas Lake, through pre-emption and purchase; by the 1880s, the rest had been claimed. Yet the White population in Sumas Valley remained low: a few hundred at most, counting men, women and children. While low in numbers, the immigrant farmers were able to transform the physical environment of their new home, with the aid of the plants, animals and technology they had brought with them. Meanwhile, White settlers were forced to adapt to the things they could not change. From this interplay—between controlled change on the one hand and adaptation on the other—emerged the distinct economic and settlement patterns of Sumas Valley.

The presence of a small number of very large landholdings was the most prominent of these patterns. By the early 1870s, a dozen individuals owned well over half the land acquired to that date. Charles Evans led with 790 acres; Donald McGillivray, Volkert Vedder, Chester Chadsey and brother James each held 640 acres, a full square mile. Thomas York (470 acres), William Campbell (420 acres) and Peter Anderson (360 acres) controlled much of upper Sumas Prairie. On the lower Sumas, William Hall and Thomas Lewis occupied lots of just over 300 acres; David Miller and George Chadsey, properties of just over 200 acres. This amounted to nearly 6,000 acres, an average of 470 acres per owner. Two decades later, all but one of these holdings was still intact.[59]

The existence of oversized properties in the middle of the Fraser Valley may come as a surprise to us. We associate such sprawling estates with the dry cattle country of the interior, and we think of valley property as so limited and valuable that only intensive agriculture can survive. The large Sumas estates defy not only our expectations—they clashed with the hopes and values of the very men who owned them. The prospect of being master of their own home had drawn White immigrants west in the first place. They rejected the British model of a small propertied class controlling

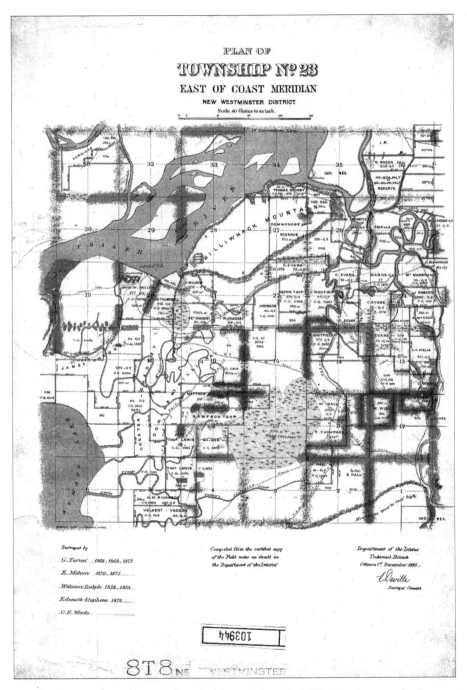

An official survey map of lower Sumas Prairie, completed in 1886. Note the sprawling properties of James and Chester Chadsey, Donald McGillivray and others. Plan 8 Tray 8 New Westminster is included with permission by the Surveyor General Division of the Land Title and Survey Authority of British Columbia.

large, inherited estates, with tenant farmers and wage labourers working the fields. Many immigrants had their first taste of land ownership in Ontario or the US, and now looked to BC as it opened up to White settlement. These newcomers were committed to the family farm ideal: each man owning his own land, equipment, house and outbuildings, running them with the help of his wife and children. On a personal level, the ideal held out the promise of material well-being, social standing and family stability. More broadly, the family farm ideal was seen as a linchpin of society, providing the basis for a prosperous, orderly and moral people.

The logic of the family farm demanded modest holdings, small enough that a family could work its property on its own, and small enough that there was enough land to go around. The quarter section (160 acres) was the standard set in government pre-emption laws. This standard was based on the model of the Prairies and extensive wheat farming; in areas of more intensive agriculture, smaller holdings were seen as ideal. Allen Wells told officials that, for Sumas and Chilliwack, "small farms—50 acres or less—are the best for the country." Yet Wells owned more than six times that amount, as did the top ten landholders of Sumas.

Why was there such a disparity between the small-property ideals of early White farmers and the large holdings they actually possessed? One reason had to do with timing. The greatest property expansions in Sumas Valley occurred in the year following passage of the 1870 Land Act, which eased the process by which you could pre-empt and purchase land. A depressed colonial economy meant few newcomers were on hand in search of land; the small number of established graziers took the opportunity to grab large chunks of upper and lower Sumas Prairie, land they were grazing on already. When the rate of immigration increased after BC joined Confederation, land seekers were shut out of the most fertile tracts on either side of Sumas Lake.

A second reason was that the physical environment of Sumas Valley created the need for oversized properties. The valley's high water table, sandy soil and yearly flooding could not sustain the White immigrants' preferred model of mixed agriculture, with its dependence on cultivated grains and intensive farming practices. The grasslands around Sumas Lake produced some of the highest yields of grass per acre in the province. The indigenous blue-joint grass that carpeted the valley, reaching four to six feet, was particularly nutritious. The problem was that horses and cattle were hulking herbivores weighing anywhere from 500 to 2,000 pounds. Huge quantities of even the most nutritious grasses were required to feed them.

Sumas graziers needed access to large expanses of grassland for pasturage and hayfields just to survive—thus the large holdings of the Chadseys, Mc-Gillivray, York and others. The demands of a pastoral economy produced these holdings, and in turn these holdings allowed that pastoral economy to dominate Sumas Valley.

Like all good farmers, Sumas pastoralists adapted their practices to suit the seasons. From early on, Sumas Valley winters were given over to grazing, by both local stock and animals driven from the interior. The season was relatively mild and wet in the Fraser Valley; grasses, rushes and other forage generally continued growing through the year. At the same time, the waters of Sumas Lake were low, opening up more land for stock to roam and graze. The amount of winter grass was never enough to last until spring, so graziers had to depend on hay that had been put up the previous fall. Wintering stock on upper and lower Sumas Prairie continued as a yearly tradition into the 20th century. The 1894–95 season provides just one example: through the chilly, wet months, three herds grazed along McGillivray Creek, another three along lower Sumas River, and a final one farther down toward Fraser River. These were in addition to herds wintering across the lake, on upper Sumas Prairie.

As temperatures rose moving into spring, Sumas grasses gained new life. Oftentimes, before letting their herds onto the land, graziers would set fire to the winter grass to make the early spring growth thicker. The *British Colonist* noted the practice as early as April 1867, reporting that there were "very great prairie fires at Sumas." The practice lasted into the 20th century, as Sumas farmer Charlie Power explained:

> Previous to the grass becoming green, someone would go out there and set fire to the old [winter] grass. They'd be firing all over the prairie. And the green growth would come up, and the water would come up. And it [fire] would die down.

Through May and June, the grazing cattle were forced from lower grassland by rising waters. Herds on upper Sumas Prairie could find refuge atop one of the sandy ridges that rose up to 30 feet from the valley floor. In one of his yearly reports prepared for BC's Department of Agriculture, Orion Bowman wrote that the ridges "were of great advantage in the establishment of cattle ranches," as they could be used to "keep the cattle during high water and winter and use the native fodder and pasture to advantage." Fritz Stromberg, who grew up on a dairy farm at the foot of Vedder Mountain, recalled tending to his father's herd. "The water came up and pushed us from one ridge to the other," where hay had been laid up. Those years when even the ridges were covered, Stromberg and his younger brother William drove the herd up the mountain slope, to feed on the leaves and shoots of vine and broadleaf maples—"they were crazy for maple leaves."

The most productive growth of grasses and forage came after the high water receded and the heat of summer set in. As Stromberg explained, farmers had to make sure the high water had gone all the way down and then "wait for a good rainstorm…because it [flood water] formed slime on the top of the grass. You get a good rainstorm, it would wash all of that off." With the grass clean and thick, cattle were let loose to fatten themselves on the rich growth. In late summer, herds were driven off the prairies to let the early-fall crop grow; this was then harvested and put up as hay for winter. Graziers often worked together, as farmer Jack McCutcheon recalled: "Big ranchers would club together and start putting up wild hay in stacks. But before they started to cut, they would buy a keg of whiskey and put it in a shack in the centre of the laying area." Hayers had to wait to the end of the day for the whisky, but it was a great spur to work.[60]

The existence and use of large tracts of "commons" land was another example of how Sumas farmers adapted their thinking and practices to suit environmental conditions. The idea of open land as a common resource

A typical scene of Sumas Valley's pastoral economy: a lone horseman overseeing a herd of grazing cattle. Chilliwack Museum and Archives 1973.034.028.

went against one of the most dearly held values of the time: the sanctity of private property. The existence of commons land had a long history in British common law and practice, although the tradition was little practiced in 19th-century North America. Oftentimes, where it was practiced, the land defined and used as commons was wetlands, on the fringe of drier, privately owned property. Such was the case around Sumas Lake, which each year expanded to cover an additional 5,000 to 6,000 acres. This seasonally flooded acreage was called "marginal land," and it defeated the usual steps needed to take ownership of it: the land was not worth the asking price, legal property surveys were difficult, and fences and other improvements were routinely washed away.

The result was that thousands of acres of rich grassland on upper and lower Sumas Prairies "lay as a common." Twice each year, Sumas graziers—White and Sto:lo alike—drove their stock onto the grasslands, where they were let loose. The cattle were branded so their owners could be identified when the time came to collect them. This was not always an easy task: cattle often became mired in swampland, lost in thick bush or stranded on small ridges encircled by rising waters.

Chilliwack stockholders also took advantage of the Sumas commons. Allen Wells had his herds "driven down to the big commonage on Sumas Prairie" near the mouth of Vedder River, where a hired hand tended to them. The commons also was harvested for its hay. "They had a kind of gentleman's agreement," Fred Zink of lower Sumas Prairie explained. "If a man went out and cut a swath around a certain tract of land, why that was his hay. And nobody would infringe on his rights to the hay." The tracts cut ranged from 25 to 40 acres; the hay would be brought back to the farmer's property or left in stacks in the field, curing under a blanket of sod. The cured stacks would then be used when graziers drove their stock to the prairies for winter.

The sharing of "marginal lands" on either side of Sumas Lake occurred because of their wetland nature, not because of past practice or traditional values, as in Britain. Sumas farmers were not budding communists. They were keenly possessive of their private property; the chance to acquire their own land had been their main reason for moving to the valley. Where they could, they threw up split-rail fences to mark it out and protect it. Cultivated portions of their property, such as orchards and vegetable gardens, were enclosed; even grassland that stayed above the yearly flooding was sometimes fenced. Sumas and Chilliwack graziers believed that clear property lines and good fences were essential for their economic well-being. One of their first collective political efforts came in 1869, when they banded together to demand that colonial fence laws be extended to their lands.[61]

Along with their own large holdings and the existence of common pasturage, Sumas farmers gained access to grazing land through pastoral leases. The 1870 Land Act permitted local property holders to lease an unlimited amount of unclaimed grassland, at very low rates. In December 1870, Thomas York applied for a lease of 2,000 acres on upper Sumas, for a term of 10 years. On lower Sumas Prairie, Donald McGillivray and Chester and James Chadsey made similar applications. Meanwhile, David Miller obtained a lease for 300 acres (at four cents per acre per year) spread over three islands in the middle of Fraser River, directly opposite Miller's Landing. Miller wintered his own stock here, as well as renting space to other graziers. Cattle were swum across to the islands at low water—as many as 100 at a time—and fed on the four-foot-high grass and rushes growing there.[62]

The farmers of Sumas Lake turned the valley's lush grasses into income in a number of ways: growing and selling feed to other graziers; pasturing the latter's stock on their land; raising beef cattle; even breeding cattle and horses. But it was dairy farming that soon came to dominate the local economy. Sumas Valley's environmental conditions made the dairy industry profitable, and it was dairying that Sumas landholders aspired to. They saw themselves as farmers, not ranchers, and running a successful dairy was closer to their dearly held family farm ideal. "This is grand dairy country," William Chadsey proclaimed, "with cool nights and no weeds to cause a taint of butter or milk." The municipal council promoted the valley's brand with the memorable slogan: "Sumas—Pre-eminently the Land of the Cow."

William's older brothers James and Chester, along with brother-in-law David Miller, had pioneered the Sumas dairy industry in the 1860s. The trio used their first years on lower Sumas Prairie to build up their dairy stock, and in July 1865 they started selling fresh butter to New Westminster stores. Soon, upriver and interior markets were tapped; in January 1867, the *Yale Examiner* reported that 3,000 pounds of Chadsey butter had been sold that season alone. The following summer, James and William pioneered a new method of marketing butter: rather than simply salting the butter, they sealed it in airtight cans of two, five and 10 pounds. In July 1868 alone, they moved 2,500 pounds to the Cariboo; another 6,000 pounds followed two months later. Into the 1870s, Miller and the Chadseys routinely garnered blue ribbons for their butter and cheese at the New Westminster and Chilliwack agricultural exhibitions.

The success of Miller and the Chadseys encouraged others. In 1874, John and David Wells began producing cheese on their upper Sumas Prairie farm, drawing on their experience in Ontario. Dairying at Sumas had grown "extensively," the *Mainland Guardian* reported a few years later; some farms were even using windmills to churn butter. Thomas York led the way on upper Sumas Prairie, having the largest stock of dairy and beef cattle. The industry grew over the next decade and a half, and in 1898, Orion Bowman opened Sumas Valley's first full-fledged creamery. Orion's creamery served 15 regular suppliers, producing 40,000 pounds of butter from the milk of 250 cows.[63]

Yet there were built-in limits to the dairy industry. Sumas dairymen did not have the technology—pasteurization or adequate refrigeration—to keep the milk fresh for any length of time. And until construction of the BC Electric Railway in 1910, they could not transport it to town markets quickly enough to prevent spoiling. Cheese making never grew past the initial start-up stage, leaving butter as the only viable product. Fresh butter had a longer shelf life than milk; salted or sealed butter lasted even longer.

Cattle were not the only animals introduced and raised on Sumas farms; pigs, horses, chickens and even sheep experienced varying degrees of success. Pigs in particular took to the fertile, mucky Sumas wetlands. As with cattle, swine were branded and allowed to roam free to graze—which, pigs being pigs, they did with gleeful abandon. "The hogs from the farms would roam the woods in the days before fences," Fred Zink recalled. During salmon spawning season, they would "feed on the fish from the streams." The swine even ventured into bogs, rooting out skunk cabbage; but this was dangerous, for they could be picked off by bears if they wandered too far. Sumas farmers were able to raise enough horses for their own needs, as transportation and draft animals; some had modest success at selling them. Chickens were a common sight around farmhouses, along with smatterings of domestic ducks and geese. Sheep, though, never took hold. George Chadsey and the Evans family brought in flocks, but after some early success grazing them on the Sumas Lake flats, the flocks dwindled and disappeared.[64]

By and large, Sumas Valley's White farmers succeeded in introducing the alien plants, animals and agricultural practices that were part of their way of life. As the indigenous grass cover was grazed off, Sumas farmers discovered that certain imported species could thrive. Red clover, timothy, reed canary grass and redtop grass were introduced and eventually replaced most of the indigenous species. Oats, barley and root crops (potatoes, turnips, mangels) also were imported and grown for feed. Of these, the mangel-wur-zel—a large, coarse beet—was the most successful and became a staple on Sumas farms. These alien species thrived because they were well suited to the natural environmental conditions of Sumas Valley.

Not everything the immigrant farmers tried succeeded. In most cases of failure, the agriculturists would step back and try something else, in a process of trial and error. But sometimes they persisted even after failure was obvious; efforts to grow wheat were the clearest example of this stubbornness. Wheat was so central to the White settlers' way of life that they found it hard to conceive of living without it. The immigrants' history books told them that Western civilization itself had been built on the cultivation of wheat; more immediately, bread remained the primary staple of their daily diet. Wheat was among the first imported crops introduced. Every year through the 1860s and 1870s, Sumas farmers seeded hundreds of acres with wheat, enjoying some early success. David Miller built the first grist-mill at Miller's Landing; in 1873, the Chadseys constructed a bigger mill on their property. Threshing machines were purchased, and newspapers touted the valley as the future "granary of the colony."

By 1880, though, crop yields had dropped dramatically; the Chadseys were forced to close the doors of their Sumas flour mill, relocating it to Mill Street in the new centre of Chilliwack city. Farm wife Mary Kipp noted the mill's failure in her diary, writing, "Alas, our wheat was too damp and soft to make food flour." The valley's high water table was one cause of Sumas's spongy wheat. Another was a growing season that started late and ended early: farmers could not sow their wheat immediately after the spring waters fell; they had to wait until the ground had dried out, putting back sowing to July. The wheat then needed to grow fast enough to be harvested before the fall rains came.

Yet it took decades for wheat growers to admit defeat. Farmers, newspaper editors and government officials stubbornly clung to the notion that the fertile grasslands around Sumas Lake could be converted into productive wheat fields. In 1892, after decades of promoting the crop, the Department of Agriculture finally declared that wheat-growing in the region was "utterly wrong from an economic point, for several reasons, the chief of which [was] the uncertainty of the harvesting weather." Local wheat might produce good-looking kernels, but these could not be made into marketable flour—their value was, quite literally, mere chicken feed.[65]

The failure of wheat aside, White farmers succeeded in transforming the Sumas Valley so that it supported their way of life. But they could not have done so without the aid of their biological allies. Through the late 19th century, the local population of imported cattle and horses dwarfed the number of White settlers. Large herds of these voracious herbivores crowded out indigenous grazers such as deer and elk. The decline of elk was particularly dramatic. Chief William Sepass and elder Dan Milo recalled elk herds "as numerous as cattle" grazing around Sumas Lake; by 1902, naturalist Allan Brooks had to report that the wapiti "was now extinct south of the Fraser." As deer and elk became ever more scarce, so did predators such as wolves, cougars and grizzly bears. But nature abhors a vacuum, and the departure of large predators made room for smaller ones. Coyotes—not seen in the valley prior to the coming of Whites—swept in to feed on the abundant supply of small indigenous mammals and plump alien species like chickens, along with domestic dogs and cats.[66]

The expansive grasslands on either side of Sumas Lake also were transformed, not by the plow but by alien grasses and large grazing mammals. Omnivorous pigs, hulking cattle and horses tore up indigenous grasses, while their hooves churned the native soil. This prepared the ground for new species already suited to the demands of pastoralism. Timothy, red clover, redtop and reed canary grass took hold on Sumas's wetland meadows, reseeding themselves each year and crowding out indigenous grasses. At the same time, noxious weeds moved in where given the chance, Canada and Scotch thistle being the most pernicious.

Along with rich native grasslands and the success of imported grasses, White settlers were quick to exploit the superabundance of fish and birds found in Sumas Valley. White fishermen took trout and sturgeon from Sumas Lake itself, while salmon were caught in the lake's tributaries or on Fraser River. After spawning season, farmers collected salmon carcasses by the thousands from local streams and used them as fertilizer for their orchards and gardens.

Most White fishing in and around Sumas Lake was for personal consumption, a convenient way to supplement a limited diet of meat, bread and root vegetables. Some efforts were made to establish a commercial fishery through the introduction of local and alien species. In 1889, 400,000 young salmon were let loose into the lake with hopes of boosting the salmon run; a second experiment two decades later saw 75,000 sockeye fry released. Nobody bothered to measure what impact these actions had on the fish stock already there. Catfish and carp also were introduced, apparently by private individuals. Catfish was a favoured catch of some anglers, while carp was mistakenly billed as a potential cash species—"to be raised on farms like cattle." The two bottom-feeding species were worse than failures. They were a bust economically, destroyed much of the lake-bed vegetation, and competed directly with indigenous trout and sturgeon.[67]

Compared with how important the lake's stock was to the Sema:th, the take of White fishermen was modest. White hunters took much more from Sumas Lake's supply of waterfowl. Sumas Valley was seen as "a hunter's paradise": every fall, ducks and geese would congregate there by the "millions," feeding along the lake's shores and wet prairies. Most Sumas households hunted waterfowl, children as well as parents. Barbara Beldam spent her childhood along the shores of Sumas Lake, and she later recalled hunting from the time she "was able to hold a gun." The Stromberg and Bellrose brothers also spent much of their youth in the valley's fields and wetlands. Men often camped on the lake for week-long hunts, sleeping in cabins or tents to be on site at the peak hours of dawn (when the birds took flight) and dusk (when they came low to land). Mallards, teal, widgeon and canvasbacks were the favoured ducks; geese and swans were coveted for their size, while grouse and pheasant were desired for their tenderness. The fowl was either eaten fresh or preserved through canning, with the rest sold in town.

The profitability of market hunting on Sumas Lake rose in the years prior to World War I, as the population of cities from Chilliwack to Vancouver rose dramatically. Allan Brooks and others made a modest but steady income supplying game birds for market. The Chadsey and Wilson brothers shot ducks and geese and sold them at Miller's Landing to steamboat stewards, who took them by the hundreds to city markets downriver. New Zealander Walter Harris eked out a living hunting on Sumas Lake, selling wild duck meat to the David Spencer store in Vancouver.

The growth of Fraser Valley towns also increased the number of those who hunted for recreation. Sport hunting at Sumas Lake had began four decades earlier, with the arrival of the Northwest Boundary Survey. Local fowl and game provided much of the food for the British and American commissions. While such practical hunting was the responsibility of enlisted men, the commissions' officers hunted for "sport," the one form of gentlemanly recreation available to them. Through the Victorian era, "sportsman" and "gentleman" were synonymous; Sumas Lake provided survey officers the opportunity of being both. During the colonial period, Sumas Lake was a favoured destination for the gentleman hunter, including the colony's highest officials. Returning from his court circuit through the interior in September 1864, Judge Matthew Begbie stopped over at Sumas

Lake, relaxing with "a few days' shooting." Begbie spread the word, and two months later Governor Frederick Seymour led a party up Fraser River to Sumas, "to enjoy a day's sport amongst the game with which the marsh lands abound at this season of the year."[68]

By the end of the 1800s, sport hunting had been democratized, transformed from a gentlemanly to a manly pastime. Hunters by the hundreds flocked to Sumas Lake from New Westminster, Vancouver and beyond. The pace quickened even more after the completion of the BC Electric Railway, with the company advertising weekend junkets of tourist hunting to city-weary men. Sumas Lake and its seemingly endless flocks of waterfowl were aggressively marketed as a "Sportsman's Eden." Sema:th elder Edward Kelly later recalled city hunters leaving Sumas Lake with "ducks hanging over their shoulders, riding the B.C. Electric tram back home to Vancouver."

The double-barrelled blasts of market and sport hunting seriously depleted the population of Sumas Lake waterfowl. Binge hunting became the norm, thanks to more lethal firearms (such as pump-action shotguns) and the migratory nature of the birds (with so many appearing suddenly, for a limited period). We do not have enough information to measure the depopulation of Sumas waterfowl in numbers, but anecdotal evidence gives us some idea of its magnitude. Win Fadden of upper Sumas recounted one tale of excess: "For an hour at dusk, why a good shot would get anywhere from 20 to 40 ducks in an evening, just shooting them in flight." Allan Brooks provided more: 45 ducks bagged in two hours one October afternoon; a month later, 34 ducks and three geese in a few hours, with only 47 shots; and 23 mallards, along with an unspecified number of other ducks, in one December evening.

Brooks himself chronicled the decline of Sumas Lake's bird population in his published articles. He wrote of the Hutchins's goose: "The vast flocks that used to remain on Sumas Lake and prairie every fall and spring mostly pass over now, as they are too much disturbed." He also reported the absence of sandhill cranes, which "bred regularly in a cranberry bog at Sumas up to 1902." Meanwhile, the various species of teals had declined precipitously; formerly the second most common duck in the valley, they had been easy prey for hunters. Despite the evidence he provided himself, Brooks rejected claims that this decline was due to hunting, putting it down to changes in habitat or natural factors such as flooding.

Brooks's opinion was not surprising, given his career as a prodigious hunter. And indeed, the man presents us with an unsettling paradox. There was the bright side of Allan Brooks, the popular view of him today:

a respected, beloved naturalist, who passed along his unrivalled knowledge of Sumas Lake's wildlife and who produced lifelike drawings of fragile songbirds. Then there was the dark side of Allan Brooks, the coolly efficient killer. For while Brooks contributed as much as anyone to our understanding of Sumas Lake's natural history, he also killed more of the valley's animals than any other individual.

Born in India to a railway engineer father, Brooks spent nearly 10 years between 1887 and 1905 in Sumas. During this time, he relied solely on hunting for his livelihood, living and working in a ramshackle cabin on the wetlands of lower Sumas Prairie. He made a modest income market hunting; he made much more killing and preparing specimens for collectors from Victoria to the American East Coast. We cannot know exactly how many animals Brooks killed, but it must have been in the tens of thousands. By the time of his death in 1946, his private collection alone numbered some 9,000 specimens. Added to this were specimens he collected for others; the birds and mammals he hunted for market or ate himself; and the fact that, in the words of his biographer, "he must have given away tons of game in his day." Not all of these animals were taken in Sumas Valley, but the Sumas years were Brooks's most productive—or destructive, depending on how you look at it.[69]

Mammals also were hunted and trapped by White settlers in Sumas Valley. Deer was the most popular game: its meat was highly prized, and large numbers of the shy creatures came down from the mountains to graze along the shores of Sumas Lake. Sumas residents often banded together in daylong campaigns, using dogs to flush out their prey. One particularly murderous hunt, led by William Campbell, left nine carcasses lying along a short stretch of Sumas Lake beach. One witness recalled the gruesome spectacle: "Campbell had 30 hounds, and he would turn them loose on the Vedder Mountain. The hounds would chase the deer, and the deer would hit for the lake; and the hunters would pick them off as they came down."

Smaller mammals such as mink, muskrats and rabbits were trapped or shot. Pelts were sold to local markets, and a few local residents made money stuffing and mounting specimens. William Hall turned to taxidermy after a debilitating injury to his left leg (he was gored by a long-tusk boar while feeding pigs on his farm). The former sapper built a workshop on the second floor of his log house and went to work preparing specimens for collectors. He became a regular contributor to the Provincial Museum, and in 1893 he supplied two cases of stuffed birds and mammals for the BC exhibit at the world's fair in Chicago. Allan Brooks made Hall look like a hobby collector. Along with bird specimens, Brooks bagged and mounted large numbers of mammals for institutions as far afield as Harvard University and the Smithsonian Institution. The BC Provincial Museum also was a customer, even though Brooks considered it "a little trumpery museum." Prices for mammal specimens were much higher than for birds: $1.50 per mink, $1 for weasel or fox, 75 cents per rabbit. Through the winter of 1899–1900, Brooks sold 25 civet cats, 17 mink, 17 rats, four skunks, three weasels, one wildcat and an unspecified number of rabbits.[70]

Sumas Valley was as rich a hunting field as any in BC. Meanwhile the three industries that drove the province's economy—fishing, logging and mining—were minor players in the valley. While fishing was central to the Sema:th way of life, it was far less important for Whites. Logging never took off for the same reasons that made the valley so suited to a pastoral economy. The yearly flood cycles kept trees off the rich grasslands, and the trees that did grow—the cottonwoods, willows and maples situated farther from the lake and along tributaries—were not marketable. White settlers even had to import the lumber needed to build their homes and barns. In 1867, the *British Columbian* reported that the steamer *Onward* had shuttled some 45,000 feet of lumber from lower Fraser River mills to Sumas and Chilliwack in just three trips. Two years later, missionary Thomas Crosby hitched a ride with "a great raft of lumber which was to be floated [up] the river to the Sumas to build barns." And when building his 14-room house on upper Sumas Prairie, Thomas York had to barge the lumber up Fraser River and across Sumas Lake. Some money was made from the wet cedar forest on the edge of upper Sumas Prairie. At the turn of the century, Orion Bowman and Charles Lamson opened a cedar mill and logging operation near the international border. But the local supply of timber soon ran out, and in 1908 Bowman moved the mill to the foot of Promontory Hill, just east of Vedder Crossing.

Dreams of mining riches proved just as elusive. Wild rumours of Sumas gold during the Fraser River rush were replaced by hopeful talk of Sumas coal. Coal was not as glamorous as gold, but in the steam-powered 19th century it was much more useful. Through the 1870s, there were a number of reports that Thomas York had found a thick seam of coal running through a ridge on upper Sumas Prairie. Surprisingly, given that York was a former coal miner, the rumours of Sumas coal were unfounded. But the search for coal continued; in 1894, the Mainland Prospecting Company received permission to prospect for and mine coal on the Upper Sumas Indian reserve. Numerous test drillings over the following decade failed to find a marketable seam of coal, but it was discovered that the mountain possessed great amounts of fireable clay. The company was not interested in clay and signed its mineral rights over to Charles Maclure, the founder of the Vancouver Fireclay Company at Clayburn. In 1911, Maclure opened the gates of the Kilgard Fire Clay Company plant, which immediately became the single largest employer in Sumas Valley.[71]

The life of White settlers around Sumas Lake was not all work, for the valley provided plenty of opportunities for recreation and play. And to an extent that was rare for its time, these opportunities were open to most everyone: girls and women as well as boys and men, those of modest means as well as the better off. Families, school classes and church groups packed meals and headed for one of the lake's beaches for a day's outing, or pitched blankets on river banks. For local newspapers, the outings were the equivalent of the teas and dances recorded on the society pages of city papers. Early in the new century, the *Abbotsford Post* reported on a party of 45 that travelled up Sumas River in two motor launches, then across Sumas Lake to "a delightful picnic ground." The children played, the men fished and the women cleaned up, before the party set out on their return journey, "a choppy sea on the lake adding to the excitement."

The long sandy beaches along Sumas Lake's western shore became favoured destinations. Growing up on upper Sumas Prairie, Neil MacKinnon recalled summer outings at Kennedy Ridge, which drew every White family in Kilgard: "There were races and games and swimming. Everyone brought food and the kids had a great treat—ice cream!" Myrtle Ferguson spent the summers of her youth at the rambling lakeshore house of her grandfather, George Bellerose. She later told an interviewer:

> There were always rowboats there. We would pack a lunch, and get in the boat, and row across to Kennedy ridge, where it was all sand. And we thought that was quite special, because we could run along the shore, and go in swimming. There was a nice place to have lunch, and return in the afternoon.

Some of the best photographs we have of Sumas Lake were taken during such outings: images of men, women and children relaxing on the fine Sumas sand, their boat pulled up behind them. While less picturesque, the rocky shore at Bellerose had the advantage of being accessible by land. The larger school and church parties travelled there along Yale Road. After 1911, the BC Electric Railway brought picnickers to the beach in the morning, and returned them home in the evening.

Two women look out over Sumas Valley toward Sumas Mountain, with Lakeshore Ridge jutting into Sumas Lake. The pair stand just above BC Electric Railway tracks on Vedder Mountain. The completion of the line in 1910 made it easier for day trippers to visit the lake. City of Vancouver Archives, Out P268 photographer Franklin Walter Hewton.

The lake's warm, shallow waters made it ideal for swimming. Ferguson recalled wonderful summer days spent in the water near her grandfather's house:

When there'd be a group of us staying there, we'd get up in the morning and have a swim before breakfast. It was just holidays. Another swim before lunch. Another swim in the afternoon. And again before we went to bed at night.

Win Fadden's sister Mary described days spent splashing along the lake's shores: "We made rafts in those days, as well as using the wooden tubs to sail in. Children had a good time playing in the high water."

Aside from rowboats and makeshift rafts, proper sailing craft took to the lake's often choppy waters. The Bowman clan's *Argo* was a common sight: a 25-foot, open-hulled sloop, its single mast supporting jib, foresail and rigging. Up to 10 people could squeeze onto the boat, which travelled by sail when the conditions were right, by four large oars when not. It was used mainly for day excursions on Sumas Lake, taking its passengers to picnics on shaded, sandy beaches. But the boat made longer journeys off the lake as well; one memorable trip in July 1897 was recorded by Ida Bowman in an unofficial "Log of the *Argo*." Leaving McGregor's ridge the morning of July 1, the crew of young sisters, brothers and cousins sailed across the lake, down lower Sumas River and into the Fraser. The *Argo* made quick time going downstream, and was in Victoria within days; on the trip back, it wound through the Gulf Islands before re-entering Fraser River. Rowing against the current, the crew arrived at the mouth of Sumas River on the 19th, where they fought their way "inch by inch." The boat finally emerged onto Sumas Lake in the dark, only to be hit by "a strong head wind....Lost our way and could hardly find the right slough." At 1:00 a.m. on the 20th, the weary crew finally struck home and trudged their way to bed.

During winter months, Sumas Lake and its tributaries regularly iced up, allowing residents to skate for miles. Charles Wilson of the Northwest Boundary Survey was the first to spot the opportunity. Returning to his frigid tent on the evening of November 12, 1859, Wilson dutifully recorded the day's temperatures: 12 degrees Fahrenheit the previous night, reaching a high of 30 degrees Fahrenheit by afternoon. The four inches of ice that had formed on the lake was "smooth and slippery as glass. I only wish I had my skates up here, should have good fun." Decades later, members of the Bowman families were avid skaters, as were George Bellerose's sons. In one delightful photograph from the turn of the last century, sisters Mary and Ida Bowman smoothly glide across Sumas ice, Nora York in tow, while brother Orion struggles awkwardly to keep up. Often, the White settlers had to improvise, as Mary Kipp's husband James explained:

Sisters Mary and Ida Bowman, brother Orion and Nora York enjoy a sunny-day skate on one of Sumas Lake's tributaries (1905). City of Vancouver Archives, Out P841.

> They made their skates in those days out of an old file or rasp or anything. They would take that sharp end and bend it up, like in the front, so you wouldn't stub your toes. Then they'd sharpen those files up…and they'd make good skates. They'd last a long while.[72]

Sleighing was another favourite winter pastime, as sled runners glided over the frozen lake and snow-covered ground. But conditions on Sumas Lake could turn deadly with little warning; the diaries of Charles Tate, the tireless Methodist minister, give us numerous examples of this. Setting out across the lake ice one afternoon in January 1876, Tate soon found himself trapped "in the midst of a snow storm which increased in volume" as he neared the centre of the lake. With visibility cut to a few feet, Tate struggled on by instinct until, well into the night, he finally reached the safety of the opposite shore. Nor could the lake ice always be counted on. Three years later to the day, while returning from Kilgard on horseback, Tate misjudged the ice's thickness: "My horse broke through. I managed to scramble on to the ice, and after considerable plunging and breaking of the ice, managed to get my horse out also."

Summer storms could be dangerous as well. Paddling across Sumas Lake in July 1876, Tate and his Sto:lo companion "were almost capsized. The wind began to blow when about in the middle, and in a short time the waves rose quite high." On a number of other occasions, the minister had to turn back because the southwestern winds were too strong. Autumn presented its own challenges: boats struck bottom in seasonally low water and horses sank in soggy trails. One Sunday in October 1878, Tate trekked 36 miles around Sumas Lake and back; he changed his mode of travel nine times, switching between foot, canoe, skiff and horse.[73]

Spring brought the mosquitoes. If Sumas residents viewed their valley as a second Garden of Eden, then mosquitoes were its serpent. Recorded complaints about mosquitoes go back to the first White visitors. Camped along Fraser River just downstream from Sumas Mountain, a grumpy Simon Fraser wrote, "Musketoes are in clouds, and we had little or nothing to eat." Fort Langley trader Archibald McDonald wrote that while his superiors might consider them "a very trifling annoyance," the annual invasion of mosquitoes made it impossible for his men to work and caused the Natives to flee. The Northwest Boundary Survey commissions suffered through the same plight, also resulting in work stoppages. Commission members ran out of adjectives to describe the yearly plague. "The musquitoes are *awful*," Caleb Kennerly wrote, closing one diary entry simply: "a day of pain and trouble."[74]

With the arrival of White immigrants, the wetlands of Sumas and Chilliwack Valleys gained the reputation as particularly fertile breeding grounds for mosquitoes. So bad were they, newspapers reported, that they frightened prospective settlers away, drove farmhands from the fields, and halted nearly all outdoor work. Locals were unanimous in describing the horrors caused by the vile insects. "I don't think that there's anybody realizes just what the people went through with those mosquitoes," Fred Zink told an interviewer. Humans could fight back with smoke pots and netting, but horses and cattle had to suffer unprotected. Charlie Power recalled that "you could wipe an animal down with your hand and it would be red with blood." As cows suffered, so did their production of milk, hitting at the very lifeline of the local economy. The only dissenting voice came from the reliably optimistic Myrtle Ferguson. She admitted that some years the mosquitoes could be a problem, but "there would be years when they weren't as bad." In either event, "they didn't last long"—most importantly, they were gone by summer, "when we were enjoying our swimming so much."

CHAPTER 7

PEOPLES DISPLACED

The arrival of White gold miners and pre-emptors through the second half of the 1800s triggered forces that irreversibly altered the lives of the Sema:th. Then the emergence of an agricultural economy, established by White farmers, changed how Sumas Valley was used and by whom. But the first and greatest assault on the Sema:th and their neighbours came from the smallest invaders. For the single most important factor in the dispossession of BC's first peoples was the introduction of disease—carried by microscopic viruses, germs and bacteria that were hidden inside the bodies of White newcomers. Just as tragic was the fact that the spread of disease was both unintentional and, at first, indirect. Measles, influenza, malaria, tuberculosis and especially smallpox: at the time, nobody knew what caused them or how they were transmitted from one person to another.

These maladies were endemic in Europe, which meant Europeans both carried them in their bodies and had some immunity to them. In the Americas the highly infectious diseases did not exist, and Indigenous peoples had no resistance to them. So when Europeans arrived, bringing the microscopic invaders with them, "virgin-soil" epidemics tore through defenceless populations, killing at a rate triple that of the Black Plague, which had ravaged Europe centuries before.

Regarding the Sto:lo in the lower Fraser Valley, scholars disagree on how many of these early epidemics struck or when they occurred. Some argue that a single smallpox epidemic struck in the fall and winter of 1781–82 or 1782–83, originating in Mexico and then travelling along Native trade routes to Puget Sound and north to the Fraser Valley. Other scholars argue that the region was depopulated by a series of smallpox epidemics. The first was introduced by Spanish explorers on the Washington coast in 1775; it was then carried by Indigenous traders north to the Fraser. Another, more limited outbreak then struck in the first decade of the 1800s, followed by another in the 1820s. The second argument, positing a series of epidemics, seems the stronger, for it captures the fluid demographic situation of the early-contact decades. In the words of anthropologist Robert Boyd, the depopulation of the lower Fraser River "may have been, not a single event, but a *process*, accentuated by several successive smallpox outbreaks, including all or some combination of the outbreaks recorded for the 1770s, 1800s, and 1820s."

Despite differences of opinion on the timing and number of epidemics, there is no disagreement that the invading diseases decimated the Sto:-lo. According to conservative estimates, two out of three Sto:lo died in what one historian has labelled "the Great Devastation." Additional epidemics of smallpox, measles and influenza struck through the mid-1800s. In 1853, smallpox ran rampant among the Nooksack and their Puget Sound neighbours; in 1862–63, a BC-wide epidemic laid waste to coastal and interior groups, and lingering outbreaks in the Fraser Valley lasted through that decade. These and other illnesses such as tuberculosis persisted through the rest of the 1800s, and the Sto:lo population continued to drop. With so many dying from disease, traditional food and resource gathering was disrupted, triggering malnutrition and outright famine, which killed many more. In the century following the first contact with White diseases, the number of Sto:lo had been reduced by as much as 90 to 95 percent: from a pre-contact population of between 25,000 and 50,000, it had dropped to an official total of 2,498 in 1882.[75]

The best sources we have on the deadly impact of the disease are elders of the Sema:th, Nooksack and other Sto:lo. Their oral histories of the Great Devastation begin by describing how their people were once so numerous they covered the Fraser Valley. Interviewed over half a century ago, Mrs. Vincent Peters of Seabird Island stated that "before the white man came, there were lots of people all over." Katzie historian Old Pierre explained how in earlier times the Sto:lo became so "crowded upon the land" that "their fires floated over the valley like a dense fog." Not once, but three times, they were struck by devastating catastrophes, only to multiply quickly afterward. More recently, Ray Silver spoke of the "thousands of people" who once lived in Sema:th territory.

Then the pestilence struck. "Once, everybody had smallpox," Bob Joe recalled solemnly. "Everything was dead and dry as if burnt. All the people were lying inside [the pit houses], dead." Nooksack elder Jack Jimmy added with emotion, "When the smallpox came, we just died like flies." Dan Milo provided the most detailed account of the depopulation of the Sema:th. "On the sand of Sumas Lake," Milo began, at the Sumas Lake right where Yarrow is, there was a group of Indians living there. They all died of smallpox. There was just one girl left. She done all the work to put away the dead. Across the lake at Kilgard, they called that Sumas tribe at that time. There was one [boy] left at that group of Indians that they called the Sumas tribe of Indians. This boy was left by himself, all the people died but him. He done all the work to put away the dead after everybody was dead. While he was out, he used to go to hunt out at Sumas Prairie, towards the lake. He hunting ducks. While he was out he saw smoke way over this end of the lake....So he went home and made up his mind that he come over the next morning. Which he did. He come around the lake on the south side of the lake, around the foot of the old Vedder mountain. When he come to this place where there [had been] a lot of people living, he got to the house....He went in and only found this one girl. He started to talk to her and ask her if all her people had died. She said "Yes, I'm the only one left." That's what the girl said. So the boy made up his mind to marry this girl. He was going to take her home to Kilgard. So he did. They lived together.

The Sema:th were hit especially hard by the waves of infectious disease and by the social and physical dislocation that followed in their wake. Because of this, much of their traditional history was lost. Ray Silver spent his boyhood on Kilgard reserve, sitting at the feet of his elders and listening to their stories. "They were a sad people, very, very sad," he later recalled. "See, they had the...smallpox that killed off thousands of them. The Native people lost everything, after the epidemic." Amy Cooper explained:

The Kilgards had a lot of stories....All the young people'd go to one house, and they'd get the older ones there to tell a story. And then they'd go to another house there the following night, and they'd tell stories there.

Cooper did not know whether anyone knew the stories anymore, since "these older people are all gone now."[76]

The Great Devastation also reshaped the human geography of the region. First, the surviving Sto:lo deserted smaller settlements to congregate in fewer, large villages. The Sema:th abandoned a number of sites that were scattered across Sumas Prairie, along the shores of Sumas Lake and up its tributaries. Villages such as Snanith disappeared, while surviving Sema:th congregated with their Nooksack cousins at Temixwtem. Second, other Sto:lo moved closer to Fraser River to more easily trade up and down the valley. Both the Katzie and Chilliwack did so; for the Sema:th, the increased focus on Fraser River enhanced the importance of Sumas Bar village.

Third, the demographic vacuum created by the epidemics triggered political instability and shifts in tribal territories. The clearest example of this was the movement of the Chilliwack onto the Fraser Valley floor and their occupation of the lower Chilliwack River all the way to its mouth. The retreat of Sumas Lake westward had made this former wetland habitable. At about the same time, disease struck the Sema:th, Pilalt and other valley peoples at what appears to be much higher rates than experienced by the Chilliwack, who were sheltered in their traditional territory among the Cascade Mountains. Elders such as Albert Louie testified to this reversal in tribal fortunes. Generations earlier, Louie explained, "the Pilalt was a big tribe....Chilliwack tribe was just a small one, just about half of that Pilalt." By the mid-1800s, the Chilliwack were the dominant group, pushing into areas previously controlled by the Pilalt and Sema:th.

The introduction of alien diseases fundamentally altered the human history of Sumas Lake. In their wake came the second most important force in the dispossession of the region's first people: government policies that shunted them off to constricted plots of land inaptly called reserves. The history of reserve-making in the Fraser Valley and BC is a complicated one, unique in Canada. In the rest of the country, treaties signed by government officials and tribal leaders designated what land was to be set aside for the use of Natives. No treaties were signed by the Sema:th or the rest of BC's first peoples. Instead, reserves around Sumas Lake were drawn, redrawn and redrawn again—even then, some of the most important issues were not resolved.

Initial efforts at reserve-making came during the term of BC's first colonial governor, James Douglas. Douglas was a former Hudson's Bay Company factor who was married to a Metis woman. He was genuinely concerned that the colony's Indigenous peoples be given the means to adapt to and survive the influx of White immigrants. In spring 1861, he ordered Col. Richard Moody to make a survey of lower Fraser River, marking out spots of occupation and cultivation; these would form the basis of "anticipatory reserves." Undermanned and overstretched, Moody's Royal Engineers could devote few resources to the job. After two years of sporadic work, the sappers had identified a half-dozen reserve sites, all along the banks of Fraser River.

One of these sites was located at Sumas Bar, described by Capt. Robert Parsons as "a village at the mouth of the Sumass River."

By 1864, the growing number of White immigrants seeking land was placing added pressure on Douglas. At the same time, Sto:lo leaders were adamant that their traditional territories be protected. The Royal Engineer surveys had done little to resolve the issue, and Douglas decided a more systematic effort was needed. That April, he appointed a former Royal Engineer sergeant, William McColl, to the task. McColl was ordered to immediately proceed up Fraser River "to lay out certain Indian Reserves at Sumas and Chilukweyuk." Settlements and cultivated spaces were to be included in reserves, with posts staked into the ground to mark "whatsoever land the Indians claim as theirs." Finally, reserves were to be set out "irrespective of the claims of settlers."

McColl spent six weeks in the field; using lower Sumas River as his base, he and his team traversed the valley from Chilliwack Prairie west beyond Matsqui. On May 16, 1864, McColl submitted his report and accompanying map to Joseph Trutch, the newly appointed commissioner of lands and works. In total, 14 reserves encompassing 39,900 acres were marked out. The Sema:th were split into two reserves. At 1,200 acres, Upper Sumas enclosed all land between upper Sumas River and Sumas Mountain, from Peter Anderson's claim in the west to the eastern shore of Sumas Lake. The Lower Sumas reserve was even more expansive: one-half of its 6,400 acres ran the length of lower Sumas River, taking in all the territory between Sumas Lake and the base of Sumas Mountain; the other half enclosed the southwest third of Nicomen Island. Villages were drawn at Sumas Bar and Papekwatchin, and a large tract of western Nicomen Island was designated as "summer potatoes."

The Sema:th and Sto:lo were satisfied with McColl's work, and from then on considered the "Douglas Reserves" the legally binding authority on the land question. White settlers were lived; with McColl still in the field, they launched a campaign to undermine him. A delegation visited officials in New Westminster to sound the alarm that "seven or eight miles square, including their ranches" had been handed over to the Sto:lo. A few weeks later, White farmers presented a petition attacking McColl's reserves as "unnecessarily large—10 acres to each family, and in several instances including lands already preempted and improved by actual settlers."

Colonial officials agreed with the White immigrants, but constrained by the lack of resources and confronted with the threat of Sto:lo unrest, they could not act immediately. Then, in 1867, Joseph Trutch turned his

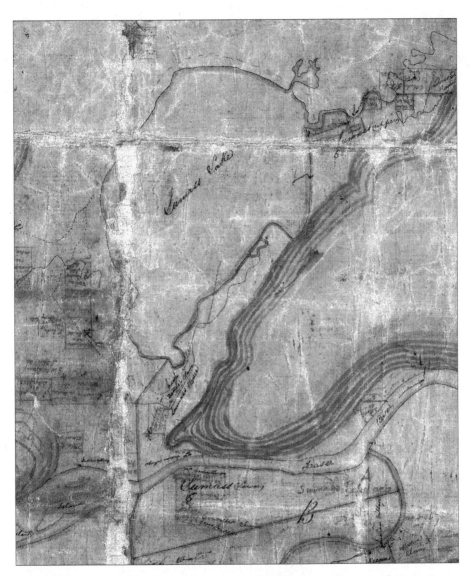

William McColl's map of the reserves he set out in 1864 (north is at the bottom). Upper Sumas reserve stretches back from the western shore of Sumas Lake and up lower Sumas River. Lower Sumas reserve includes all of the land along the lake's north shore to Fraser River, and then across to take in half of Nicomen Island. 31 Tray 1 Land Reserves is included with permission by the Surveyor General Division of the Land Title and Survey Authority of British Columbia.

attention to the issue, crafting a radically new reserve policy. Trutch started by rejecting McColl's reserve allocations as unauthorized and "excessive." He drafted clear instructions for surveyors to set aside only a bare minimum of land for Natives; then he reversed Douglas's policy, ordering surveyors to "leave out as far as may be found practicable such lands as have been settled upon, and improved by White persons." In 1868, Assistant Surveyor General Benjamin Pearse was sent into the field to carry out Trutch's instructions. Pearse visited each of McColl's 14 reserves, setting the size and location of new reserves. Pearse then passed along detailed instructions to former Royal Engineer sapper James Launders, who marked out and mapped the new allotments.

The results were breathtaking. The Sema:th received one additional reserve, but their total acreage plunged from 7,600 acres to 515 acres. McColl's Lower Sumas reserve was left with just 1.2 percent of its former land—and this was split into two isolated plots. Sumas 1 sat along the northern bank of Fraser River, on the southwestern point of Nicomen Island. McColl had noted large potato patches here; Launders likewise reported that "considerable land has been cultivated on this reserve" and drew a village on the site, but he and Pearse allotted only 32 acres. Pearse also instructed that a village reserve be set aside at Papekwatchin, but Launders dismissed the site as liable to flooding and claimed the Sema:th showed no interest in it. Close by, the surveyor found a half-dozen cultivated plots, which the Sema:th insisted be staked out. Launders refused, most likely because Pearse had not mentioned the patches. The Sema:th protested vigorously and the surveyor gave up trying to convince them, instead recommending that "some further enquiry be made or something done to secure to them in some way these patches."

After consulting his boss, Launders assigned Sumas 2 as compensation. The 43-acre plot sat nearly two miles up lower Sumas River, on its eastern bank just south of McGillivray Creek. Launders described the site as "chiefly wet prairie with a belt of stunted willow along bank of river." But he did not explain how Sumas 2 could be considered compensation for the cultivated patches and village site of Papekwatchin, several miles to the north on the far side of Fraser River. What he did report was that "the Indians were not well satisfied, they wanted all their original claim": that is, all the land on either side of lower Sumas River, from its mouth upstream to Sumas Lake. Even more curious, neither Pearse nor Launders made note of Sumas Bar, which continued to be the main settlement of the lower Sema:th and which was identified as an "Indian Reserve" on official land survey maps from the 1870s on.

The Upper Sumas reserve also was reduced, to one-third of its former size. Situated two miles off the western shore of Sumas Lake, its 440 acres stretched northward from upper Sumas River to the first rise of Sumas

Mountain, straddling Marshall Creek. "Three-fourths of this reserve is prairie," Launders reported; the remainder climbed above the flood plain, covered in pine and maple with clearings made for Sema:th houses and barns.[77]

Trutch's reserve system of 1868 was arbitrarily designed and imposed in a high-handed, often incompetent way—not surprisingly, its results were staggering. Using Trutch's own conservative population figures, the Upper Sumas reserve encompassed 55 acres per adult male (13 acres per person). The Lower Sumas reserves were reduced to 3.4 acres per adult male (0.75 acres per person). The latter fell well short of even Trutch's own tightfisted target of 10 acres per family. The new reserve boundaries also pushed the Sema:th back from the shores of Sumas Lake and granted only limited frontages along the banks of upper and lower Sumas River.

Sto:lo and Sema:th leaders protested loudly against Trutch's handi-work. They immediately petitioned Governor Seymour to voice their concern: "The white men tell us many things about taking our lands," they wrote; they called on the Governor to stop the theft. More petitions followed with each passing year.

In 1874, more than 100 chiefs—once again including leaders of the upper and lower Sema:th—wrote the federal government to express their anger at being "trampled on" and to assert their belief that the goal of White settlers and officials was "to exterminate us as soon as they can." The chiefs stated pointedly:

> Our gardens have not been protected against the encroach-
> ments of the Whites....All prairies have been taken from us
> by White men. We see our White neighbours cultivate wheat,
> peas, etc., and raise large stocks of cattle on our pasture lands,
> and we are giving them our money to buy the flour manufac-
> tured from the wheat they have grown on the same prairies.

These were precisely the problems confronting the Sema:th as White im-migrants built their pastoral economy in Sumas Valley. The petitioners noted, "Sumass, at the junction of Sumass River and Fraser, with a pop-ulation of seventeen families, is allowed 43 acres of meadow for their hay [Sumas 2], and 32 acres of dry land [Sumas 1]." This amounted to 4.5 acres per family. At the time, the average size of the top 12 White farms on upper and lower Sumas Prairies was 470 acres, together tying up near-ly 6,000 acres.[78]

The piecemeal reserve system put in place by colonial officials met further opposition after BC joined Confederation in 1871. Responsibility for Native peoples and their lands now rested with the federal government, which was determined to bring the new province in line with the rest of the country. No treaties had been signed on the mainland, and the size of reserves in BC fell well short of the guidelines followed east of the Rocky Mountains. But the province refused to hand over any Crown land for reserves, remaining adamant that it be kept open for White settlers alone. A joint Indian Reserve Commission was set up in 1876 to resolve the issue, although it took three years for it to turn its attention to Sto:lo territory.

In spring 1879, the sole remaining commissioner, Gilbert Sproat, arrived in Sumas Valley with a team of assistant surveyors and immediately set to work. Sproat recognized immediately that the existing reserves were inadequate; at the same time, he knew that most of the good land surrounding them was already taken up by White settlers. Struggling to reconcile these conflicting factors, Sproat managed to increase the number of Sumas reserves to seven and more than double their total acreage to 1,343. Sumas 1 was wholly new: the 284-acre Yaalstrick Island sat in the middle of Fraser River, opposite Miller's Landing. It was the largest of three islands David Miller had leased as pasturage, and the Sema:th requested that they be allowed to use it for the same purpose. Sproat agreed, noting that there was no place on existing reserves for the lower Sema:th to graze their cattle and that White farmers had tied up the remaining grassland of lower Sumas Prairie. Sumas 2 added five acres to the old Lackaway reserve, and Sumas 3 approved the small timber reserve land surveyors had assigned on the western slope of Chilliwack Mountain.

Gilbert Sproat getting some much-deserved rest in front of his tent. Sproat did his best to balance the competing interests of the Sto:lo and White landholders. Royal BC Museum and Archives, A-01771.

Papekwatchin (Sumas 4) was another new reserve, located on Nicomen Island across from Sumas Bar; it was created as a replacement for the small lot Launders had set aside some miles downriver. Sproat decided the new 235-acre site was a more suitable size and location for the Sema:th's potato fields than the flood-prone property to the west; the Sema:th agreed to surrender the latter in exchange for the former. Papekwatchin had the added advantage of being a traditional settlement occupied for generations.

Back across Fraser River, Sproat reaffirmed the boundaries of Aylechootlook (Sumas 2 on Launders's map, now Sumas 5), as the Sema:th continued to harvest it for hay. The commissioner rejected a Sema:th request to establish a reserve on the opposite side of lower Sumas River; the tribe wanted to log it for cedar, but Sproat considered it too sparsely wooded for a timber reserve. On upper Sumas Prairie, Sproat had the lines of the old 440-acre reserve "squared up," adding 126 acres of treed mountainside to the new Sumas 6. Finally, Sproat created a third new reserve two miles south, a quarter section just short of the American border that had not been pre-empted. Sumas 7—initially referred to simply as the Sumas reserve, but which came to be known as York's reserve—straddled upper Sumas River and the old Whatcom Trail, to the south of Thomas York's property. Sproat decided the land would support the upper Sema:th's potato fields, despite the fact it was heavily timbered and partially covered by water, and its soil was acidic.

Sproat was satisfied with his work at Sumas. The Sema:th, he wrote, had "their potato land, their hay patch and their stock run, arranged so as to be of the least inconvenience to the Somass white settlers." Sproat was unique among his peers for his sincere concern for the plight of Indigenous peoples, and for his determination that the reserve system actually help those it was designed for. But even Sproat's heartfelt sympathy was not enough to overcome the failings built in to that system. The reserve and land system constructed by White authorities was just that—a *land* system. It proved to be a poor fit for Sumas Lake and its wetlands, where the line between water and land was blurred and ever changing.

Sproat arrived at Sumas Valley in the spring of 1879 and witnessed the yearly rise of flood waters. "The season was wet," he reported. "In places the water was so high as to cover the land which the Indians wish me to look at." The Sema:th had adapted to this annual cycle by travelling to seasonal resource sites. They believed they had a right to both these seasonal sites and land they occupied the rest of the year, even if that land was annually flooded. Sproat and other reserve-makers disagreed. Sproat believed he knew what was best and focussed on sites above the high-water line; he rejected Sema:th claims for flood-plain land, seeing it as unsuitable for agriculture. This had the effect of leaving the Sema:th and their neighbours with more heavily treed property, harder to clear than prairie and lacking the latter's lush grasses. It also pushed the Sema:th back from the shores of Sumas Lake, constricting access to their primary resources.[79]

Despite its limitations, Sproat's 1879 work provided the basis for the reserve system we have today. A set of detailed, official maps of the reserves was drafted, and promptly approved by the federal government. Characteristically pigheaded, the province dragged its feet for a decade before signing off. But the issue was far from settled. Through the late 1890s and early 1900s, the BC government added its voice to a rising chorus of White public opinion that clamoured for a reduction in reserve land, which, in their eyes, was not being properly used. Meanwhile, the federal government was hearing from Native leaders that the reserves were too small for their people's needs, leaving them destitute. At a stalemate, Victoria and Ottawa agreed to set up the Royal Commission on Indian Affairs to decide whether each of BC's existing reserves needed to be enlarged or reduced. Through 1915, the commission travelled the province to hear testimony from Indigenous leaders and the occasional White representative, before handing down its decisions. While valuable territory was opened up for White settlement and development elsewhere in the province, the lines of the Sumas reserves were not touched. The Sema:th actually succeeded in gaining a new reserve that enclosed land they were using as a burial ground. The six-acre Sumas 12 was located just above the bank of Fraser River, to the west of lower Sumas River.

More remarkable was the testimony of scores of Native elsders, dutifully recorded and published by the commission in 14 bound volumes. These sessions were the rarest of events: chiefs speaking directly to representatives of the provincial and federal governments, at length and in public. Leaders of the upper and lower Sema:th were among those who voiced their thoughts on how the land question had been dealt with over the past half-century. Both Selesmlton (chief of Upper Sumas, also called Chief Ned) and Johnnie Lewis (subchief of Papekwatchin and Aylechootlook) rejected claims that their people were not making full use of their lands. They argued that the existing system—of both reserve land and the right to fish and hunt—failed to adequately provide for their people.

Selesmlton spoke with passion in defence of Sema:th territory:

> This is [our] land, and that is what the old people know and
> used to say....The old people used to say that the White peo-
> ple will be shoving you around all over this open prairie to get
> our food....When I first come up to be a grown boy myself,
> they fixed up this place and surveyed it for us people. They
> owned it, and that is what is worrying me all this time, be-
> cause I am always poor. I don't get satisfactory food for my
> children to eat.

The chief voiced his suspicion that the commission was designed as part of
the decades-long campaign to reduce reserve land. "I want to find out—
what is the meaning of this Commission?" he challenged the chair before
being cut off.

Subchief Lewis testified next, expressing anxiety over the future of the
Papekwatchin reserve:

> My old parents belonged to this place, and I don't know how
> long I am going to own that place....My old parents have
> had very hard feelings over that piece that we have and there
> was one man came along and told us he was going to survey
> it up for us, and then I thought I was all right on there. Not
> long after, White people came and settled right alongside the
> reserve.[80]

Through the decades of reserve-making in Sumas Valley, White settlement grew steadily and the Sema:th worked hard to adapt and survive.
During the 1860s and 1870s, few Whites lived in the valley and the Sema:th
were able to stay on fairly equal terms with their new neighbours. By the
1880s, the ground had shifted; the Sema:th increasingly found themselves at
a disadvantage in the face of a bumptious, often hostile White population.

This altered balance of power was starkly illustrated one chilly night in
February 1884, when local authorities handed over a 15-year-old Sema:th
boy to an American vigilante mob. Louie Sam was hustled off by the mob
and hanged, just a few hundred feet south of his home on Sumas 7 reserve.
Sam's lynching was triggered by the murder of Nooksack merchant James
Bell on Sunday, the 24th. Sam was seen walking away from Bell's place the
afternoon of the murder, and Bell's neighbours hastily fastened on him
as the guilty party. Sam wisely returned home; three days later, he was

arrested by magistrate William Campbell and detained in Thomas York's house, which served as a makeshift prison. That night, between 60 and 100 mounted men showed up at York's door, entered the house and spirited Sam away. Riding swiftly south, the mob stopped short of the border, just long enough to hang Sam from a nearby tree, leaving his lifeless body twisting in the cold night. Strong evidence pointed to leaders of the lynch mob itself as the guilty parties in James Bell's death. It also suggested that York and Campbell helped plan and carry out the plot to seize Sam. Not surprisingly, legal authorities on both sides of the border did nothing: the vigilantes got off scot-free, while York and Campbell never had to answer for their failure to protect Sam.[81]

The establishment of reserves and increasing White settlement created a new reality for the Sema:th. Their land base was radically reduced and they were pushed back from their most important resource, Sumas Lake. At the same time, the pastoral economy established by White farmers altered how the lake and its surrounding prairies were used. But the Sema:th did not passively accept these changes: they modified old ways and took up new as they adapted to the shifting ground rules. Throughout, the Sema:th continued to rely on the natural abundance of Sumas Lake and Valley, even while their access to that abundance was increasingly limited.

By the 1870s, the Sema:th were heavily involved in the pastoral industry that had come to dominate the valley's economy. This despite a deeply held prejudice among Whites that Indigenous peoples were unable and unwilling to adapt to more agricultural pursuits. On visiting Upper Sumas chief Tsiseemitston in 1870, missionary Thomas Crosby was impressed by the herd of horses kept by his host. During the summer, the herd grazed on the grasses of Sumas Prairie, "and in the fall [Tsiseemitston] had a lot of his young men cut enough wild hay to keep them through the winter." When he took over from Crosby, Charles Tate regularly visited Upper Sumas to hold services there. But every October, he arrived at empty villages as the Sema:th were out in the hayfields bringing in the winter's feed crop. An 1877 inventory revealed the extent of the Sema:th livestock holdings: Upper Sumas alone had 50 head of cattle, 30 pigs and 20 horses.

As with their White neighbours, the Sema:th found no need to sow forage crops, relying on wild grasses. The Sema:th also made good use of the seasonally flooded grassland that was treated as a commons. "All the stock ran out, on Sumas Prairie," Edward Kelly recalled. "No one bothered with fences. You just went out to look for the cattle morning and evening. And it was the same with horses when you needed them for work." The practice of the commons had its downside, though. White farmers routinely let their cattle and pigs run free; the liberated stock often made their way onto Native land, uprooting potato patches and other cultivated plots. In response, the Sema:th threw up fences and lobbied their Indian Agent to help stop the marauding animals.

The Sema:th continued to rely on stock-raising and dairy for much of their livelihood into the early 1900s. In 1915, Chief Selesmlton stated that most of his people's produce—from butter and milk to pork, chicken and eggs—was not sold but consumed by the Sema:th themselves. At the time, a tally of upper Sema:th holdings included 60 head of cattle, 30 horses and nearly 200 pigs. The local Indian Agent concluded that the Sema:th went in "more for stockraising than anything else, and at that they [were] very successful."

The Sema:th also adopted many of the food plants imported by White immigrants. The most important of these was the potato, one of the most nutritious vegetables known to humans. Introduced by the Hudson's Bay Company in the 1830s, the potato quickly spread throughout the Fraser Valley; by the1850s, it was a staple of the Sto:lo diet, replacing indigenous

Pete and Sarah Silver—of the Upper Sumas reserve Silvers—stand in front of their home. Their son, Ambrose, sits atop the family's horse, very much in charge. The picture gives us some idea of the adaptation made by the Sema:th in the face of social and economic changes brought about by widespread White immigration: the move to single-family homes, the ownership of horses and other stock, and involvement in the pastoral economy. The Reach P164.

root crops such as wapato. Members of the Northwest Boundary Survey marvelled at "the elegance of the Irish potatoes cultivated here and elsewhere in the territory by the Indians." Government officials were explicitly ordered to include existing potato patches when laying out reserves. In 1879, Gilbert Sproat went to great pains to provide for adequate potato fields for the Sema:th. The potato was still a mainstay of the Sema:th diet four decades later, when Selesmlton listed the plants his people cultivated: "potatoes, some oats, fruit trees and all kinds of vegetables."[82]

Even with these changes in their diet and way of life, fishing and hunting remained essential to the Sema:th's survival. Fishing alone provided one-half of their livelihood well into the 20th century. In petition after petition, from the 1860s on, Sema:th and Sto:lo chiefs stressed that their people could not survive if denied their traditional rights "to hunt, fish and travel over" their country. Moves by White officials to curtail these rights were, in the words of one historian, "at least as decisive for most Native people in BC as the loss of their land." For the Sema:th, the reserve system pushed them back from the shores of Sumas Lake and denied them direct access to most of its tributaries. Government regulations then restricted when, where and how they could fish and hunt, and increasing numbers of White fishermen and hunters depleted existing stocks.

The sturgeon fishery was a case in point. In the decades after the arrival of Whites, the Sema:th continued to catch large quantities of sturgeon in Sumas Lake: for their own consumption, for trade and for sale. White fishermen quickly realized why the sturgeon were so prized and set about catching the massive fish in alarming numbers. By the 1890s, Chief Selesmlton and other Sto:lo leaders voiced their alarm over "the wholesale slaughter of sturgeon." Within years, even the federal Department of Indian Affairs was warning about the near extinction of the fish around Sumas.[83]

Another assault on the Sema:th fishery was the targeted seizure of nets and gear in the two decades prior to the lake's draining. Charging that Sema:th fishermen were interfering with salmon spawning, officials in powerboats carried out raids and confiscated nets set up on Sumas Lake and River. The Fisheries Department was adamant that nets be limited in size and used primarily on Fraser River. Just as regularly, Selesmlton protested to the local Indian Agent; to his credit, the agent contacted his colleagues in Fisheries and saw to it that most of the nets were returned. The agent echoed Selesmlton's arguments that the Sema:th had always netted fish on Sumas Lake, and that without the catch they would be left destitute.

The government clampdown on fishing in Sumas Valley brought rare expressions of support from the Sema:th's White neighbours. William Hall wrote to the Indian agent, protesting both the seizure of Sema:th nets and the ban on the sale of fish to local Whites. The agent responded that the nets would be returned and that the Sema:th could continue to sell fish to local residents, although not to commercial dealers. Reacting to a seizure of nets in 1905, the *Chilliwack Progress* charged the government's actions were "nothing short of a calamity," because they took away the Sema:th's "only means of livelihood." The paper added that the government was violating a local understanding: "The Indians can at all seasons of the year both hunt and fish when such are to be used as food for themselves." Indian Agent F. Devlin agreed, stating the Sema:th and other Natives had the right to "fish in any river or lake in B.C., at any time for food" to feed themselves and their families.

The protests from Chief Selesmlton, Indian Affairs and local Whites were ignored; instead, Fisheries officials became even more aggressive in imposing regulations. "If I go out and catch a fish, the policeman comes out after me with a gun," Selesmlton stated in 1915. "Every year that we use a net, they come out and take it away from us." One year, an armed Fisheries official had confronted Selesmlton and taken his nets. The chief claimed the official fired a shot at him; the official responded that he had fired a shot over the chief's head. Samuel Cromarty, whose father was Sema:th, recounted another dramatic incident involving his father and uncle:

> They bought a boat in New West and they were fishing on Sumas Lake, making pretty good money, until one night a provincial fish boat come along and chased them. Well the only thing they could do was head for the bluffs...at full speed, and they run the boat right up on the rock bluff and jumped off and run up in the bush. The boat bounced back off the beach and turned and went out into the lake, and the fish wardens chased the boat instead of chasing Dad. And that's how come he got away.

Regulations on hunting waterfowl were even more restrictive as government officials belatedly scrambled to stop overhunting by White sportsmen. A string of provincial game laws and international treaties in the early 1900s sought to conserve BC's dwindling flocks of waterfowl by restricting when they could be hunted. The creation of hunting seasons came too late to check the damage done by White market and tourist hunting, but it did cause serious problems for the Sema:th.

Once again, Selesmlton described his people's predicament: his people could not get enough ducks and geese for food because the hunting season was too short. "If I go out and take my gun"—either out of season or outside reserve boundaries—"there is always someone to round me up and have me arrested." Yet White hunters still "flock in here so much" and roam free, the chief added, even hunting on reserve land. Moreover, traditional Sema:th hunting grounds were being turned into private land owned by White farmers and organizations such as the Lakeside Gun Club. Decades of White overhunting, Selesmlton concluded, took a heavy toll: "Years ago these ducks used to be so thick around here that we could kill all we wanted, but now there is hardly any."[84]

Meanwhile, the mammal population of Sumas Valley was relatively untouched by government regulations. The Sema:th continued to trap the fur-bearing mammals that thrived in the Sumas wetlands, and hunt the deer that favoured the slopes of Vedder and Sumas Mountains. Joseph Cole at Kilgard and Burns Mussell at Lackaway were well-known for their skill as trappers and hunters. Ray Silver remembered the days when in a matter of weeks he could bring in "150 muskrats, three to four dozen mink...and beaver, otter. I'd be trapping really hard." What ended these days was not government regulation, but the depletion of mammal populations due to increased White hunting and the transformation of Sumas Valley into farmland.

Through the later decades of the 1800s, as White immigrants built this new agricultural economy, they relied on Sto:lo labour to do much of the work. One of the few early Whites to acknowledge this was Charles Evans Jr., the younger son of Charles and Jane Evans. In a four-part memoir printed in the *Chilliwack Progress*, Evans tried to stir his neighbours to a better appreciation of the debt they owed to the local Sto:lo. He wrote with heartfelt sympathy: "The Indian was the pioneer's live capital. He was the man who...cleared all these first fields; he helped cut the hay and grain that grew on them. He baled hay, made roads and bridges, and did all manner of farm work." Three decades earlier, when Charles Tate found empty Sema:th homes during spring and late-summer visits, many of the men were at work on White farmers' fields.

White farmers also hired Sto:lo canoes and crew to haul their grain to market in New Westminster, particularly when steamboats could not do so or were too costly. The Sto:lo recognized their importance in the supply chain: in July 1872, they went on strike for higher pay; in December, they again demanded better wages, "thinking the steamer had stopped for the season."

Much of the timber required by White settlers was supplied by Sto:lo loggers. The latter bucked and split cordwood for steamboats and White farmers' stoves, and milled planks, fence posts and railway ties. They even rafted the lumber used by Whites for houses and barns up Fraser River and across Sumas Valley waterways.

Much of Sumas Valley's early road and railway systems were built with Sto:lo labour. Through the 1860s and 1870s, Sto:lo and Chinese work-men cut and graded roads through Sumas and Chilliwack Prairies. In the early 1900s, Sema:th men found work constructing the BC Electric and Vancouver, Victoria and Eastern Railways; Gus Commodore, Jimmy Poole and Francis Kelly were among them. At some point in their lives, most of the upper Sema:th men found employment at the Kilgard Fire Clay Com-pany plant. Brothers Edward and Albert Kelly, and cousin Francis, spent much of their working lives there, performing a wide range of jobs from kitchen to kiln. Ray Silver was only 15 years old when he began at the plant and worked there on and off for years.

Unfortunately for the Sema:th, new opportunities for wage labour did not make up for the loss of their traditional land and resources. Even the reserves themselves were not safe from the demands of White settlers and companies. The Kilgard clay plant sat on 12 acres of reserve land, and owner Charles Maclure held the mineral rights to the mountainside plot. At the same time, the Vancouver, Victoria and Eastern Railway was being constructed, running from Abbotsford through Sumas 6 reserve to the Can-nor station east of Sumas Mountain. The railway secured 31 acres of the reserve for its right-of-way, bringing the total of alienated land to 43 acres (10 percent of Sumas 6). When the railway abandoned the Kilgard line in 1927, the alienated land was supposed to revert back to the band. Instead, the railway company sold its interests to Maclure, robbing the Sema:th of its rightful claim.[85]

The other Upper Sumas reserve—Sumas 7—fared even worse. For generations past, a Sema:th village sat along the banks of upper Sumas River here. In 1879, Gilbert Sproat set up the 160-acre reserve as potato land, despite its thick cover of trees, mostly cedar. But most families left in the 1880s after the murder of Louie Sam, leaving only Sema:th elder Jim York and his family; in the early 1900s, they too moved away. The Sema:th continued to log cedar and other timber from the site, using it for houses, outbuildings and firewood. Some lumber was sold to the BC Electric Rail-way during construction of the line, while a later contract produced an order of cedar shingles. Meanwhile, Gus Commodore had moved in with his wife and three children; Commodore built a small shingle mill and fed it with the reserve's cedar.

Over the years, the reserve's White neighbours had convinced themselves that the land was unoccupied and unused, and that it should be taken out of Sema:th hands and sold. In 1903, Sumas Municipality offered to buy the quarter section, hoping to use it as a park or to sell it as farmland. Between 1913 and 1915, a more concerted campaign was spearheaded by the municipality and the Upper Sumas Women's Institute. Their vision was to turn this "wild and uncontrolled" land into a public park, a scenic venue for civic events such as Empire Day picnics. Indian Agent Peter Byrne fired back: he pointed out that the majority of White-owned land on upper Sumas Prairie had not been cleared or cultivated either, and that there were too few White families in the area to justify a park.

The municipal park proposal failed, but that did not end the pressure on Sumas 7 reserve. Through 1918, as World War I ground to its grisly end, there were increasing calls throughout BC that "unused" reserve land be opened up to returning soldiers for settlement. In the Fraser Valley, the campaign was spearheaded by F.B. Stacey, minister of the Chilliwack Methodist Church and local representative on the Soldier Settlement Board. In April 1919, Stacey informed Indian Affairs in Ottawa that eight returned soldiers had applied to the board for the right to homestead the quarter section comprising Sumas 7. Stacey, whose son had been killed in the war, demanded that the reserve be surrendered and the veterans' application approved, stating emphatically, "I want to get them settled there."

Unlike Sema:th concerns, the reverend's demands were acted upon. In June, Indian Agent Byrne was ordered to visit the Upper Sumas reserves for the purpose of obtaining the approval of band members for the surrender of Sumas 7. Byrne reported back that while some members were in favour, "others strongly object, and it is doubtful if the consent of a majority can be obtained" It took Byrne nearly six months to wear down the opposition, a task made easier by the money he was able to bring to the table. On November 15, the land was officially surrendered to the Soldier Settlement Board and Sumas 7 ceased to be. But the eight veterans whose application triggered the reserve's surrender never moved there; and when the land was publicly offered for sale, no preference was given to returned soldiers.[86]

In the face of the multipronged assault on their lands, resources and way of life, the natural abundance of Sumas Valley provided the Sema:th with some relief. They could still draw upon the richness of the valley's grasslands, vegetation, berry bushes and trees—to sustain their livestock, supplement their diet and build their houses and canoes. They also could feed upon the still-considerable supply of fish, waterfowl and game in and around the lake.

Sumas Lake also provided the Sema:th with ample opportunities for recreation. Edward Kelly recalled a favourite family pastime during spring and summer:

> The people had the small canoes in those days. And for a Sunday outing, they would go out from the small slough [at Kilgard], to the big slough, and into Sumas Lake. And had a picnic. Mother used to make up the lunches, and my Dad would bring his rifle along; if we needed deer, he killed the deer. Then Dad always brought his fishing line, and would be trolling around, up and down. Mother would be knitting, and us kids would be swimming in the lake.

Cornelius Kelleher and his wife remembered similar outings, travelling from Matsqui to the lake's sandbars and beaches: "And a whole bunch of us, on a Sunday…would go up there…and have a whale of a time, swimming and laying in that sand, that beach."

In winter, Sumas Lake turned into one large skating rink. Again, Edward Kelly pulled up cherished boyhood memories:

> Sumas Lake used to freeze over to the point where a team of horses and a bobsled [could travel] over it. A group of us boys and one elderly grown up, by the name of Gus Commodore, he was very good to the kids. He was always with us. And we would skate from Kilgard, in the creek, to the small slough, then into the big slough, and the big slough emptied into Sumas Lake. And we'd skate right across Sumas Lake to what is called Pumptown [today], where the pumps are. And on the way back, Gus Commodore [would say], "Alright kids, it's time to go home." So we'd start for home. The north wind was blowing so hard it was very easy to get home, because we'd just put out our coats, for sails. And sail back home again on the ice.

Winter also was the time for dances and other social events. The Upper Sumas reserve emerged as a centre of social life that drew people

Gus Commodore was popular among the boys of Upper Sumas reserve, leading them on many adventures on and around Sumas Lake. The Reach, P154.

Chief Ned (Selesmlton) seeing off guests in front of his smokehouse on the Upper Sumas reserve. The smokehouse was the centre of social activities like winter dances, which brought together Sema:th, other Sto:lo and Nooksack from miles around. The Reach P1410.

together from across reserve lines. As with other Sto:lo villages, the Kilgard reserve's most prominent building was its smokehouse, the site of events such as winter dances and potlatches. The largest smokehouse we know of was erected by Selèsmlton a few years after he became chief in 1903. Kilgard's cemetery was rundown, and the chief sent out invitations to extended relatives of those buried there to come and rebuild it. Arriving at Kilgard, the assembled kinfolk—Nooksack, Chilliwack, Swilhcha, Chehalis and Matsqui—set to work on the smokehouse. Master carpenters Johnny Lewis, Jimmy Poole and George Swanaset oversaw construction of the building, which measured 50 feet wide by 100 feet long, and stood 25 feet high. "This was late fall and dances were held in the house while the fence was being built," Swanaset later explained. "The smokehouse was used for winter dancing for years."

The winter dances were major events in the lives of the Sema:th and their neighbours. Francis Kelly recalled how he and his father "ran several teams hauling the dancers and their families from the B.C.E.R. station near Huntington to Kilgard reserve. People came from all over and stayed a week. They were put up in Chief Ned's smokehouse and fed communally twice a day." The last great winter dance took place in December 1926, when 200 people from the lower Fraser, Vancouver Island and Washington State converged on Selesmlton's longhouse. For three days and nights, dancers donned "headdress, feathers, claws, anklets and ceremonial decorations" as they assumed the identity of eagle, wolf, snake, bear, owl or kingfisher. They then took to the floor, performing to the accompaniment of a dozen drums and the audience's rhythmic chanting. Selesmlton's smokehouse burned down some years later, and a smaller replacement was built a short distance away.[87]

CHAPTER 8

REDEEMING SUMAS LAKE

No sooner had White immigrants settled into their new homes around Sumas Lake than they began thinking of ways to get rid of it. The history of efforts to drain the lake and dewater the valley is long and tortuous: a half-century of false starts and disappointments before the dream was finally realized. From the start, White settlers, officials and planners spoke of how they might "reclaim" or "redeem" Sumas Lake and Valley and transform the new land into productive farms. But Sumas Lake had been there since the time of the last ice age, and every year flood waters covered the valley. There had never been a time when the valley was dry land. To us the question is obvious: how can you reclaim something that was never there? And what had Sumas Lake done wrong that it needed to be redeemed?

These questions never occurred to Sumas's White population. The reasons why not were buried deep within their fundamental views of nature and humanity's place in it. These views were themselves the results of two powerful traditions of thought. The concepts and words used in the reclamation discourse were based first in the Christian tradition. The ideal of the truly natural world was the Garden of Eden: tamed and fertile, giving humans all they needed. When Adam and Eve sinned, they fell from grace and were expelled from Eden. And with their Fall into sin, nature fell with them, for God had created nature to serve man. Now the natural world was filled with weeds, hostile animals and other unwanted things; man had to toil on it, struggle with it to feed himself. Just as man had to redeem himself from sin, so the land had to be redeemed from its fallen state.

The second tradition of thought was built upon the first. The British and American tradition distinguished between the physical world as it existed and the physical world as nature intended it to be. The existing world could be faulty, possessing flaws that prevented it from fulfilling its true purpose of serving man's needs. The image of the truly natural world was that of the Garden: cultivated, tamed, transformed by man. And this world was split into two fixed elements: water and land. Water that was silted up with land, or land that had too much water on it, was faulty and had to be fixed. This was the thing wrong with the aging, shallow Sumas Lake and its surrounding wetlands. Sumas Lake and the yearly flood waters were preventing the Sumas lands from being what nature meant them to be—fertile agricultural fields. The task then was to reclaim those lands, to bring them back to their proper purpose.

This may seem too abstract and general to be of use to us; but these very concepts and words were used by drainage promoters and Sumas residents when they considered the state of Sumas Lake. One of the clearest expressions of this world view came from the pulpit. In spring 1894, in the midst of the greatest flood on record, local Presbyterian minister John Logan challenged his flock: "If this fertile land is ever to be settled, if it ever comes to what God or nature intended, there must be a strong and united effort made to reclaim it from its watery grave." The flooded Sumas Valley was "paradise lost"—it was up to them to get rid of the unwanted waters so that God's people "may have paradise regained."[88]

The ever-practical Volkert Vedder avoided such lofty words when he came up with the first plan ever made to "reclaim" the flood lands of Sumas Valley. In autumn 1867, he and a handful of neighbours hatched a scheme by which "many thousands of acres, now flooded during the spring freshet, will be effectually reclaimed and rendered highly productive." Vedder provided few details of the plan, other than to say it would involve cutting "a ditch through a small ridge near the boundary line."

Nothing came of Vedder's ill-formed idea. Four years later, a more formal plan was proposed by an English-born engineer who had just completed the first land surveys of upper and lower Sumas Prairies. Edward Mohun witnessed the valley's high waters and plagues of mosquitoes, and heard from local White farmers of their struggles. In June 1871, he submitted a plan to Surveyor General Benjamin Pearse "for reclaiming and draining this Valley." The plan's first stage involved construction of a "substantial dyke" along the southern bank of Fraser River between Sumas and Chilliwack Mountains. Lower Sumas River would be dammed near its mouth, with a floodgate open most of the year to let Sumas water into Fraser River, but closed during the spring freshet to stop Fraser water from flowing up the Sumas. Mohun estimated the cost of the project at $10,000, to be paid for by a government land grant of the same number of acres. If successful, a second stage would set about "reclaiming the Lake, should it be considered advisable."

Pearse was impressed, and he recommended the scheme to his superiors. But Victoria was just then in the midst of negotiating its way into Confederation and could not commit to the scheme. Meanwhile, Sumas farmers had caught wind of Mohun's proposal; in early 1872, they convened the first meeting of its kind to consider the draining of Sumas Lake. The assembly called for a government survey to consider the feasibility of dyking the valley to reclaim "a large tract of valuable land supposed to contain from 15,000 to 25,000 acres, fit for agricultural purposes." Mohun also was busy. In 1873, he returned to Sumas Valley for more surveying. He then submitted a new proposal aimed at "redeeming by dyking" 15,000 acres of Sumas Valley, which was "in large part valueless and unfit for occupation." He committed himself to raising the $15,000 needed; in exchange, he would receive "a free grant of Sumas Lake and 5,000 acres of land," plus the right to buy the remainder of drained land for a dollar an acre.

The *British Colonist* publicly supported the scheme, and the provincial government sent its own man into the field to investigate the design's feasibility. Henry Edmonds concluded that the Mohun design did not address a number of serious issues, including what was to be done with streams flowing into Sumas Valley from the south. He also balked at the suggestion of ceding the rights to Sumas Lake, "as the exact boundaries of Sumas Lake [had] not been defined." More positively, he found that lower Sumas farmers unanimously supported the plans; he had not consulted upper Sumas farmers, but presumed they too would back such efforts.[89]

Edmonds's cautionary words did not pierce the bubble of optimism that surrounded drainage proponents; the latter were convinced that draining Sumas Valley would be a fairly straightforward job, and that its cost would be recouped many times over by the value of the newly dewatered lands. One reason for this misplaced optimism was that White settlers had lived around Sumas Lake for a very short time. They had experienced the yearly rise and fall of Sumas waters, but had yet to witness a truly historic flood. A second reason was that, at the time, most of the volume of upper Chilliwack River was kept off Sumas Valley, flowing north through the lower Chilliwack River and Luckakuck Creek. Drainage proponents did not know just how far Sumas Lake could and did expand if the conditions were right.

This changed in 1875 and 1876, when consecutive flood seasons broke all previous recorded levels. Through winter and most of spring 1875, cold, wet weather built up a large snowpack in the mountains. Quickly rising temperatures through May melted the snow and sent torrents of water into swelling rivers. The Fraser River peaked on June 26, several feet higher

Looking to the southeast across Sumas Lake, two small boats make their way during high water. At low water, the area in front of the boats was muddy land (1915). The Reach P 188.

than anything seen by White immigrants. Most of Sumas Valley was under water—roads and trails were inundated and nearly all bridges washed out.

Even after the waters receded, the valley soil stayed saturated. Another cold, wet winter was followed by another late spring in 1876. From mid-May on, Fraser River rose ever higher until June 29, when it crested nearly four feet higher than the year before. The Fraser pushed up Sumas River into the lake, swelling its water. Across the valley, upper Chilliwack River—which most years peaked before Fraser River—reached its freshet at the same time. Turned aside by a blockage at the head of lower Chilliwack River, the swollen stream rushed northwest onto lower Sumas Prairie through Luckakuck and Atchelitz Creeks, and due west into Sumas Lake through Vedder River. For the first time, White settlers witnessed the return of greater Sumas Lake. One witness wrote: "At Sumas, the entire valley from mountain to mountain is one vast sheet of water, probably 8 to 10 miles wide." At its centre, the lake reached nearly 30 feet deep. Only a handful of houses stayed dry, perched on the valley's ridges. The high water lingered for three full weeks; when it finally receded, it left behind several feet of mud, coating roads, fields, trees and buildings. James Chadsey wrote of the "terrible destruction" wrought by the waters: "Desolation and dreariness have usurped their sway over our beautiful prairie."

Stunned by the scope and power of the 1876 flood, Sumas farmers pressed the provincial government to act. They demanded that "some practicable scheme be at once set on foot to reclaim the large tracts of most valuable land from annual and destructive inundation." Only the government had the resources needed for such a project, they argued; the money spent would pay for itself through sales of the newly drained lands, plus reasonable levies on their own improved properties. The White farmers' immediate demand was that a competent engineer be sent to examine the problem and come up with a workable solution. Victoria agreed, and in September it dispatched renowned surveyor Edgar Dewdney to study and report on "the feasibility of dyking and draining the lowlands situated between Cheam and Sumas Mountains and lying to the south of Fraser River." For six weeks, Dewdney criss-crossed the Sumas and Chilliwack Valleys, meticulously examining their topography, soils and watercourses. He also spoke with local residents, Sto:lo and White alike, to draw on their knowledge and listen to their concerns.

Dewdney submitted his report in late November, along with three blueprint-quality maps that showed the components of his proposed plan. Dewdney's scheme was designed to protect Sumas Valley against an 1876-level flood. Like Mohun, he proposed the construction of dykes between Chilliwack and Sumas Mountains, but these were to be considerably higher. The section east of Miller's Rock rose eight feet, seven inches above the ground, while the western stretch averaged 14 feet, six inches; floodgates at the Sumas River dam, as well as at McGillivray and Wilson Creeks, allowed for off-season drainage. Unlike earlier proposals, Dewdney's plan provided detailed specifications and instructions on the dykes' construction, and argued forcefully that it could be done. He also added another levee on the northeastern edge of lower Sumas Prairie, running along the eastern bank of Atchelitz Creek, which was to hold back Fraser water coming from Chilliwack.

This system of dykes and gates would protect Sumas Valley against Fraser River waters. But Dewdney knew this would not be enough, that something had to be done about the wild torrents of Chilliwack River. He was the first to recognize that any effort to drain the valley would be futile unless the Chilliwack "could be returned to its old channel or diverted from the Sumas District." An "impenetrable dam" of drift material—reinforced by the work of local Whites and Sto:lo—had diverted all the water from the old Chilliwack River bed. Half of the upper Chilliwack water now pushed due north down Luckakuck Creek, with the other half divided between

Atchelitz Creek and Vedder River (the last flowing west into Sumas Lake). Dewdney concluded that while it was "almost impossible to open the original channel, it would be feasible though very costly to make a new one, or utilize either the Luckakuck or Atchelitz." As it provided the shortest, most direct path from Vedder Crossing to Fraser River, Dewdney favoured a dredged and straightened Luckakuck channel.

Here, Dewdney raised an issue that would bedevil drainage efforts for decades. Locals were split over what route any diversion of the Chilliwack River should take. On one side were White settlers along Luckakuck Creek and Chilliwack River, who were adamant that the proper channel for Chilliwack water was due west into Sumas Lake. Sumas farmers countered that this was not so, that the Chilliwack had only recently been diverted into the lake. Alone among his peers, Dewdney made an effort to get the Sto:lo perspective, finding a similar rift: Chilliwack elders backed the claims of their White neighbours, while the Sema:th denied that the Chilliwack River's original course was into Sumas Lake.[90]

Despite the hefty price tag for his design—an estimated $137,690—Dewdney's proposal was well received. City newspapers and local residents alike pressed the government to act on it; Dewdney had shown how Sumas Lake could be drained, they argued, and all that was needed was someone to do it. The man who stepped forward was an unknown engineer from Ontario named E.L. Derby. Derby's past was shrouded in mystery; it was reported that he had worked on dyking projects in California and had ties to railway and financial interests in Seattle and San Francisco. In late summer 1879, Derby spent a fortnight surveying Sumas Valley before travelling to Victoria to make his pitch. His initial proposal was to drain Sumas Lake and dyke the surrounding prairies, then settle a colony of 100 Ontarians to farm the newly "reclaimed" land. These plans soon grew into "one grand scheme" that would see the dyking and draining of the entire flood plain south of Fraser River, from Matsqui to Cheam.

Government officials and valley residents were smitten. The *Mainland Guardian* reported: "The farmers are so engrossed with dyking and draining, that it has almost become a mania with some. Public meetings are all the rage." Derby presented his proposal to a pair of well-attended meetings in early November—one at Sumas, another at Chilliwack. The provincial government showed its support of the scheme by having Finance Minister William Smithe appear onstage beside Derby. The engineer had been told to expect "a good deal of opposition," but he was pleasantly surprised when both assemblies expressed overwhelming support. A lone, unidentified

Sumas farmer refused to play along, saying "that he was quite satisfied with his farm as it was, and thought if he could fight mosquitoes, the other settlers should do so as well."[91]

Upon closer examination, public support was not as unified as it seemed. At their meeting, Sumas landowners voted in favour of seceding from Chilliwack to form their own municipality, "in order to carry the dyking scheme more successfully into effect." For their part, Chilliwack landowners demanded a guarantee that any drainage plan—which necessarily would involve the diversion of Chilliwack River—not cause undue damage to their properties.

In Victoria, Derby's scheme sailed through the legislature, and in April the Sumas Dyking Act of 1878 came into effect. It committed Derby to dyking and draining the Sumas, Chilliwack and Matsqui Prairies. Once he had done so, he could levy charges on landowners who benefited from the work; he would also be granted 51,000 acres of Crown land, including the bed of Sumas Lake itself. Some isolated voices warned that it was dangerous to hand over such a large block of land to a private individual, but most saw no threat in it. They argued that the overflowed valleys were "wasteland," of no use in their current state; better they be given to someone who could "redeem" them and turn them into productive agricultural land.

For those who wished to see them, there were early signs that Derby was not up to the massive task before him. Through 1878 and 1879, the engineer focussed on the easiest part of the job: constructing a low dyke along the northern edge of Matsqui Prairie. But the dyke failed its first test, giving way before the freshet of 1880. The failed Matsqui dyke would be the sum total of work completed by Derby. Not a single shovel of soil was turned in Sumas or Chilliwack Valley during the 10 years the Sumas Dyking Act of 1878 remained in force. There is no evidence that Derby had even drawn up plans for Sumas, although it was assumed he would use Dewdney's design. Public opinion turned sour as Derby stalled. "The people of Sumas have been expecting that work would commence on Sumas dyke in July [1879]," one resident wrote. "But since the latest news arrived, they have lost all hope of Derby ever striking a blow."

Frustration mounted higher through the 1880s: it was obvious Derby was never going to tackle the Sumas and Chilliwack Valley sections; and as long as he held his charter, 45,000 acres there remained locked up. As more and more White immigrants looked to settle in the area, they either were turned away or resorted to squatting. A growing chorus called for repeal of the act. In 1887, a few months after Derby's death, the BC government finally relented. It nullified the Sumas Dyking Act and provided ways for squatters to legally register property they occupied.[92]

The Derby fiasco hampered land settlement in Sumas Valley for a full decade—it undermined any new plans for the valley's drainage for even longer. Nobody else could take up the project while Derby held his original charter, and it took Victoria a full decade to change that. Provincial officials had been burned by their early, public support of Derby. In 1877, then finance minister William Smithe had sat shoulder to shoulder with Derby, selling the merits of the latter's scheme to the assembled landowners of Sumas and Chilliwack. By spring 1883, Smithe was premier and he was putting as much distance as possible between himself and the failing project. The premier found a convenient escape in the newly established Railway Belt: 20 miles on either side of the planned route of the Canadian Pacific Railway. Smithe told the legislature that the Sumas Dyking lands now fell "within the Railway Belt conveyed to the Dominion government, and ought therefore to be dealt with by that government."

Nobody believed the distant federal government—just then committed to building a transcontinental railway—would or could undertake the draining of Sumas Lake. But the creation of the Railway Belt gave federal officials some say in the matter, further complicating drainage efforts. Ottawa now owned all unalienated land around Sumas Lake, along with the lake bottom itself. Since the only way cash-strapped governments could pay for any drainage project was through the grant of public land and the drained lake bed, any proposed scheme now needed Ottawa's approval.

During the first half of the 1890s, the provincial government stepped back from any active role in promoting the draining of Sumas Lake, forcing local landowners to take the initiative. In early 1891, a small group of shareholders headed by Donald McGillivray founded the BC Dyking and Improvement Company, and obtained provincial approval to undertake surveys and call for tenders. Everybody expected McGillivray would get the contract; instead Victoria awarded it to brothers Frank and John Lumsden, dairy farmers and stockbreeders who had purchased Volkert Vedder's sprawling property at the foot of Vedder Mountain. After obtaining the right to buy the bed of Sumas Lake from the federal government, the Lumsdens received provincial approval for their own firm, the Sumas Reclamation Company, in early 1892. Financial backers of the new scheme included David Miller, who raised $10,000 by mortgaging his property. Sumas farmers promptly abandoned McGillivray and threw their support behind the Lumsdens. All McGillivray could do was point

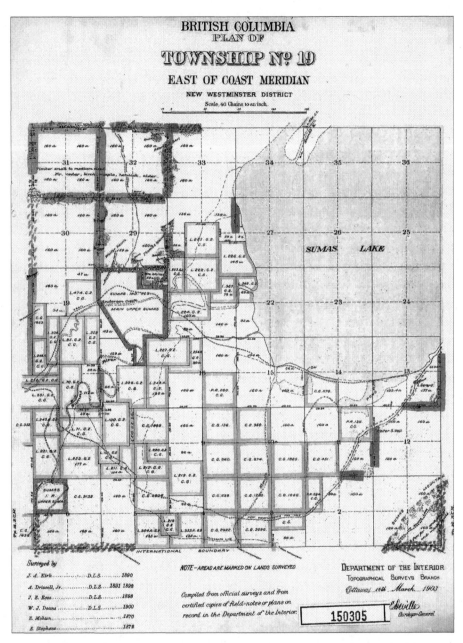

An official survey map of upper Sumas Prairie, completed in 1892. White settlement there remained sparse because of yearly flooding. Note the location of Upper Sumas reserve, pushed well back from the shore of Sumas Lake. Plan LTSA5725-150304 is included with permission by the Surveyor General Division of the Land Title and Survey Authority of British Columbia.

out the absurdity of having two companies legally incorporated for the sole purpose of draining Sumas Lake.

Through most of 1892, the Lumsden scheme generated much talk but little work. Months were wasted waiting for the arrival of a consulting engineer from Holland. Finally, the Dutchman arrived, surveyed the scene and gave his recommendations; these were incorporated into a plan unveiled in September. The design included the usual dykes between Sumas and Chilliwack Mountains and southward along Atchelitz Creek, as well as a large dam on lower Sumas River. It also called for something new: a tunnel to be drilled through Sumas Mountain near the mouth of lower Sumas River; large pumps would carry Sumas water through the tunnel into Fraser River. A bustle of activity followed through fall, as workers' quarters were built, right-of-ways excavated and initial dyking begun. As 1892 came to a close, the *British Colonist* praised the Lumsden brothers for "carrying out the work in a thoroughly practical way and so rapidly." The paper concluded that residents "believe they have seen the last overflows in the Sumas valley."

The high hopes were dashed in early 1893 when the Lumsdens ran out of money. The brothers had grossly underestimated the cost and sheer scope of "reclaiming" Sumas Lake; they also lacked any previous experience overseeing such a project. Their efforts were surely doomed from the start, and it is difficult to understand why they had been chosen for the contract. The Lumsdens asked Victoria to guarantee interest payments so they could secure a private loan, but were turned down. Facing personal bankruptcy, they were forced to sell their livestock and farm equipment at public auction. David Miller lost his entire investment; broken and aged, he sold his beloved homestead a few years later.[93]

The collapse of yet another drainage scheme reinforced the provincial government's determination to keep its distance from the troublesome enterprise. Sumas landowners now realized they needed to organize if they wanted to see their dream of a dewatered valley come true. These two trains of thought came together in June 1893, with the establishment of a board of commissioners for the Sumas Dyking District. The province gave the commissioners the authority to enter into contracts with developers for dyking and drainage projects within the district. It was a sweet moment for Donald McGillivray when Victoria chose him as chairman; Asa Ackerman, John Atkinson and William Maher were the other appointed commissioners, with George Chadsey serving as secretary. The following spring, the Sumas Dyking Act of 1894 was passed, granting the commissioners broader powers. Along with authorizing dyking works in general, the act gave specific approval for the diversion of water from Chilliwack River through Luckakuck Creek.

The new act sparked heated debate that revealed a growing rift among valley residents. A petition supporting the bill was signed by 280 landowners from Upper Sumas, Lower Sumas and parts of Chilliwack. It argued that the diversion through Luckakuck Creek had to take place for the project to succeed. An equally forceful petition against the bill was submitted by 55 landowners from Chilliwack and the eastern edge of lower Sumas Prairie. These petitioners stated, "The diverting of waters of the Vedder Creek into either the Atchelitz, Luckakuck or the Chilliwack would do very serious injury to our farms." The Sumas lands could be effectively dyked without such a diversion, they claimed. The spirited opposition failed to stop the bill; however, to allay their concerns, an additional clause was added, ordering that the banks of Luckakuck Creek be strengthened to protect adjacent lands before Vedder River was diverted through it.[94]

In the meantime, the Sumas Dyking Commissioners hired the well-known engineering firm Keefer and Smith to come up with a workable plan. Submitted in May 1894, the Keefer-Smith report was the most detailed and technically competent design yet produced. It also was the first to show some understanding of the complexity and scale of work required. While many of its components were familiar, the devilish details were new. Two dykes averaging between 12 and 17 feet would close off the opening between Chilliwack and Sumas Mountains; a third, lower dyke would run south from Chilliwack Mountain, along the western bank of Atchelitz Creek. Lower Sumas River would itself be dyked; a mile back from its mouth, a massive dam would be built and a 90-foot tunnel drilled through Sumas Mountain to divert water into Fraser River. During high water, floodgates on the north side of the tunnel would keep water from flowing upward from the Fraser. During low water, the gates would open and a system of powerful pumps would turn on to drain excess Sumas water. Finally, the plan called for the diversion of Vedder River into a dredged and protected Luckakuck Creek. The engineers argued that if the Vedder were allowed to flow into Sumas Lake, as it was then doing, the whole scheme could not succeed.

While none of the work outlined in the plan would be attempted, the Keefer-Smith report laid the foundation for others to come. It also introduced the Sumas Reclamation Datum as the yardstick for measuring the height of flood waters on Sumas Lake and Fraser River. Engineers now had a single measuring tape—on a scale of 100 feet—by which to measure the height of each year's waters. Keefer and Smith chose the highest flood level yet experienced as the official yardstick, from then on known as the Sumas Datum.

That level was reached in spring 1882, when Fraser River and Sumas Lake peaked at a foot higher than the 1876 mark. Just as in 1876, heavy winter snows and early spring rains were followed by a rapid spike in temperatures in late May and early June. The water rose with alarming speed, cresting on June 14. "Sumas prairie looks like a gulf," the *Mainland Guardian* reported. "The orchards and farms are all under water. As far as the eye can reach there is nothing to be seen but water. Several houses are submerged to their second stories."

Like the residents of Sumas Valley, Keefer and Smith could be forgiven for thinking they had seen the worst nature could offer. But they were proven wrong in May 1894, just one month after submitting their report. Once again, a sudden rise in temperature through May caused an exceptionally heavy snowpack to melt quickly, sending water rushing down to Fraser River. On May 25, the thermostat climbed past 90 degrees Fahrenheit in Quesnel; at Hope the Fraser rose 18 inches in just 24 hours. The mounting crisis was made worse when Thompson River peaked within a day of the Fraser. The Fraser River crested on June 5, at two feet higher than in 1882; the entire flood plain of lower Fraser Valley lay under water.

The 1894 flood remains the greatest ever recorded, an event scientists say happens once every 200 years. Sumas Lake reached a Sumas Datum of 102 feet: 31 feet deep at its centre, it spread over 47 square miles (30,000 acres), reclaiming the territory and size of its former glory days. From the foot of the bluffs marking the western edge of upper Sumas Prairie, through the four-mile gap between Sumas and Vedder Mountains, past Chilliwack to the foot of the Cheam slide, Sumas Valley was one great sea. A young Jack McCutcheon marvelled at the sight: "Looking south and west, Sumas Prairie looked like the Pacific Ocean." The *Chilliwack Progress* reported grimly, "Few have suffered more than the residents of Sumas district." What only days before had been happy homes and productive farms was now "a muddy lake with here and there a deserted building cropping up from the dreary sea."

The devastation of 1894 had an immediate and lasting impact on plans to drain Sumas Lake. On occasion, previous floods had spurred officials into action—the cataclysm of 1894 had the reverse effect. Even as the high waters were receding, the Sumas Dyking Commission adopted the Keefer-Smith design and put out a call for construction bids. Some weeks later, the commissioners asked the government to back a bond issue of

$340,000 to finance the works. The timing of the request could not have been worse. The flood stretched Victoria's resources to the limit: on top of the bill for emergency measures taken during the flood, it faced further costs for supplying seed and other supplies to farmers after the flood. The commissioners' request was denied.[95]

Over the following decade, in the words of an official report, the Sumas Lake drainage project was "practically abandoned." First, the attention of the public and resources of both provincial and federal governments were diverted elsewhere. The 1894 flood demonstrated the vulnerability of all the lands lying along the lower Fraser River, from Hope to Vancouver. A grand scheme was proposed to protect the Fraser Valley: construction of an unbroken chain of dykes along the whole length of the Fraser. Ottawa agreed to pay most of the cost (it retained responsibility for the lower Fraser River as a waterway that could be navigated to the ocean), and Victoria happily followed along. Work on the five-year project began in 1898; remarkably, it was finished on time and on budget. Yet there was one conspicuous hole in the new lines of levees running along either side of Fraser River: the 2½-mile gap between Chilliwack and Sumas Mountains. The thinking was that dyking the Fraser here would do little good until something was done about Sumas Lake itself.

A second reason the Sumas Lake drainage cause lost momentum was that the long-simmering dispute among local farmers over the course of Chilliwack River erupted into open hostilities. Lower Chilliwack River was effectively blocked by this time, and farmers along both Vedder River and Luckakuck Creek had built jams to control their streams. As the flood waters rose in spring 1894, Sardis and Vedder farmers took turns destroying each other's jams. The combatants wound up in court, and the judge decided in favour of the Vedder landowners. He ordered that the Chilliwack water be diverted away from its westerly run into Sumas Lake, to a northerly course down the Luckakuck or lower Chilliwack; and he set a two-year deadline to complete the work.[96]

The judge's orders were never carried out. Led by Allen Wells, Sardis farmers held the local levers of power and could stop any action. Indeed, over the following decade, local officials used money freed up by Victoria in the wake of the 1894 flood to reinforce upper Vedder River as the sole carrier of Chilliwack River water. The Vedder was systematically cleared of obstructions and its banks were hardened with rock and gravel. Then a substantial network of rock and timber cribbing was built at the heads of Chilliwack River and Luckakuck Creek. The work provided effective protection for Sardis and Chilliwack farmers and safeguarded the newly completed Big Prairie project, which drained Chilliwack Prairie. But it made it much harder to undertake the draining of Sumas Lake. For the first time since the arrival of White settlers, the entire volume of Chilliwack River water ran due west, swelling the lake. At the opening of the new century, Sardis and Chilliwack landowners had gotten most of what they wanted; they now had less reason to join with Sumas farmers in a common front to press for the drainage of Sumas Valley as a whole.

It took until 1905, more than a decade after the cataclysm of 1894, for the Sumas drainage dream to be revived. That year, three Chicago investors established the Sumas Development Company (SDC). The SDC and its president William Lewis were hailed as a saviours by the *Chilliwack Progress*, and in April the BC legislature passed the Sumas Development Act. But the provincial government offered no backing for loans or bond issues and promised no lands, stating for good measure it was not "in any way connected therewith." Instead, the federal government provided the lifeline, pledging in July that it would hand over thousands of acres of the Sumas Lake bed once the SDC drained the lake.

The company's first order of business was to come up with a plan to get the job done. Assistant engineer Stirling Hill of Seattle oversaw field surveys through fall 1905 and spring 1906. That summer, he sat down in Chicago with chief engineer Daniel Mead to draft a formal official design. The plan's basic components included: a high dyke between Chilliwack and Sumas Mountains to hold back Fraser River; the rerouting and containment of lower Sumas River; a large dam and pumphouse near the latter's mouth; and a web of interception ditches on the lake bed and valley floor. The most significant innovation was the engineers' proposal for a new diversion channel for the Chilliwack River. Like other engineers, Mead and Hill believed the Luckakuck diversion to be the best and cheapest. This was the route called for in the 1905 act, but Mead and Hill conceded that there was too much local opposition to it for it to work. Seeking to "reconcile conflicting interests," the engineers proposed that Chilliwack water be carried farther down Vedder River, to a point midway between Vedder Crossing and the eastern shore of Sumas Lake. Here it would be turned sharply into a newly constructed Vedder Canal, flowing due north and entering Fraser River at Wilson Creek. The increased velocity of the water—flowing more directly and dropping elevation more rapidly—would be slowed by three dams built inside the canal.

Despite strong support from the Sumas Dyking Commission, the SDC scheme sparked a firestorm of opposition. Leading the charge were Thomas

Lewis, Charles Richards, Tom Hall and Jacob Zink: all first- or second-generation White settlers living on lower Sumas Prairie. In letters to the press, petitions to Victoria and raucous landowners meetings, the group questioned the financial estimates given them and argued that local landowners would be left holding the bag for the inevitable cost overruns. They were deeply distrustful of the SDC, an American enterprise that had not even been incorporated yet; they dismissed it as a "company of ghosts" and characterized its plans as "a grafting scheme pure and simple." It was left to the Sumas Dyking Commission to defend the project. Commissioners Donald McGillivray, J.A. Atkinson and Wendell Bowman rejected the opposition's criticisms outright, and dismissed the naysayers as "false prophets" and "don't-want-a-dyke-unless-the-other-fellow-pays-for-it class of obstructionists."

Previous drainage proposals had sparked public meetings and spirited debate, but none matched this volume and animosity. Nor was all this simply hot air; for the first time, landowners in the Sumas Dyking District had the power to approve or reject proposals put before them. The 1905 law stipulated that any scheme required the approval of 60 percent of landholders attending duly organized public meetings. The first meeting was held on September 19, 1906, at Upper Sumas town hall. The Mead-Hill plan was presented and discussed, and a vote was taken: 104 in favour, 53 against. A second meeting was called in the face of charges that the first vote had been rigged. On June 19, 1907, Upper Sumas town hall was again filled to capacity. The Mead-Hill plan was retabled, with a revision that moved the crucial diversion back to Luckakuck Creek. But the change only alienated farmers adjacent to the Luckakuck and support dropped: 94 voted for the new scheme, 52 against. The 60 percent threshold had been reached, but with only 0.3 percent to spare. Donald McGillivray conceded that the result "was so close in numbers that it may be unsatisfactory."[97]

We do not know whether the commissioners would have gone forward with the SDC scheme or not, because within months the company collapsed on its own. As its opponents charged, the SDC was a paper company: it lacked a pool of capital of its own, did not possess physical assets it might use as collateral for a loan and was unable to raise money by leveraging land it had yet to drain. Victoria refused any assistance, and William Lewis negotiated the sale of the SDC to the British Columbia Electric Railway (BCER). In March 1908, the BCER paid $70,000 for the company's only assets: the engineering surveys and plans prepared by Mead and Hill; the federal grant of Sumas lands once they had been dewatered; and the provincial charter to undertake such a project.

The British Columbia Electric Railway Company—London-owned
and Vancouver-based—was one of the province's most successful and in-
novative corporations. It built, owned and operated the electric light and
streetcar systems of Victoria and greater Vancouver, and it was expanding into interurban rail service. In 1907, it launched yet another ambitious project: construction of an electric rail line from New Westminster
to Chilliwack, to be completed by November 1, 1910. From the start, the
company's Vancouver managers viewed Sumas Lake as the most daunting
obstacle to the new railway. They were convinced that the line could be
completed on time only if the lake was drained. Accordingly, they kept a
close eye on the progress and pratfalls of the SDC scheme. They also ordered their surveyors to map out a projected route through the middle of
Sumas Lake—running four miles due northeast, midway between Vedder
and Sumas Mountains. The survey teams reported back that the dewatering of Sumas Valley was doable and that "the reclamation of these lands
will be a very profitable undertaking."[98]

Local artist Louise Alexander seated above the newly finished BC Electric Railway line on Vedder Mountain, making field sketches for a painting of Sumas Lake. In the final painting, Alexander omitted the telephone poles and railway tracks (1916). The Reach P5655.

Thus, the BCER was ready to step in when the SDC faltered. In March 1908, it officially took over the drainage project; by early May, its chief engineer, Francis LeBaron, had prepared an initial plan. LeBaron was an American hydraulic engineer with extensive experience in drainage projects south of the border. Over the following year, he fine-tuned his design and submitted a final version on May 14, 1909. LeBaron's design differed fundamentally from all that had come before. His key innovation tackled the most intractable problem: what to do with the Chilliwack River as it rushed out of Vedder Crossing and onto the valley floor. For decades, planners and proponents had struggled to find a way to tame and divert the torrential stream, only to tie themselves up in rancorous squabbling over which route was best.

This was the Gordian knot nobody could cut, so LeBaron untied it. He wrote that the Chilliwack-Vedder "is so rapid and powerful a stream that it is dangerous to try and divert it." Channelling the water through the Luckakuck or Wilson Creek diversions was "too hazardous and costly"—water would rush down "at the speed of a railroad train" because of the elevation drop. The solution was "not to meddle with the Vedder or Chilliwack, but let it run in its chosen channel, banking it so as to hold it in where it shows a tendency to spread out, and helping it discharge into the Sumas as soon as possible." LeBaron proposed to run the Vedder in a more or less natural course four miles due west from Vedder Crossing, dropping some 80 feet before hitting the Sumas flats. Then it would be turned northward into a new canal dug between high, widely spaced dykes; skirting along the eastern shore of Sumas Lake, the canal crossed the gently sloping valley floor to join lower Sumas River near the mouth of McGillivray Creek. Most of the hydraulic energy of the Vedder thus would be spent *before* the diversion; in the canal itself, "the current of the Vedder would have less velocity, and [dykes] would be easier to build and maintain."

LeBaron's plan incorporated a second key innovation: the partition of the whole design into self-contained sections or units, which would function just as bulkheads do in a ship's hull. With the planned network of dykes, he explained, the land subject to overflow was "divided into three parts, and if the dykes should break only one of these parts would be flooded." LeBaron recognized the fatal flaw inherent to every drainage plan from the 1870s on: their reliance on a high dyke between Sumas and Chilliwack Mountains to hold back Fraser River waters. Should this dyke break, "the whole territory would be flooded." In LeBaron's scheme, the high Vedder dykes split Sumas Valley in two, forming a dividing line along the old eastern shore of Sumas Lake. Dykes to the east (at Atchelitz) and north (back from Fraser River) created a protected triangle. To the west, the Sumas River dyke and Vedder Mountain created a much larger triangle; the latter was itself bisected by the planned BCER railbed, which would rise 80 feet from the valley floor.

At first, LeBaron had rejected the idea that a dam and pumphouse were required on the lower part of Sumas River; but he soon realized that gravity alone would not take Sumas water to the Fraser. LeBaron's dam would sit "just above the proposed new mouth of the Vedder River," back from McGillivray Creek. During those months when Fraser water was higher than Sumas River, pumps would lift Sumas water into the Fraser; for the rest of the year, the Sumas would flow freely through gates opened in the dam.

Historians have overlooked LeBaron's contributions, giving credit to others for the proposals and innovations he introduced. Yet the ultimate success of the Sumas drainage project owes more to LeBaron than to any other planner or engineer. LeBaron laid out the core components that went into the final Sumas Lake drainage design and set down the operating principles that made it work. He did so by turning the established thinking on its head: orthodox engineers such as Mead and Hill sought out the line of least resistance in plotting new channels and dykes. This line was invariably the most direct route between two points, and since such straight lines rarely exist in nature, they had to be created. Engineering works became complex systems, immaculately conceived on a draftsman's table and imposed on the landscape.

Faced with the same problem, LeBaron chose simplicity over complexity. "It is wise to design it as simply as possible," he wrote:

> It is always good practice to substitute constructions of a simple, strong character, requiring little or no skill, for complicated, risky and delicate works requiring skilled labour of a high class to construct and repair.

Natural forces were altered as little as possible, and wherever possible those forces were to be harnessed or redirected to do the desired work themselves.

Local landowners responded favourably to both the BCER's involvement and LeBaron's plan. In July 1908, Sumas residents again assembled at Upper Sumas town hall; 73 voted in favour of the BCER scheme, while 13 opposed it (nearly all naysayers were non-residents voting by proxy). The next day, west Chilliwack landowners filled the city courthouse, voting 109 to 12 in favour. The collapse of the previous year's opposition vote was due in part to the greater trust felt for the BCER: its competence, local knowledge, physical assets and access to capital. The other factor was that LeBaron's design resolved the vexatious problem of what to do with the raging waters of Chilliwack and Vedder Rivers. The new channel was taken much farther west, along the edge of Sumas Lake; very little of this wetland was owned, effectively defusing any not-in-my-backyard opposition.

Meanwhile, LeBaron's fellow engineers harshly criticized his unorthodox approach. In spring 1908, Stirling Hill was hired by the BCER to supervise its survey teams and to work with LeBaron on plans for the drainage project. LeBaron had rejected Hill's 1906 design; now Hill returned the favour. Smarting from the fact he had been passed over for the post of chief engineer, Hill charged that LeBaron did not know enough about local conditions, leading to "several serious errors." First, Hill claimed, the length and height of dykes required for LeBaron's Vedder diversion would make the plan too costly; the shorter route through Luckakuck or Wilson Creek was superior. Second, LeBaron failed to see that much larger pumps, operating through most of the year, would be required to lift Sumas water into the Fraser. Early in 1909, Hill submitted his own proposal, which was a rehash of the plan he and Daniel Mead had drafted for the Sumas Development Company.

With two conflicting designs in hand, the BCER called in consulting engineer James Schuyler. In engineering terms, Schuyler was unable to choose between the two plans, saying each had its advantages. He was much clearer in his assessment of the financial costs. LeBaron placed a price tag of $1,152,561 on his final design; Schuyler argued the pumps needed for the plan would cost much more, raising the price to $1,550,000. Hill's planned budget of $1,001,007 was even less realistic; Schuyler pegged the real cost at $1,796,000, once again because the cost of the pumping plant would be far greater.

Schuyler's estimates were telegraphed to the BCER's head office in London, where the board of directors pored over them. The hard-headed directors knew from experience that even such second looks tended to underestimate the final costs of a project. Re-examining the work required, they concluded the scheme could hit the $2 million mark. They promptly decided to abandon the project, publicly announcing the move in early April 1909: the cost of building a safe and permanent structure "on the lines proposed" greatly exceeded both the original estimates and "the amount the company was prepared to contribute." Privately, company managers expressed an equally compelling reason for dropping the scheme. The BCER had to begin construction immediately on the Sumas leg of its Chilliwack rail line or risk losing its franchise "through failure to comply with the time limit" of November 1910. With the drainage project abandoned, crews began work on a line running along the foot of Vedder Mountain. On October 3, 1910, with a month to spare, the first BCER train rumbled along the shores of Sumas Lake on its way from New Westminster to Chilliwack.

Yet another scheme to drain Sumas Lake had come to nothing. Drainage proponents reacted with disbelief at what they saw as the blunt, ruthless abandonment of the project. Yet it is unfair to fault the BCER directors for their decision, and the company's involvement in the Sumas drainage scheme was far more positive than recognized at the time. Unlike those who came before, the BCER made its decisions quickly and acted on them promptly; it did not tie up the project for years on end, with nothing done. The company held the reins of the drainage project for just over a year, from March 1908 to April 1909. During this time, it spent over $100,000 on surveys and engineering plans, producing studies and designs that would provide the basis for the final scheme a decade later.[99]

Moreover, during the time they held control, the BCER directors were committed to seeing the project succeed, and they could have raised the capital needed to see it through. The directors concluded, and rightly so, that the project was simply too expensive—indeed, they were the first to appreciate the true scope and cost of the enterprise. The $2 million price tag they foresaw was not far off where the actual construction bill would be at the end of 1924, particularly when we translate the estimate from 1909 to 1924 dollars (World War I caused considerable inflation).

Finally, the BCER's brief but intense involvement clearly demonstrated that the Sumas drainage project could not be done by a private company for profit. No private corporation was better suited to carry out the project than the BCER, with its local knowledge, physical assets, personnel and access to capital. But its directors' calculations were correct: the risk was simply too high, the odds that post-drainage revenues would cover the massive investment needed too low. Success required direct government involvement, an argument many proponents had been making for years; likewise, returns or benefits needed to be seen in terms of the public good, not just private profit. These were truths even those who would successfully oversee the draining of Sumas Lake dared not speak.

CHAPTER 9

A LAKE DEWATERED

Those who wished to see Sumas Lake dewatered were stunned by the news that the BCER would no longer be involved in any drainage scheme. This was the closest proponents had come to achieving their hopes and they refused to give up; over summer and fall 1909, the Sumas Dyking Commissioners and the *Chilliwack Progress* launched a campaign to revive the project. The commissioners enlisted the help of four engineers who had worked on the BCER scheme to come up with a new plan. Led by Daniel Mead and Stirling Hill, but excluding Francis LeBaron, the group banged together a plan, which was submitted to the commissioners and then published verbatim over seven editions of the *Chilliwack Progress*. The new plan was a warmed-over version of the old Mead-Hill proposal. But it took two giant steps *backward*: it resurrected the argument that the Luckakuck diversion was "greatly superior" to any other; and it claimed the whole project could be completed for a mere $932,000, "about one-half of that estimated by the BCER."

James Schuyler had shown definitively that Mead and Hill were wrong on these two points, but the power of wishful thinking kept their plan alive. In 1911, L.M. Rice and Company of Seattle stepped forward with a proposal to drain Sumas Lake using the Mead-Hill design. Rice and the dyking commission signed a contract that fall; when Rice failed to start work within the allotted one year, the commissioners granted an extension and called a public meeting to drum up support. On January 15, 1913, landowners crowded into the Upper Sumas town hall to consider whether Rice should continue with the scheme: 104 owners voted in favour, 37 against. Even this vote of approval failed to stir Rice to action. By the end of 1913, the only accomplishment the company could point to was its submission of a formal design for the project. The December plan was a copy of the 1909 engineering group design, right down to nearly identical cost estimates. The one important difference concerned the Luckakuck diversion, although here too Rice borrowed from earlier reports. While the Luckakuck was "the most natural and direct course" for diverting the Chilliwack River, local opposition to the route was so strong it would be "futile to try to overcome it." In its place, Rice suggested a lower diversion ending at Wilson Creek, an option first advanced by Mead and Hill.

Through this whole time, not a shovel of Sumas soil was turned and not a dollar of financing raised. As public opinion grew ever more restive, landowners cast about for alternative proposals. In 1913, a group of upper Sumas farmers got behind a plan advanced by William Fadden that would have seen the partial draining of the lake: the western half of the valley would be protected from flood waters by a massive dyke running along the western edge of Sumas Lake, from Vedder to Sumas Mountain. The idea had been circulating since 1889, when it was put forward as a way to salvage the drainage project in the wake of the E.L. Derby fiasco. The proposal to partially dewater Sumas was not given serious consideration at either time, but it would be revived five years later, again in response to delays in the project.[100]

Also that year, a former BCER engineer named Frederick Sinclair put together a more comprehensive design and launched a personal campaign to have it adopted. Sinclair was an American railroad engineer who had done preliminary fieldwork on the Vancouver, Victoria and Eastern Railway. Early in 1907, he was hired by the BCER to survey a possible rail line through the middle of Sumas Valley. When the company abandoned the Sumas drainage scheme, Sinclair was put in charge of the crew constructing the last leg of the railway to Chilliwack. Let go by the BCER, Sinclair moved on to other work, but the prospect of draining Sumas Lake continued to intrigue him. The idea that he could draw upon his experience to devise his own scheme was first suggested to him by an American colleague some years earlier. By October 1913, Sinclair was ready to put his thoughts to paper in a preliminary report.

Sinclair's report was based on the exhaustive fieldwork, reports and plans produced by the BCER. Most importantly, his plan incorporated the core innovations of Francis LeBaron's design. First, the water from Chilliwack River would be allowed to run westward through upper Vedder River onto Sumas Prairie, then turned northward into Vedder Canal. Failing to credit LeBaron, Sinclair wrote immodestly, "I have taken the water from the Vedder after it has become a quiet stream and out through a section of the Valley...where there could be no opposition." Sinclair added that the slow-moving Vedder Canal—corralled between widely spaced outer dykes—also would serve as a massive reservoir for water entering from both the Fraser and Chilliwack Rivers. Second, Sinclair proposed rechannelling Sumas River and centralizing the dam and pumphouse in one location. And third, he described in detail the compartmentalized "unit system" of his design. The East Prairie unit was enclosed by the Fraser River, Atchelitz Creek and east Vedder Canal dykes; the lake-bed unit was formed by Sumas and Vedder Mountains and the west Vedder Canal dyke; and the West Prairie unit stretched west of the upper Sumas River dyke. Sinclair favoured proceeding with the whole design as one project; if that proved financially impractical, he noted, then the work could be done unit by unit, over a longer period of time.

Sinclair's report was significant in its own right. To be sure, LeBaron had introduced its core components four years earlier; and Sinclair's cost estimate of $733,660 represented a giant step backward in the effort to put a realistic price tag on the drainage project. But the former BCER engineer succeeded in putting LeBaron's ideas, if not his name, back on the agenda. From summer 1914 on, Sinclair attended public meetings of Sumas landowners and submitted his plan to the Sumas Dyking Commissioners. In early 1917, the Sumas Land Owners' Protective Association passed a resolution strongly in favour of Sinclair's plan, sending it off to the provincial government. That March, Sinclair attended a high-powered meeting in Victoria that included Premier Harlan Brewster, future premier John Oliver, federal interior minister Mackenzie King and the Sumas Dyking Commissioners.[101]

The March 1917 meeting was convened to consider the fate of the Sumas drainage project in the wake of two developments from the previous fall. The first was the expiration of Rice's charter, which had at last run out of extensions. The second was the landslide victory of a reform-minded Liberal government in the 1916 provincial election. One of the new government's earliest moves was to establish the Land Settlement Board (LSB) as an arm's-length body within the Agriculture Department, headed by a chairman and five directors. The brainchild of activist lands minister Duff Pattullo, the LSB's mandate was to promote modern agricultural development in the province. New lands were to be opened up to settlers, with preference given to returned veterans. John Oliver, then agriculture minister and future premier, was the strongest advocate for soldier settlement in the new administration. For him, the LSB was the instrument by which the government could meet its "need for land on which to settle the returned soldier." The Sumas drainage scheme was one of a handful of projects Oliver and Pattullo had in mind for the LSB. Specific provision was made for board directors to take over as Sumas Dyking Commissioners, which would give the LSB direct control over the drainage project.

In summer 1917, with the Sumas scheme drifting, Pattullo decided to act. He penned a confidential letter to Edward Barrow (the Member of the Legislative Assembly for Chilliwack), suggesting that the dyking commissioners instigate a petition from Sumas landowners requesting that the LSB take over. The commissioners, now led by long-time Upper Sumas resident John Atkinson, had become convinced that only direct government involvement could save the project. Through the fall, a majority of Sumas landowners signed the orchestrated petition, the commissioners tendered their resignations and directors of the LSB were duly appointed in their place. The former commissioners were permitted to linger on as members of a newly created advisory committee. In early 1918, the provincial cabinet officially approved the takeover.

The speed and apparent ease with which these events took place should not obscure their significance: the move by the LSB to take control of the Sumas Dyking Commission was the most decisive event in the decades-long campaign to dewater Sumas Lake. The key opening the deadlock was a change in the policy and actions of the provincial government. It created the LSB for just such a purpose, then orchestrated the board's smooth assumption of control. As the Sumas drainage project proceeded through the following years, the premier, cabinet and relevant ministers would be involved in key decisions. And when the project threatened to founder, the government made it possible for the LSB to obtain funding to keep the work going.

The involvement of the provincial government—at the highest levels—created a broad consensus among Sumas officials and landowners that Victoria now firmly backed the scheme and that success was thereby ensured. Yet "Honest John" Oliver, the new premier, went out of his way to pierce the optimistic bubble that surrounded the project. Striking the tough-talking, "tell it like it is" pose of so many politicians before and since, Oliver was adamant that his government's policy had not changed: the dyking commissioners, not Victoria, were responsible for the project; and the scheme would have to pay for itself through levies on landowners who benefited from it and through sales of drained lands. At a meeting of Sumas landowners in November 1919, when the decisive vote on the LSB scheme was taken, Oliver explicitly rejected "the general impression that the government was backing the scheme….The provincial government is taking no responsibility whatever for this scheme: understand that clearly." But Oliver later contradicted himself by stating that, after drainage, the

A group of beach-goers enjoys a sunny afternoon on the western shore of Sumas Lake. They have armed themselves with branches to beat back persistent mosquitoes and sandflies (c.1900). The Reach P1394.

provincial government would "be given power to dispose of these lands for the benefit of liquidating the debt of the district."

Caught in the middle of this was Edward Barrow, recently appointed the Minister of Agriculture with ultimate responsibility for the LSB. As a member of cabinet, Barrow could not publicly disagree with the premier; but as local provincial representative, he desperately wanted to see the drainage project succeed. Behind the scenes, Barrow used his ministerial position to lobby for the project in cabinet and caucus. He also took every opportunity to build public support for the scheme.

In 1918, an old villain presented him with a golden opportunity to do just that. In spring and summer, as Sumas residents fretted over the lack of progress in the drainage scheme, the lower Fraser Valley suffered through a particularly bad plague of mosquitoes. Winter flooding had been followed by an exceptionally high spring freshet, which deposited mosquito eggs far and wide. When the waters receded, the summer sun and heat hatched countless swarms of bloodthirsty insects. Newspaper headlines screamed "Mosquito Must Be Exterminated," and "Mighty Mosquito Must Migrate." The situation presented in the press was dire. The winged invaders had brought the valley's economy to a virtual standstill: fruit pickers, lumbermen and other outdoor workers were forced inside during peak season; and milk production dropped as cows suffered through the affliction. This was on top of the general torture visited upon all residents.

Scores of local politicians, businessmen, prominent citizens and scientists convened at a pair of "Mosquito Conferences"—the first in Mission, the second in Chilliwack. Barrow was the keynote speaker at both meetings, and he promised passage of a new Mosquito Control Act, which focussed on insect control through methods such as oiling. But the minister realized the limits of his own legislation; he echoed the statement of one senior federal scientist that "oil was not a cure all. Reclamation and drainage were the only true remedies for the mosquito." Barrow himself did not claim that draining Sumas Lake would eradicate the mosquito threat in the area, but the implication was there. Meanwhile, a meeting of upper Sumas farmers expressed the hope that "the dyking of the lake would do away with the mosquito pest to a great extent." The *Chilliwack Progress* added its view that the drainage project would "incidentally wipe out one of the worst mosquito breeding grounds in the Fraser Valley."

The view of mosquitoes as a clear and present danger was not a significant factor in the campaign to drain Sumas Lake. Even the *Chilliwack Progress* admitted that eradicating the menace was only a secondary, "incidental" benefit. But the mosquito threat did help galvanize public opinion as the scheme moved through the final planning stage. During the early construction years, the mosquito question was kept alive by federal entomologist Eric Hearle, who was sent to the lower Fraser in summer 1919. Hearle spent three seasons criss-crossing the valley—by canoe, motorboat, automobile and airplane— seeking out mosquito breeding zones. His reports corroborated earlier claims that the numbers and virulence of mosquitoes hurt the region's economy. He concluded that spreading oils provided some relief, but that the only effective long-term solution was "the elimination of flood-water breeding areas by dyking and pumping." Of the 30 such breeding areas from New Westminster to Hope identified by Hearle, upper and lower Sumas Prairies were the most prolific. However, his solution to the mosquito problem at Sumas fell well short of draining Sumas Lake. "The draining of a mile of the lake shore," he concluded, "would soon result in the elimination of the greatest mosquito breeding ground in the Lower Mainland."[102]

While Barrow led the public-opinion campaign, out of the spotlight the LSB engineers soldiered on. In September 1918, engineers Harvey Brice and Chester Smith drafted the first *Key Map of the Sumas Reclamation Area*. Four months later, after nearly a year of study, they submitted their much-awaited report. Brice and Smith stressed that their January 1919 submission was not a final plan, that many details still needed to be worked out. Nevertheless, the 63-page report was the most exhaustive to date and would provide the blueprint for the project as it moved forward.

Brice and Smith began with the thorniest problem: what to do with the waters of Chilliwack River as they spilled onto the valley floor. They demonstrated conclusively that diversion of the stream down the Lucka-kuck was unworkable from an engineering perspective (not because of local opposition to it). Dropping some 35 feet per mile at its steepest, the Lucka-kuck water would reach dangerously high velocities, placing great stress on its dykes. The downward pressure of the water and the fact that it ran over higher, more porous ground would cause seepage and flooding outside the dykes. The yearly cost of maintaining the diversion rendered the option too expensive, and the threat to surrounding farmlands made it too risky. A diversion beginning farther west, running through Wilson Creek, had similar problems: the grade was lower but still significant, bringing fast water and seepage.

The superior option was a new Vedder Canal even farther to the west. As in LeBaron's and Sinclair's plans, the Vedder River was allowed to run to the eastern edge of Sumas Lake before being diverted. The canal then took "a direct course from the end of the curve at the point of diversion, to the mouth of McGillivray Slough." The large outer dykes to the east and west ran in parallel lines, 350 feet across from each other, and averaged 20 feet high. The low gradient of the canal bed—1½ feet per mile at low water—produced a channel with a "slow, uniform velocity" that was more easily controlled; the valley floor's mucky soil meant less seepage; and the location of the canal's mouth meant it would not interfere with the drainage of McGillivray Slough. Another advantage of the Vedder Canal and its substantial dykes was that it divided the whole drainage design into self-contained units. Following LeBaron and Sinclair, Brice and Smith constructed their design on the "unit system."

The components needed for draining the 6,500-acre East Prairie unit were fairly straightforward. The East Vedder dyke, built from soil excavated for Vedder Canal, protected the unit on the west. To the north lay the Fraser River dyke, pulled back from the Fraser and running along the northern edge of the Canadian Northern Railway bed. The Atchelitz dyke to the east and high ground below Vedder Mountain to the south completed the enclosure. A dam, floodgates and pumphouse at the mouth of McGillivray Creek drew the water out into lower Sumas River. The lake-bed unit itself comprised just under 12,000 acres. Dewatering it involved construction of a new channel for Sumas River, with a high dyke on its south bank and Sumas Mountain to the north. A large dam complex on the river—with floodgates and an expensive plant of pumps—and a network of canals and ditches moved water from the lake bed and upper Sumas River. It also held back the flood waters of Fraser River.

What made the Brice-Smith plan unique was its handling of the West Prairie unit, which encompassed 11,800 acres from the western shore of Sumas Lake to the international boundary. It was here that the pair examined the viability of draining only the western part of Sumas Valley, leaving Sumas Lake itself intact. This was a response to a proposal put forward the previous year by Upper Sumas municipal council that would have dewatered only upper Sumas Prairie. That plan would have built a dyke along the western shore of Sumas Lake, from Vedder Mountain to Sumas Mountain, complete with appropriate sluices and gates. Chester Smith attended the spring 1918 council meeting; according to newspaper coverage, he rejected plans for the wholesale drainage of the valley as impractical and expressed support for the "smaller dyking scheme." Over the summer and fall, a group of local landowners formed the Marshall Creek Dyking Association and approached a Vancouver engineering firm to carry out the scheme. The firm expressed interest in the project, and in December, Upper Sumas council gave its backing. While no work was ever done, the initiative showed how seriously the partial draining action was being taken, at least in the western half of Sumas Valley.

In January 1919, realizing they had to address the issue, the LSB directors instructed Brice and Smith to give the partial drainage option serious consideration. "In the event of it not proving to be economic to reclaim all or any considerable part of the bed of Sumas Lake," the LSB stipulated, the engineers were ordered "to devise plans for the reclamation of the... East and West Prairies, leaving the lake bed unreclaimed for the present at least."

Accordingly, the West Prairie unit components proposed by the pair left Sumas Lake intact, but enclosed it between dykes to the west and east. A low dyke ran along the western edge from Vedder to Sumas Mountains, "following the lake ridges, [to] confine the lake to its normal shore line." A small dam and pumphouse at the mouth of upper Sumas River moved its water into the lake. Across the lake, Vedder Canal kept the waters of Chilliwack River out of Sumas Lake, diverting them directly to lower Sumas River, then on to the Fraser. The high west Vedder Canal dyke doubled as the lake's eastern shore. A large dam at the head of lower Sumas River kept back the Fraser freshets; sluice gates would permit Sumas Lake water to drain northward, but pumps would not be needed to lift water out of the lake itself. The engineers' conclusion was that this design was the "only one worthy of consideration" should the LSB decide to proceed with the partial draining of Sumas Valley. The plan required no major pumping and fit in with designs for draining other parts of the valley. It could be undertaken now, with other work—draining the East Prairie unit and/or Sumas Lake itself—coming later.

Brice and Smith demonstrated that the option of partially draining Sumas Valley—building the East and West Prairie units but leaving Sumas Lake intact—was a viable one from the engineering perspective. Despite this, the pair strongly recommended the LSB proceed with "the reclamation of the entire district"—built on the unit design, but undertaken as one project. The partial drainage design, they argued, would end up costing more per acre reclaimed and "the lake lands would still be left unreclaimed." The "whole project" dewatered all three units—30,000 acres in total—at a cost of $1,249,430 (or $41.70 per acre). Draining the East Prairie unit on its own would cost $442,733 ($68 per acre); the West Prairie unit alone would cost $331,786 ($28 per acre). If combined, the east and west units would run to $774,519 ($42.32 per acre).

Brice and Smith's own numbers, though, demonstrated that the per-acre cost of draining only the flood lands on either side of Sumas Lake was the same as draining the lake and valley as a whole. Indeed, the partial drainage option had distinct advantages: the overall cost was much less, which would have saved considerable money in eventual financing costs; and there was no need for a complex dam and pumphouse on the lower Sumas River, cutting both the initial and yearly costs. The subsequent decision to go with a total drainage scheme was not made solely on objective facts of what could be done and how much it would cost. The decision came down to what the LSB, its political masters and the majority of landowners desired and imagined. The mindsets of all the key players were so fixed that they simply could not picture a future of the region with Sumas Lake in it: the complete draining of Sumas Valley had come to be seen as a matter of necessity, not choice.

There also were more concrete factors at work. From 1917 on, the mandate of the LSB virtually guaranteed that it would seek the draining of the lake bed. As Agriculture Minister Edward Barrow explained, the board's policy was "not to buy lands already under cultivation. Our policy is to add to the production of the province by bringing into cultivation as much virgin soil as possible adjacent to transportation and markets." The LSB took over the Sumas drainage scheme for this very reason: by draining the lake, it created *new* agricultural land, ready for the plow. Indeed, the need to dewater all of Sumas Lake was built into every major drainage scheme from the very earliest on. For half a century, the provincial government refused to treat the "reclamation" of Sumas Lake as a public, or even semi-public, project. It provided no funding up front and stubbornly insisted that the project pay for itself. The only way companies could make the project pay was through the future sale of *new* land—that is, the 12,000 acres that lay beneath Sumas Lake. And the only way companies could raise the capital needed up front was to use the grant of yet-to-be "reclaimed" lands as collateral.

We have gone through this extended discussion of the partial drainage option—a proposal that was never seriously considered by decision makers—to show that there was nothing inevitable about the draining of Sumas Lake. Under different circumstances, the lake could have been saved, even while the expansive flood lands on either side of it were dyked and drained. This would have met the overriding goal of transforming thousands of acres of wetland into fertile agricultural land. But saving Sumas Lake would have required the provincial government to take over the project, financing and controlling it from start to finish just as it was doing with other infrastructure works. Only the government could undertake the project without relying on the promise of a drained lake bed to raise capital or later sell off to pay for the project.

To their credit, Brice and Smith recognized this underlying truth: that the dewatering of Sumas Valley was an inherently public project. The pair believed that draining the entire valley was the best option, but they were clear-headed enough to see that it could not be done without direct government involvement. They were the first and only project engineers to make this case:

>The Sumas Reclamation Project is a feasible and economic
>engineering project, and worthy of the most hearty support
>of the government. The enterprise is distinctly not one to
>be undertaken by private interests. The magnitude of the
>project, the difficulties of properly financing from the private
>standpoint, and the very considerable public nature of the
>enterprise, combine to make it distinctly a public function.

The call for direct government involvement was met with a resounding silence. The LSB and provincial government felt the engineers should stick to their plumb lines and slide rules, and leave the messy financial matters to them.[103]

Nevertheless, within weeks of receiving the Brice-Smith report, the LSB and provincial cabinet gave it their stamp of approval. Ignoring the call for direct government backing, they decided to move forward on the recommended draining of the whole valley, using the report as a blueprint. The vexing diversion question was settled definitively in favour of a newly constructed Vedder Canal; a major Sumas River dam and pumphouse would take care of Sumas Lake water; and the massive work would be broken down into self-contained units. The LSB's engineering team was then instructed to come up with a final design to accomplish this. However, in March, chief engineer Harvey Brice was taken ill and died, robbing the board of his expertise. Curiously, Chester Smith was not promoted to take his place, but remained an associate engineer; instead, Frederick Sinclair was quickly hired, with the same title and salary as Smith.

The two-headed arrangement did not work well. Personal tension between Smith and Sinclair existed from the start. Smith resented not being promoted to head engineer; Sinclair harboured his own resentment at not being taken on as engineer in the first place, and at what he considered Brice and Smith's pilfering of "his" plan for the project. By summer 1919, the pair had stopped working together. Unable to unite behind a single final plan, they drafted and submitted separate reports.

Yet the plans turned in by Smith and Sinclair in July agreed on all the main points. Differences of opinion existed only "on nonessential matters," wrote Smith in his report. Sinclair noted in his that the plans' principal components were "identical...and only in a few instances, vary in location." Both plans diverted Vedder River at the same point, through a wide, high-dyked canal to the lower Sumas River. The mouth of Smith's canal was just above McGillivray Creek, while Sinclair moved it some 800 feet upstream. Both plans also relied on a large, centralized dam and pump-house on Sumas River, which Sinclair placed half a mile above his Vedder Canal mouth. Originally, Smith and Brice had located the dam more than a mile to the west; in his July proposal, Smith moved the plant well down Sumas River, but still 3,000 feet above Sinclair's plant. The final difference was over the Fraser River dyke. Smith stuck with his and Brice's initial proposal, placing the dyke to the north of the Canadian Northern Railway line. Sinclair pulled it even farther back from the Fraser, running it along the southern edge of the Canadian National Railway bed.

Smith and Sinclair completed their reports in early July; on the 15th, they were in Victoria to present their designs to an ad hoc committee consisting of the premier, Barrow, all five LSB directors and the Sumas Advisory Board. Smith spoke first, but when he began outlining the location of his Fraser River dyke, he was unceremoniously stopped by Oliver. "Young man," the premier interrupted, "you mean to tell me that you're protecting the Canadian National—a forty million dollar corporation—at the expense of the farmers of Sumas?" Oliver and Barrow then swept out of the room, leaving a stunned Smith behind. The pair were convinced to return, this time to hear Sinclair's proposal. Before the engineer could start, the premier asked where the Fraser dyke would be; when Sinclair answered south of the Canadian National Railway, he was allowed to continue. Upon finishing, Sinclair was complimented by Oliver for a "very comprehensive scheme."

The committee convened again the following day, this time to hear from P.M. Smith, a junior engineer who had been given the unenviable task of passing judgment on the designs of his two bosses. The younger Smith had worked directly under Sinclair and was more familiar with the latter's work; rightly protesting that his task had "not been a pleasant one," Smith gave the nod to Sinclair. The decision was promptly made: the project would proceed on the basis of Sinclair's design, with Sinclair in charge of the next step (although not yet promoted to chief engineer). At the same time, the LSB informed Chester Smith that his plan had been rejected and that his services were no longer required.

Yet again, Chester Smith had been cheated by an unpredictable turn of events. Smith was undone in part by Premier Oliver's childish pique at funding a project that might benefit a federally chartered railway company. More substantively, the engineer dared to say things the LSB and Victoria did not want to hear. In January, he had forcefully called for the government to step in and treat the drainage of Sumas Lake as a public project. Smith's July report was more muted, but it still argued that "the government might properly be expected to bear a large part of the necessary expenditure." It was unfair to expect Sumas landowners to bear the full cost of a project that benefited others as well as them. Most particularly, Chilliwack landowners had solved the threat posed by the Chilliwack River by pushing it into the laps of Sumas residents; the former also should be asked to contribute.

All of these things were true, as would be borne out over the following decades, but they did not help Smith's case. Nor did the fact that Smith submitted a more realistic and honest cost estimate: $1,447,706 to Sinclair's $1,152,795. What was more, Sinclair made no mention of government funding or involvement in his 1919 final report. Through the previous half-decade, while promoting his own plan, he had stuck to the specious argument that no government funding was needed, that the project could be financed solely by private capital.

The LSB moved quickly to put this tempest behind it. Through summer and fall 1919, Sinclair was given the task of ironing out details of the plan, and an outside expert was consulted to give a final appraisal of the design. The LSB was now satisfied it had the right plan and the right man, officially appointing Sinclair as the chief engineer. The board also called a meeting of Sumas landowners, as required by law. On Saturday, November 22, Sumas landowners crammed into the Huntingdon tavern, which, thanks to Prohibition, could not quench the thirst of the jam-packed crowd. After hearing from the LSB chairman, MLA Barrow

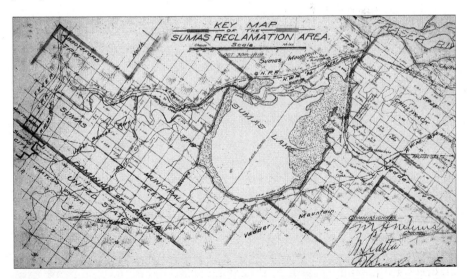

The final, official map used in the construction of the Sumas Lake drainage project. Notice how the lake is made to look even smaller, with its shores shrunken back and surrounded by large muddy flats (1919). Royal BC Museum and Archives, CM/A 1855.

and the premier himself, it was left to Frederick Sinclair to explain the finer points of the proposed plan. He concluded with the most important detail, stating confidently, "$1,500,000, which included interest for five years, could about cover the cost of the work." Based on this figure, landowners voted 144 to 21 in favour of the plan. Four months later, the LSB convened another public meeting to get approval for a new cost estimate of $1.8 million. This second vote was even more lopsided: 102 for, five against.

With a strong vote of approval, the LSB forged ahead. In January 1920, it placed notices in newspapers calling for bids from private companies to undertake the first phase of construction. The contract included the bulk of the earthworks: the Vedder Canal and all its dykes; the Fraser River, Sumas River and Atchelitz Creek dykes; the Sumas Lake drainage canal; various interception ditches; and bridges. (Construction of the Sumas and McGillivray dams and pumps would be covered in later contracts.) Four qualified bids were received by the deadline, all of which exceeded chief engineer Sinclair's estimate of $980,245. The provincial cabinet balked at the high tenders and ordered the LSB to have the companies bid again. The new bids were identical to the first: two of these were on a commission basis and thus put aside, leaving the Marsh Construction Co. (at $1,182,063) and the Northern Construction Co. (at $1,527,657). On Sinclair's recommendation, Marsh was awarded the contract as the lowest bidder—30 percent below its competitor. After presenting the company's proposal at the late-March meeting of Sumas landholders, the LSB and Marsh signed a contract on April 29.

That same month, the provincial government rushed through the Sumas Drainage, Dyking and Development Act. The new legislation belatedly repealed the 1905 Sumas Development Act. It also retroactively ratified the LSB's takeover as dyking commissioners three years earlier, and validated all actions and decisions it had taken since. Meanwhile, the LSB itself was streamlined into a one-man show: its board of directors was reduced to one member, R.D. Davies, who in turn became the sole Sumas dyking commissioner. A former colonel during the Great War, Davies capably directed the project through its critical construction years.

At long last, everything seemed in place for work to begin. By the end of May 1920, Marsh was in the field clearing the right-of-way for the planned dykes, canals and ditches. Then Fraser River began to rise, climbing for six full weeks before peaking at its highest level in nearly two decades. All work was put on hold, and would not continue until the end of August. Delays due to the yearly freshet had been foreseen and written into

From the left: Col. R.D. Davies, an LSB director and sole commissioner of the Sumas Dyking Commission; Frederick Sinclair, chief engineer; and D.D. Munroe, another LSB director. The men are posed in front of the Sumas drainage works. Davies and Sinclair are dressed for the field, with knee-high rubber boots and protective coats. Royal BC Museum and Archives, D-09675.

Marsh's contract, which specified that all the necessary machinery was to be on the ground and ready to start work as soon as the flood waters receded. But going in, no one fully appreciated the impact Sumas Lake's yearly flood cycle would have on the work. As Frederick Sinclair later explained, they were "at the mercy of the high water." Construction could take place only during a shortened working year: each work year commenced "with the fall of water in August, and terminated with the rise of flood water again in the early Summer." Some of the heavier work—such as parts of the Vedder Canal and dykes—required the land to be completely dry, which further reduced the work year to seven months. On the other hand, the high waters of the freshet period made it easier to move the massive suction dredges from one place to another.[104]

Construction of the Sumas Lake drainage project took place over four such working years, with the large majority of construction done in the middle two years. Year One ran from high water 1920 to high water 1921; Year Two, high water 1921 to high water 1922; Year Three, high water

1922 to high water 1923; and Year Four, high water 1923 to high water 1924. The seasonal flood cycle also set yearly deadlines for work to be completed—a component had to be far enough along and strong enough to withstand the spring freshet, or risk being washed away. And work had to proceed at full pace through the winter, when the days were shorter and the weather at its worst. Heavy rain, snow, ice and the yearly winter freshet also slowed progress. Fortunately for the drainage builders, the "unit system" upon which the drainage design was built made it possible to work within the seasonally defined schedule. By splitting up the design into self-contained units, each work year could focus on one unit, putting all efforts into completing it before the flood waters arrived. Work then moved on to the next unit the following year.

Construction Year One got under way on August 30, 1920, when a No. 205 P&H dragline shovel broke ground for the McGillivray Creek interception ditch. The target for the first year was to have enough of the East Prairie unit completed—including the crucial Vedder Canal and east dyke—in time for high water 1921. Marsh knew it could not meet that goal with the lone P&H excavator and its ¾-cubic-yard bucket. The company had ordered a much larger steam shovel, the *Bucyrus*, but the machine was tied up in Vancouver harbour because Marsh did not have the money to pay for it. The *Bucyrus* was a behemoth: its 3½-cubic-yard bucket sat at the end of a 100-foot boom, and its 35-foot housing enclosed a massive coal-fired steam engine. The machine's Ohio-based manufacturer had supplied 77 of the 102 steam shovels used to excavate the Panama Canal; the *Bucyrus* most likely was one of them. Through fall 1920, chief engineer Sinclair became increasingly anxious, and he pressed the LSB to take action. The board responded by securing $45,000 from the provincial government to buy the *Bucyrus*, then leased it back to Marsh.

Loaded on two barges, the *Bucyrus* made the perilous journey up the Fraser River into lower Sumas River. The flotilla got snagged on pilings near the Canadian Northern bridge, nearly capsizing, and workers had to use dynamite to free it. Finally, on November 18, the reassembled steam shovel began work on the Fraser River dyke. Through that winter and into the following spring, the *Bucyrus* and P&H dragline made progress on the Fraser and Atchelitz dykes, as well as the McGillivray ditches. At the same time, a line of electrical poles and high-tension wires was run from the BC Electric Railway's Woodroofe station northward along the foot of the future East Vedder dyke to the main construction camp at the mouth of Vedder Canal. During construction, the 34,000-volt line carried power to dredges and excavators (some originally electric, others such as the *Bucyrus* converted to it) and to the various construction camps; after construction, it would supply the Sumas dam and pumphouse.

As the freshet of 1921 brought construction Year One to a close, the view from the ground was disheartening. The hulking *Bucyrus* had made a start on the East Prairie dykes, but it toiled with little help, its work slowed by harsh winter weather. Then spring brought historically high waters, cresting 1½ feet above the previous year; much of the work already done was washed away, and lower and upper Sumas Prairies were inundated. At the same time, it became increasingly clear that Marsh Construction Co. did not have the resources to complete the contracted work; the project was doomed to failure if things proceeded as they were. At first, the LSB tried to push the company in the right direction. It arranged an agreement between Marsh and the A.S. McDonald Company of Tacoma to supply the additional draglines and suction dredges needed. When the machines started arriving in March, McDonald himself was appointed superintendent of construction. Soon after, McDonald employee Art Strong took over from his boss; through the critical years of construction, he remained in "complete charge of the work," reporting directly to Sinclair.

Not even this was enough to save Marsh. When the company found itself unable to pay the bill for McDonald's machinery, the LSB decided it was time to take direct control. Commissioner Davies sent a sternly worded letter to Marsh president John Duncan demanding "a definite statement admitting their inability to continue and asking the Land Settlement Board to assume control." Duncan had no choice but to comply. Beginning August 1, Marsh would continue as the construction company of record, but the LSB took direct control of financing "in full," making monthly payments to Marsh as work progressed. The board also clarified the chain of command: from R.D. Davies down to Sinclair, to Strong, to Marsh.[105]

Thus, while little progress was made on the ground through Year One, behind the scenes crucial changes were made to put the project to drain Sumas Lake back on track. The LSB was now firmly in control, and as the high water of 1921 receded and construction Year Two got under way, it had the equipment, organization and men in place for work to begin in earnest. Davies and Sinclair set a firm goal of completing the East Prairie unit before the 1922 high water, while progressing far enough on the West Prairie unit to keep back the Fraser River waters.

The main part of this work was the excavation of Vedder Canal and construction of the massive dykes protecting it—this was the linchpin that

The soil excavated from the Vedder Canal was used to build dykes on either side. The work proceeded from south to north, as seen here. Note the power lines stretched out behind the eastern dyke being built. Royal BC Museum and Archives, D-09674.

held the whole design together. Work on Vedder Canal began in late August 1921, when the electric suction dredge *Col. Tobin* floated up lower Sumas River to the main camp. A.S. McDonald arranged the lease of the *Col. Tobin*—a 100-foot-long scow worth $150,000—from the Puget Sound Bridge & Dredging Co. of Seattle. Floating on high spring water to the point where Vedder River was diverted, the *Col. Tobin* turned around and worked its way north, the massive screw mounted on its bow cutting into the unbroken ground. The soil was then saturated with water and pumped out through 20-inch piping. The liquefied soil was carried over imposing wooden bulwarks constructed on either side of the canal, where it was dumped. The *Bucyrus* dragline shovel then took this material and began shaping the canal's eastern dyke. Conditions through September were ideal; that month, the *Col. Tobin* moved some 400,000 cubic yards of soil and completed one-quarter of the three-mile Vedder Canal.

At the end of October, heavy rain triggered a flash freshet down Vedder River, washing out some of the work. This was followed by one of the worst winters on record. An ice storm in November halted work for a week; another in December did the same. Frigid temperatures froze the ground two feet deep and dynamite had to be used to break it up; the canal also froze, momentarily trapping the *Col. Tobin*. The bad weather continued through January and February, but the *Col. Tobin* and *Bucyrus* soldiered on.

It was, of course, the construction workers who bore the brunt of the harsh winter conditions and accelerated pace. Crews on the power shovels and suction dredges put in 10-hour shifts, six days a week, plus a half day every other Sunday. During pushes, extra day hours and full night shifts were added. The work itself was hard, messy and dangerous. Clad in hip boots and short raincoats, workers slogged through the mud, manhandling sodden timbers to build the bulwarks or wrestling the large suction pipes into place. The most heart-racing job was laying dynamite to loosen frozen ground. Art Van Meter recalled working the graveyard shift that winter, "out in the middle of Sumas Prairie in freezing weather." With a sledge-hammer and metal stake, he would dig holes every four feet, five holes a row, several rows at a time:

> I'd make up 30 to 50 charges and insert them in the holes….I would start lighting my charges consecutively until the first would go off. Then I would take off out across the prairie in that cold northeast wind with kerosene lantern swinging like mad. It's lucky I didn't fall in a hole. When the blasts stopped for a while, I'd take a chance and go back to finish the ones that did not discharge.

For this, Van Meter earned 75 cent an hour, from which he paid $1.40 a day for room and board at the workers' camp.

Fortunately, conditions in the camps were good: hot showers, proper bathrooms and decent food. On top of that was a regular supply of liquor, a don't-ask, don't-tell arrangement, since the construction contract explicitly barred alcohol from the site. Kilgard store owner David Matthews obtained the lucrative liquor concession, making daily runs to the camps to satisfy the workers' thirst.[106]

March 1922 brought much-needed relief, as the harsh winter weather broke and crucial reinforcements arrived. Two new suction dredges were put on the job: the *Robson*, an ungainly 150-foot scow leased from the Pacific Construction Co.; and the *King Edward*, a converted paddlewheel steamer owned by the federal government. Also, A.S. McDonald provided two electric-powered Lidgerwood dragline shovels, with booms measuring 88 feet and 65 feet. The larger of these immediately joined the *Bucyrus* on the East Vedder dyke. By early April, the "complete diversion" of Vedder River into Vedder Canal had been accomplished; by the end of May, East Vedder dyke had been built up to 15 feet. The other components of the

East Prairie unit—the Fraser and Atchelitz dykes, and the McGillivray dam and pumphouse—were also completed. Now, all eyes turned to the rising Fraser, memories of the devastating 1921 floods still fresh in everyone's mind. The water peaked on June 9, 1½ feet lower than the previous year and less than two feet below the top of the East Vedder dyke. The dykes held, thanks in part to frantic sandbagging to stop seepage through the freshly compacted levees. For the first time in its history, lower Sumas Prairie stayed dry through the spring freshet.

While the LSB proclaimed victory in the East Prairie unit, it was facing defeat farther west. By spring 1922, the West Prairie unit was nowhere near complete; but considerable work had been done on the Sumas River dykes and parts of the West Vedder levee, in the hope that they could hold back the rising Fraser waters that June through August. The biggest gap in these defences remained Sumas River itself, and the decision was made to construct a temporary dam upriver from the Vedder Canal mouth. That May, the LSB pulled out all stops in a race against the freshet. It positioned the *King Edward* and *Col. Tobin* on either side of the dam site, working the machines around the clock to build up the barrier. But the soil at the site was too sandy and would not hold, so the *Col. Tobin* returned downriver to the denser material of Vedder Canal; from here it pumped a steady stream of mucky soil 5,000 feet back to the dam.

With the waters rising, it became apparent that the dredges had got onto the job too late—the previous harsh winter had kept them on the Vedder Canal much longer than planned. Fearing the pressure of backed-up water would threaten existing dykes and banks, Sinclair decided to dynamite the temporary dam and let the freshet flow westward. The direct cost of the failed dam was $48,920; the indirect cost was the damage of yet another year of flooding in the West Prairie unit.

As the drainage project moved into Year Three, plans and deadlines were once again determined by the inevitable approach of the following spring's high water. The season's goals were ambitious and urgent: completion of both the West Prairie unit and the main dam and pumphouse on lower Sumas River. "Failure to keep out the 1923 high water," wrote its director, would be "disastrous." But the dual task required intricate planning: the dam had to be closed before the arrival of the 1923 freshet; but it had to stay open until the hulking dredges finished on West Prairie or the machines would be stranded there.

Work began on both components in summer 1922. After putting the finishing touches on Vedder Canal, the *King Edward* moved to the lake bed and began work on the Sumas Lake drainage canal. At the end of No-vember, the federal government recalled the dredge and the *Robson* took its place. Beginning at the head of the channel and moving south, the *Robson* worked through the winter and into spring. Meanwhile, *Col. Tobin* excavated the Sumas River canal and threw up material for its dykes. The *Robson* and *Col. Tobin* toiled to complete their components before the spring freshet, but the soils and waters of Sumas Lake conspired against them. The soft, sandy soil excavated along the Sumas River and Lake channels was poor material for dykes; it had difficulty settling and much of it simply slid back through the bulwarks. Nor was it easy to maintain a stable channel with a high water table and soft soil, which had a tendency to seep in behind the dredges and fill in the newly dug channels. The spring and winter freshets brought in new sediment, which was deposited as the waters receded.

Sumas Lake's low-water season caused problems of its own. As on the Vedder in Year Two, in Year Three the *Robson* and *Col. Tobin* were forced to dig below the planned grade to keep enough water below them to float. Through the winter, the *Robson* repeatedly ran aground on the sandy lake bed; by the beginning of spring 1923, it was effectively stuck. The lake canal had silted up behind the massive machine, and it was forced to turn around and re-dredge its way north. At the northern end of the canal, where it entered Sumas River, a natural dam of soil and debris had formed, block-ing access in and out. Fortunately, the *Col. Tobin* had completed its work on Sumas River and escaped downriver before the closing of the main Sumas dam at the end of March. It immediately rushed to the *Robson*'s rescue, clearing the lake channel from the river southward. After meeting up, both dredges then steamed out of the canal before the arrival of the spring freshet.

While other, smaller dragline shovels worked alongside the suction dredges to build the Sumas River and Sumas Lake canal dykes, the *Bucyrus* was toiling away on West Vedder dyke. The excavator had started the con-struction season on East Vedder dyke, topping it up to its full height. After completing that task in mid-November, it moved across the canal to tackle the final major component of the West Prairie unit. Largely unaffected by low-water conditions and working with the Vedder's mucky clay, the *Bucyrus* finished the job on schedule.

The earthwork features of the West Prairie unit were finished in time for the freshet of 1923. Meanwhile, work on the main Sumas dam and pum-phouse had proceeded at breakneck speed over the course of Year Three. Planning for the structure started in summer 1922, and in September, G.P.

Moe was put in charge as construction engineer. Moe had been working as an assistant engineer under Sinclair; his task now was to locate, design and oversee construction of the dam and installation of its pumps. The new construction engineer was given a free hand on these: the dam complex was not included in the original construction contract with Marsh, and Moe did not feel constrained by Sinclair's official design of 1919. On the crucial matter of location, Moe rejected Sinclair's proposed site and opted for a spot nearly 3,000 feet farther up Sumas River, a mile from the mouth of Vedder Canal—exactly where Chester Smith had placed it. Moe concluded that the rock and soil underneath the latter site were much harder, "forming an excellent base for the concrete dam and sluiceways."

Moe also changed the original design of the structure itself. Instead of spanning the whole width of Sumas River with a reinforced concrete structure, the cement dam would extend only half the distance, with reinforced earthwork making up the rest. Ten sluiceways within the dam would handle the water of the Sumas River and Sumas Lake canals: four of these passed water out by gravity, the remaining six by pumps. For Moe, a critical feature of the dam's design was its flexibility: "By opening or closing the different gates, either all pumps, or a combination of the different pumps, may be used to pump from either the high level or low level areas, or from both areas at once."

Excavation for the dam's foundation began in early fall 1922, and construction work soon followed. By the end of the year, 150 men were employed on the site under the watchful eyes of Art Strong. The workforce doubled through the early months of 1923 as an all-out push was made to finish on time. By the end of March, the concrete structure was completed; in total, 36,000 sacks of cement, 300 tons of steel rebar and thousands of cubic yards of rock, gravel and sand went into the dam. The *Col. Tobin* and *Robson* arrived on the spot in April, and by early May the earthen portion of the dam was ready, just in time for the spring freshet. The water rose until mid-June; at its peak, the level on the downriver side of the dam was 13 feet higher than on the upriver side. The dam held, as did the other components of the West Prairie unit. For the first time, the invading waters of the Fraser and Chilliwack Rivers were thwarted, diverted or blocked from their age-old courses into Sumas Lake.

The lion's share of work on the Sumas drainage project was completed during building Years Two and Three—Year Four was devoted to finishing the job. The first task was to rid Sumas Lake itself of its remaining waters. Installation of the Sumas dam's pumping plant proceeded rapidly through May and June 1923. Each of the four 54-inch vertical spiral pumps was driven by a Canadian Westinghouse electric motor, and could be operated at varying speeds. On July 4, Westinghouse technicians started up pump number one and ran it through the month. A shutdown in August allowed the technicians to hook up the remaining motors, and by the end of the month, all four pumps were running. While the Sumas pumping plant hummed along, crews worked to complete the remaining components of the project. Dredging of the southern half of the Sumas Lake drainage canal moved ahead as more and more of the lake bed was exposed; the Marshall and Saar Creek canals were excavated, along with a network of smaller drainage ditches. Most of this work was done by the Northern Construction Co., as the LSB moved to cut all ties with Marsh. The board also sacked Frederick Sinclair as chief engineer and promoted G.P. Moe in his place. Both Marsh and Sinclair responded by suing the LSB.

The spring 1924 freshet brought construction Year Four to a close. The waters crested early, on May 22, and rose to a few inches above the historical average, a relief after the unusually high levels of the previous years. All components of the design held, and the only water left behind the flood defences was a shallow pool sitting atop several hundred acres at the lowest stretch of Sumas Lake. The following month, the LSB announced "that on Thursday, the 26th June, 1924, the last of the water remaining in the Sumas Lake basin was pumped out." The *Vancouver Province* proclaimed, "Sumas Lake is no more." Closer to home the *Chilliwack Progress* rejoiced:

> Sumas Lake is now dry. Three years of work met its reward almost overnight, the way the final sheet of water in the lake area disappeared....In place of thousands of acres of wave tossed water, there is now a vast agricultural land spread out from mountain to mountain.[107]

The edifice constructed to achieve this was monumental: 15 miles of high dykes, 13 miles of lower levees, 19 miles of canals 30 feet or wider, and 41 miles of smaller diversion ditches. But in many crucial respects, the victory celebrations were premature; the half-century-long quest to dewater and transform Sumas Valley was not yet complete. The expanse of wave-tossed water may have been gone, for now, but the promise of vast agricultural land was still some way off.

CHAPTER 10

NEW LAND

On a sunny morning in May 1928, a stocky, balding man in well-tailored tweed disembarked at the Bellerose station of the BC Electric Railway. Leonard Frank, the province's pre-eminent photographer, paused to assemble his cumbersome equipment, then trekked up the side of Vedder Mountain to a clearing overlooking the valley floor. Frank set up his camera and from this vantage point snapped a series of shots that captured the dewatered expanse of Sumas Valley. The photographic panorama showed a flat plain of budding vegetation, free of water; a smattering of houses, barns and dirt roads marked the beginnings of agricultural settlement. More than six years earlier, in late winter 1922, Frank had photographed the same scene, from the same spot. The Sumas Lake and Valley captured then was an eerie landscape of shallow water broken here and there by mud and debris, a marshy wasteland devoid of any human presence.

Frank's panoramas were instant classics, the iconic images of the "Sumas Reclamation Project." Set side by side, they presented the official story of the lake's draining: a before-and-after tableau that documented Sumas Valley's transformation from a muddy wasteland to a fertile new land. While they recorded the profound reshaping of the Sumas landscape, the photographs' contrast of before and after was deceptive. For one, Frank's 1922 panorama was not taken before the construction of the drainage work, but during. The project was three-quarters of the way through construction Year Two by this time: most of Vedder Canal and the East Vedder dyke had been completed, and water was already being diverted. Sumas Lake in Frank's portrait—shallow, muddy and lifeless—was in truth half-drained. People accepted the image as an accurate portrayal of an untouched Sumas Lake because that is how they wanted to see it, as a dreary wasteland that needed to be reclaimed.

For another, a closer look at the 1928 panorama reveals flaws in the budding agricultural scene it was intended to portray. The cover of vegetation was not the rich carpet of crops promised by proponents, but was riddled through with thick growths of invading thistles and willows. The human presence was scarcely more encouraging, with only a handful of buildings and the most rudimentary dirt roads.

The gap between the official picture and the reality on the ground—between the promises made and the results delivered—plagued the post-drainage years. For half a century, drainage proponents had predicted that the land beneath Sumas Lake would be ready immediately for cultivation once the unwanted waters were banished. In 1913, Frederick Sinclair stated that the Sumas lands would be "clear and ready for the plow as soon as unwatered." A decade later, after declaring Sumas Lake dry, the Sumas Drainage Commission promised that any land offered for sale was "guaranteed to be at least ready for the plough, if not already ploughed and cropped."

These words were premature at best, for Sumas Valley was neither wholly dewatered nor ready for cultivation. Meandering streams and placid pools remained over most of the lake bed and prairie land. The ground was saturated with water rising to the surface from below, due to the high water table and seepage under dykes. And the soil itself lacked elements essential for fertility. In 1925, the province's chief agronomist concluded that the newly drained lands were low in nitrogen and potash. The report also found the western portion of the old lake was too sandy, exposing it to "drifting and erosion at a rapid rate." Upper Sumas resident Edith Lamson remembered the sand well. One hot summer day that same year, her family ventured onto the lake bed by car: "It was dry sand all of the way, just ripples of white sand like an ocean beach when the tide goes down, only cleaner and evener." Lamson's neighbour Jean recalled, "All you could see was sand and clamshells."

Meanwhile, the rest of the drained land was rapidly covered by a thick blanket of thistles and willows. As early as August 1924, the *Abbotsford, Sumas and Matsqui News* reported, "On every hand and in the most fertile fields are to be seen high banks of sow and Canadian thistles, choking down crops, and at this season casting their seeds to the wind." The Canada thistle was a non-indigenous species, inadvertently introduced with the new cereals and livestock brought in by White farmers. Efforts to eradicate the plant had been unsuccessful, and now the opportunistic weed rushed in to the newly opened expanse of the Sumas Lake bottom.[108]

Willows presented an even greater problem. As first the East and then West Prairie units were drained, the fast-growing bush immediately

Leonard Frank's panorama of Sumas Valley "before" drainage was actually taken during Year 2 of construction, in the winter of 1921–22. This was how drainage proponents wanted people to see Sumas Lake: a muddy wasteland in need of "reclamation." The Reach P5659 and P5660.

moved in. Starting as low bushes, the willows reached as high as 10 feet and were so dense it was impossible to force your way through them. "The willows were—holy Moses they were high," Charlie Power recalled. "You could stand on the back of one of those old Model T Ford seats, and you couldn't see over the top [of them]." Local farmer Fritz Stromberg was equally amazed by the growth: "If things had stood for another five or six years, this whole country would have been wilderness." Initially, the Land Settlement Board hired horse and tractor teams to mow down the unwanted saplings, but this had the effect of pruning them, and they came back even thicker the following year. Then the willow stands were plowed under, cutting them at their roots, and new covering crops such as timothy grass and red clover were sown to occupy the open ground and deny the weed species the chance to take root again.

Willows were indigenous to Sumas Valley, and at the time their invasion was blamed on nature. But the willows that invaded the drained lands were introduced by man. Workmen planted willow bushes along the base

of every dyke built from 1921 to 1924, to protect the levees from the full force of running water and wave action. In a June 1923 progress report, Frederick Sinclair sang the praises of the prolific willow:

> Nothing better in the way of rapid growth can be found, and it is not necessary to plant more than the slope lying between elevations 82 and 90. The growth of the willows will protect the remainder of the slope to the highest water.

The willows refused to stay in their allotted place, and before long the dyking commission was regretting its chief engineer's misplaced enthusiasm.

While waging war against thistles and willows, the commission moved ahead with plans to cultivate the first crops on the drained lands. In spring 1924, it sowed 6,000 acres in timothy and a further 800 acres in a mix of timothy, red clover and oats. The fall harvest was disappointing; the following two years, equally ambitious plantings produced markedly improved yields, particularly when timothy was replaced by red clover as the main crop. Clover was such a success that politicians and press predicted Sumas soon would become the clover capital of Canada. But disaster struck in

Frank's "after" panorama, taken in 1928, was equally deceptive. What appears to be a lush covering of crops is actually a mix of stubborn weeds and willow bushes (1928). Leonard Frank photo, Vancouver Public Library, 13257 and 12532a.

1927: heavy rains in late summer and early fall destroyed half the clover crop. The following years brought only modest harvests.

For the dyking commission, these were frustrating years: plants they did not want to grow flourished, while plants they did want struggled to gain a foothold. These failures were setbacks in the commission's larger mission of transforming the former lake lands into a new agricultural landscape of modest but prosperous family farms. The family farm ideal had been the linchpin of White society in Sumas Valley for half a century. But while the lake existed, only extensive farming on large holdings could make any money; properties this size were beyond the means of all but the most successful farmers. Using modern technology, the Sumas drainage project had banished the yearly high waters and pumped off the lake water. Thousands of acres of new fertile soil lay open; intensive farming was now supposed to be possible, on lots small enough to be within the reach of most families.

Even as construction was still under way, the dyking commission moved to put its family farm model into place. In 1923, it produced the first post-drainage map, which divided the Sumas Lake bed into rectangular lots, 40 acres in size, offering them for sale. "It is felt that a farm of that extent of Sumas lands," Edward Barrow explained, "is sufficient to enable a man with a certain amount of capital to raise a family and to maintain a proper standard of living." A dairy herd of 15 or so cows, along with a mix of food and cash crops, would sustain the family farm.

Nothing came of these initial efforts. Then in 1926, the commission drafted a new official map, reorienting the property grid to existing township lines but keeping the same lot size. It also launched an advertising campaign, producing slick pamphlets to entice buyers. The cover illustration of one pamphlet captured this vision for the "Sumas Reclaimed Land," evocatively and in colour: perfectly geometric 40-acre properties spread out evenly across the valley, each with a substantial red-roofed barn, silo and comfortable family home. In an inset to the lower right, a farmer walks into his field to drive a band of cows home for their supper-time milking.[109]

No amount of advertising could make these visions of Sumas Valley as an agricultural Eden—home to contented farm families and even happier cows—a reality. Through the 1920s, despite policy shifts and aggressive campaigns, efforts to sell drained lands lagged well behind expectations. By 1930, the Conservatives were in government and Victoria decided to try a new tack. It outsourced the job to the Vancouver real estate firm Fell and Scharfe: the firm handled all Sumas land sales in exchange for a commission on each sale. With aggressive advertising and new easy financing, the firm succeeded where the commission had failed. By the end of the year, over 8,000 acres had been sold, all but a few hundred acres of the former lake bed. On paper, the sales totalled just over $800,000, almost half the original cost estimate for the drainage works.

Fell and Scharfe's sales miracle, though, was an illusion. With very little money down, buyers had obtained title to their land, but only by taking on substantial mortgages. At just this time, the Great Depression shook the economy, driving down the value of land and the demand for agricultural goods. Most Sumas buyers could not make their payments and soon were left with properties worth less than their debts. By 1936, nearly half of the properties bought in 1930 had reverted back to the dyking commission, and many of the rest threatened to follow. A report prepared for the commission pointed to the recklessly inflated value placed on Sumas lands as the root of the problem. Easy financing and slick pitches by Fell and Scharfe lured buyers in; when reality hit, owners were left with debts that far exceeded the real value of their properties.[110]

The failure of small property holders was not the only unexpected development. In the 15 years between the draining of Sumas Lake and the start of World War II, corporate agriculture practiced on very large properties came to dominate the economy of Sumas Valley. Tobacco and hop growing were the earliest agribusinesses. The tobacco industry got its start in 1928, when a combine of Hungarian immigrants bought 40 acres of lake-bed land. Two years later, tobacconist and department-store mogul Victor Spencer secured 1,362 acres and put it into tobacco. In 1932, the Totem Tobacco Company became the second large corporate operation in the valley. Tobacco enjoyed a measure of success through the 1930s; it then declined rapidly and did not survive World War II. Wet, nitrogen-poor soil was the main culprit. A provincial tobacco specialist concluded that the proportion of premium-grade flakes in Sumas tobacco was "too low for profitable production."

By that time, hop growing had established itself as Sumas Valley's leading agribusiness. Beginning in 1926, Oregon-based interests purchased

640 acres at the very centre of the valley (the lowest point of the lake bed). The newly incorporated Canadian Hop Co. then erected hundreds of rows of crop vines; it also installed an extensive network of drainage pipes to fight the high water table. Two large processing plants and a string of bunkhouses were built along the Sumas Lake drainage canal. By 1928, the company reported a harvest worth $100,000. Production dropped through the Depression, but picked up with World War II, as hop-exporting centres in Germany, Czechoslovakia and Poland were cut off. At its peak, the Canadian Hop Co. employed up to 2,000 pickers during harvest. Scores more worked next door, in the fields of Harry Ord, the former manager of Canadian Hop's Sumas operations.

Despite this success, hop growing lost its leading economic role in Sumas Valley with the arrival of Buckerfield's Ltd., one of the province's leading agricultural companies. Buckerfield's specialized in the production and marketing of feed for livestock and chickens. In 1940, it purchased a 1,000-acre spread lying between the Canadian Hop operation and Spencer's tobacco fields. The land had been used for low-intensity haying and pasture; many of its owners were financially pressed, and Buckerfield's was able to drive down prices, paying from $60 to $75 an acre. The feed company expanded to 2,500 acres when it acquired Spencer's holdings directly to the west. By 1948, Buckerfield's was responsible for one-quarter of the entire agricultural output of Sumas Valley.

One hundred percent of this production came from one crop. Vita Grass was not a single plant but a blend of 10 different legumes and grasses: red, white and wild clover; timothy; redtop; New Zealand browntop; perennial and Italian rye; and meadow and creeping red fescue. Local graziers had been growing many of these species for decades, so they were well suited to the valley soils. Buckerfield's set about cultivating its patented blend on an industrial scale, at a hyperaggressive pace. Instead of taking the usual three crops a year, the company deployed its large fleet of combines to clip the Vita Grass every two weeks. While still in the field, the shorn crop was put through 50-foot dryers and then transported to on-site plants, where it was processed into feed pellets for poultry. The secret to Vita Grass's quick growth was heavy use of chemical fertilizers, along with summer irrigation from the Sumas Lake canal and ditches.[111]

The success of Buckerfield's marked the high point of corporate agriculture on the former Sumas Lake lands. Its operations—along with those of hop and tobacco companies—contrasted sharply with the family farm model envisioned by drainage proponents and promoters. Property holdings in the thousands of acres; mass production of a single, highly processed cash crop; heavy use of chemical fertilizers and irrigation water; a workforce of wage-earning employees; heavy investment in machinery and the operating plant—these were the hallmarks of the agribusiness model.

At the time, little was said about the threat agribusiness posed to the small family farm or to the environment. Instead, most criticism of post-drainage developments—and at times the criticism was loud and strong—focussed on the project's ballooning cost and what measures were needed to pay for it. In March 1920, Sumas Valley landholders had authorized $1.8 million to be spent on the project, the final official estimate submitted to them by Frederick Sinclair and the Sumas Dyking Commission. Four years of construction followed, and at the end of 1924 the commission completed an official tally. It announced that the full cost of draining Sumas Lake and dewatering Sumas Valley was $3,357,085. A decade later, the declared price tag had nearly doubled; by the end of 1944, it had reached $9,104,357—five times that of the project's official budget.

Faced with these numbers, landowners, newspapers and opposition politicians unleashed a storm of criticism in the years after Sumas Lake was drained. More recently, historians have been just as harsh in their assessments of the drainage project: the Marsh Construction Co., they charge, "was guilty of sheer incompetence," and engineers, of "bad planning." The whole deal was "hastily arranged," set up to benefit Liberal party insiders. The result was that "the Sumas project quickly became an enormous financial disaster."

A closer look at the books reveals that such damning assessments are unfair and off target. The first step to take in this closer look is a calculation of the actual building costs on the ground. The best source for this is the commission's own tally as of December 31, 1924 (after deducting non-construction items such as interest on loans and post-drainage land development). The Vedder Canal system (with dykes and diversion) was the largest item on the bill, at $821,764; next was the Sumas main dam and pumphouse, at $752,998. The mid-sized canals on upper Sumas River, Goose Lake and Sumas Lake, along with the Fraser River and Atchelitz dykes, totalled $656,097. Adding the smaller components, engineering expenses, right-of-way purchases and maintenance through 1924, the direct cost of the Sumas drainage works was $2,915,015.[112]

True, the real price tag was 62 percent higher than the figure approved in March 1920—considerable, but only a fraction of the eventual fivefold increase. Also true, Marsh Construction has to shoulder some of the blame: its bid was unrealistically low, and it was not ready to start the job in Year

One. But for years Sinclair and the commission had been guilty of underestimating the project's cost; pressure from landholders on one side and Victoria on the other led to their creative accounting. The losses caused by Marsh's ill-fated first year were, R.D. Davies concluded, "comparatively trifling." Marsh received payment only for work that was done; as little was accomplished that year, little was paid out.[113]

After Davies took control of the project in spring 1921, Marsh stayed on as the general contractor for the crucial Years Two and Three. Through this time, there is no evidence that the work was incompetently done, nor that it could have been completed for less money, nor that a different plan would have been better. The work that was done cost what it cost. The problem was that the project required much more work and money than commission engineers such as Sinclair had predicted.

First, there was a massive increase in the amount of soil moved in excavating canals and building dykes. On the Vedder Canal, dredges had to dig up to 12 feet below the projected grade to keep themselves afloat. Dykes had to be more substantial than planned: greater mass, with a bigger base and more gradual slope. The extra cubic yards of soil that needed to be moved was substantial: 562,000 cubic yards for the Sumas River canal and dam system; 523,000 for the Vedder Canal and dykes; and 124,000 for the Fraser River dyke. Including smaller components, more than 1.5 million cubic yards of extra material had to be moved, at a cost of $533,000. To do this, additional suction dredges were procured, once again raising costs.

And second, the Sumas River dam complex cost three times the $285,000 Sinclair had initially earmarked. The project required a far more substantial structure than Sinclair had thought. The final cost of the concrete dam, massive pumps and supporting plant was $754,747; the small McGillivray Creek dam and pumphouse rang in at $39,250. Taken together, unforeseen increases in the two components—the Sumas River dam complex and movement of extra yardage of soil—amounted to over $1 million. This represented nearly all of the difference between the project's original budget and its final costs. Further losses were caused by the exceptionally bad winters of Years Two and Three, the failure of the temporary Sumas dam and the challenges of working around the yearly flood season.

The yawning gap between original budget estimates and final construction costs was caused by unrealistic early estimates, not by wasteful construction or a bad design. Yet even greater increases in final costs were caused by banks and—at the bottom of it all—the provincial government. By 1944, the project's price tag stood at $9 million, fully two-thirds of which was due to the interest charged on loans. The dyking commission was forced to finance the project as it went along; this required various forms of lending, from public bonds, to bank loans, to borrowing from the provincial treasury. After completion of work, expected revenues from land sales failed to materialize. A complicated system of levies was imposed on existing landholders. While sparking rancorous resistance, the system garnered token payments so meagre they did not even cover the yearly cost of maintenance and operation. There was, in short, no money to pay back the loans. The amount of interest owed compounded rapidly, charged on both the principal and outstanding interest.

In the end, the "financial disaster" of the Sumas drainage project was a creation of the provincial government. Throughout, Victoria had followed a two-faced policy. In public, it denied any responsibility for the scheme and rejected any pleas for financial assistance. Privately, the premier and cabinet wielded veto power over all major decisions from 1917 on, dictating the terms by which the project was funded. These terms rigidly adhered to the principle that the project pay for itself. It soon became obvious this was a wholly unrealistic demand; the government refused to budge, and the dyking commission was forced to pile debt upon debt.

All this could have been avoided if Victoria had accepted the fact that the magnitude, financial requirements and benefits of the Sumas drainage scheme made it an intrinsically *public* project. The commission's own engineers, Harvey Brice and Chester Smith, dared to say as much in their official plan of January 1919. Within months, Brice was dead and Smith lost his job for speaking truth to power. If Victoria had heeded the engineers' advice and treated the draining of Sumas Lake as a government infrastructure project, millions of dollars in interest charges could have been saved. A half-century later, in the mid-1960s, the bloated drainage tab was charged against the province's taxpayers when Victoria quietly shuffled the debt from the dyking commission to itself in a bureaucratic sleight of hand.

After discussing the long-term finances of the Sumas drainage project, we can return to the valley itself and consider the impact of the works on the ground. First off, did the works succeed in their primary task, to pump the water out of Sumas Lake and Valley and to keep it out? Fortunately for us (but not for those who experienced them) two historic floods provided real-life tests of the drainage design's ability to protect the new land it had created.

Through January 1935, five feet of snow fell on Sumas Valley and frigid temperatures clogged canals, ditches and streams with ice. Then the snow turned to freezing rain, coating every surface with ice; transmission lines were brought down and the Sumas pumphouse lost power. To the south, a rising Nooksack River breached its banks and spilled northward into upper Sumas River. The snow, ice and flood water overwhelmed the drainage network, and by the end of January more than 12,000 acres were inundated. The headline from the *Chilliwack Progress* summed it up: "Sumas Lake is a fact again." Some 350 people were evacuated while crews scrambled to stem the tide, shoring up dykes and clearing watercourses. By this time, the Sumas pumps had regained power; for five weeks they ran at full speed, until March 2, when the last of the flood water was lifted from the former lake bed.

The 1935 ice storm and flood shook the confidence of Sumas residents. Many left the valley for good, and many others clamoured to know whether the drainage works had failed them in their hour of need. A government report asserted that the system had not. "This flood could not have been kept out of the lake area by any works which would be within the limits of economic feasibility," the province's Water Branch concluded. Even if the Sumas River dyke had held and the pumps had worked throughout, the old lake bed would still have returned to its natural state. It was a reminder that the environmental forces that created and sustained Sumas Lake were still there—and that when they were determined, they could overwhelm the defences constructed by humans.[114]

This sobering truth was demonstrated more than a dozen years later, when the Fraser Valley was hit by the highest waters since 1894. The 1948 flood was caused by a near-perfect storm of spring freshet conditions: a heavy winter snowpack, a cool spring and a rapid rise in temperatures in late May and early June. By May 26, the Fraser River at Sumas was already at dangerous levels, and it continued to rise for two weeks. On June 1, the Fraser dyke gave way at Cannor (1½ miles east of Sumas River) and water rushed through. More than 5,000 acres of lower Sumas Prairie were flooded—between the East Vedder and Chilliwack dykes—reaching a depth of 25 feet in low areas. The flood waters peaked nine days later at a full foot below the 1894 mark, and hovered there for a full week. One-tenth of the entire Fraser Valley, some 50,000 acres, was inundated before the water gradually retreated in late June and early July.

Through it all, the East and West Vedder dykes stood firm and the Vedder Canal remained intact. The Fraser dyke proved to be the weak link in Sumas Valley's chain of defence, for a number of reasons. The soils from which it was built were composed of the silt left behind by earlier Fraser

Two men in a rowboat at the eastern foot of the Vedder Canal Bridge during the 1948 flood. This area east of the canal was flooded because of the breach in the Fraser dyke at Cannor. The drained lands west of the canal stayed dry and the canal itself remained intact. Royal BC Museum and Archives, NA-09540.

floods; they were less dense and more sandy than the heavy clay deposits used in the Vedder Canal and Sumas River dykes, which came from the margins and floor of Sumas Lake. Also, trees had been allowed to grow to great heights on the outer slopes of the Fraser dykes. According to eye-witnesses, the Cannor break was caused by "a large tree [that] fell and up-rooted a section of the dyke." A quarter-century earlier, willows and other saplings had been planted on the outer banks of levees to hold the newly mounded soil in place. This had worked at first, but as the trees grew they became more top-heavy, while their root system remained shallow. They were easily toppled by wind or erosion, and when they fell their roots took huge chunks of their dyke with them.[115]

The Cannor breach was a disaster for those fighting the flood. Yet this very failure demonstrated the underlying success of the Sumas drainage design. Because the drainage works were divided into units, a break in one of the major dykes did not flood the whole area but was contained in a

single unit, the East Prairie. This was precisely what Frances LeBaron had in mind when he first proposed the concept; he had rejected existing plans that were built around a diversion well east of Vedder Canal, which left a single dyke between Sumas Valley and the Fraser. If any of these designs had been adopted, the Cannor break would have flooded the entire valley. Indeed, the water delivered by a more eastern diversion would have reached Fraser River just above the dyke break; it would then have flowed directly back onto Sumas Valley, raising the flood level even more.

In the years following 1948, nearly $1 million was spent shoring up the Vedder, Sumas and Fraser River dyking system. While everyone focussed on the question of whether the drainage works succeeded or failed in keeping flood waters off Sumas Valley, no one asked the reverse: had the dewatering of Sumas Lake contributed to the size, intensity and devastation of the flood?

The short answer is yes. The Sumas drainage project disrupted the natural drainage system of the Fraser. The mighty river's waters had to go somewhere; prior to 1920, massive quantities flowed into Sumas Lake and Valley. For centuries, the Sumas flood plain functioned as a spillway for Fraser River water, at 30,000 acres the largest in the region. The holding capacity of the Sumas spillway can be calculated in units of acre-feet: the amount of water needed to cover one acre of land with one foot of water. When it was needed most, in 1894, Sumas Valley held an estimated 300,000 acre-feet of water—enough to cover the entire Fraser Valley in more than a foot of water. It thereby mitigated the effects of the flood in the rest of Fraser Valley, lowering water levels downstream and absorbing much of the raging water's energy. In 1948, with the exception of the Cannor breach, access to this expansive spillway was denied. The inevitable result was to make matters worse downriver: the full volume of the flood waters rushed past Sumas Mountain and battered against flood defences farther west, increasing the devastation there.

Planners and engineers of the Sumas drainage project did not foresee the impact of the works on the natural hydrology of the Sumas and Fraser Valleys. Nor did they foresee their effect on Sumas Lake's rich and complex web of plant and animal life. Like others in their profession, the drainage engineers were largely blind to this organic world, what we today call its ecosystem. They viewed the natural world not as a living organism, but as a machine. Their focus was on how the various inorganic parts of this machine—lakes, rivers, mountains—worked together, and their concern was how to manipulate these parts to get the end they desired. The problem of Sumas Lake was seen in terms of water being where it should not be; the solution was to reshape the earth to control this water. What this did to plants and animals that were in the water or on the land did not enter into their calculations. Of course, the engineers were very much creatures of their time and place. With the notable exception of the Sema:th and their neighbours, most everyone from high government officials down to local farmers viewed Sumas Lake and Valley through much the same mental framework.

No serious thought was given to the ecological impact of draining Sumas Lake. In the reams of records produced from the time the Land Settlement Board took over the drainage project in 1917 to the works' completion in 1924, only three letters from middling bureaucrats in Ottawa could be found. Here, Department of Fisheries officials asked the dyking commission whether draining Sumas Lake would harm the important salmon runs up the Chilliwack and Sumas Rivers. The commission answered that the Chilliwack run could use the new Vedder Canal; it also promised to build a fish diversion or ladder around the Sumas dam. No federal officials followed up to see if these promises were kept. In the case of the Sumas diversion, nothing was ever built.[116]

It is no surprise, then, that Sumas Lake's disappearance hit the valley's salmon hard. The migrating fish could no longer spawn along the edges of the lake, nor use it to access its numerous tributaries. While Vedder Canal provided a substitute route for the Chilliwack River and Cultus Lake runs, the Sumas River run was halted at the main dam. Sema:th elder Francis Kelly explained how the spring salmon run was disrupted: "Formerly, the Springs would enter the lake and pass through it in a certain way. The drainage canal changed all that.…A fish has its path and if this is changed, he won't go up."

Fortunately, while the Sumas River run was halted by the main dam, the Vedder Canal did allow the crucial Chilliwack River and Cultus Lake runs to survive. But this was an unintended consequence. None of the engineers who had proposed the Vedder Canal solution—from Francis LeBaron to Chester Smith—had thought of or foreseen it. Plans put forward by other engineers—with diversions along Luckakuck or Wilson Creek—required steep grades and dams that would have killed the Chilliwack and Cultus runs. By contrast, the gentle slope and slow current of the Vedder Canal made it easy for salmon to travel up from Fraser River and into the four-mile-long upper Vedder River. The latter was allowed to take a more natural form within set borders; its looping curves, meandering side channels and plentiful gravel bars provided new spawning areas for salmon. An exhaustive study covering the 12 years after the draining of Sumas Lake showed that the Cultus Lake run—which now had to go through the new Vedder channels—was healthy and thriving.

Meanwhile, the draining of Sumas Lake had an immediate and calamitous impact on the local stocks of fish. Flying over the freshly dewatered valley, Sumas resident and professional pilot Earl Macleod looked in awe at the "tens of thousands of fish on the mud-and-sand lake bed, including many sturgeon weighing hundreds of pounds. Nearby farmers loaded large quantities of dead fish onto wagons for use as fertilizer." Others, White and Sto:lo alike, recalled the huge corpses of sturgeon left behind by the retreating waters. The *Chilliwack Progress* reported the grim fate of even more:

> While the pumps were working some days ago, it was seen that sturgeon six feet or more long had been drawn to the grids of the intake, their heads were held to the bars by the strong suction of the pumps, which prevented them from turning to escape.

For countless generations, Sumas Lake had been "a natural breeding ground for sturgeon"—now the lake was gone and its sturgeon gone with it.[117]

Moving from water to air, untold millions of birds were lost to Sumas Lake because of its draining. In the decades prior to the lake's disappearance, the flocks of ducks, geese and other fowl that used to darken the sky had been reduced by overhunting and the spread of agriculture. But large numbers still came, resting, feeding and breeding on the Sumas wetlands, until those wetlands disappeared. The "hunter's paradise" of Win Fadden's youth was only a memory: "Since the lake was drained the ducks don't come this way anymore." Sema:th elders also lamented the loss: "All the ducks were gone," said one. "There's no longer any ducks around Kilgard now," said another.

It is impossible to put an exact figure on the numbers of waterfowl lost. One scientific study estimates that in 1820, the lower Fraser Valley as a whole supported billions of waterfowl, most of which migrated seasonally; by the end of the 20th century, that population had dropped to half a million. The draining of Sumas Lake was responsible for only a part of this, of course, but it was a significant part. And the impact of the lake's disappearance was continental in scope. Because of its lush wetlands, Sumas Lake was a crucial link in the Pacific Flyway, where massive flocks would lay over on their way from summer grounds in California to winter haunts in Alaska. The Sumas flocks were so large and diverse because fertile stopovers like Sumas Lake were few in number. When one of these stops disappeared, the birds searched desperately for somewhere else to go. When other stops along the flyway were destroyed at the same time by the same forces—drainage, agriculture, urbanization—the effect was catastrophic. One environmental historian concludes: "By the early twentieth, the tapestry of wetlands along the southern portion of the Pacific Flyway largely disappeared....By the early 1930s, migratory bird populations were plummeting."[118]

The ecological changes brought on by the draining of Sumas Lake caused a profound, irreversible disruption in the way of life of the valley's first people. Yet the Sema:th were never given a say in whether the lake should be drained or not. Sema:th leaders had been voicing their concerns for as long as there had been plans to dewater Sumas Valley—and for just as long they had been ignored. When Edgar Dewdney surveyed the valley in the aftermath of the 1876 flood, local elders made sure to present their views to him. Two years later, they found a more sympathetic ear in Gilbert Sproat of the Indian Reserve Commission. Faced with the passage of the Sumas Dyking Act and the proposed plans of E.L. Derby, the Sema:th protested the proposed draining of "their lake."

Sproat's field surveyor reported in May 1879, "The Indians say they are in the habit of catching large quantities of sturgeon in Sumas Lake. And if Mr. Derby succeeds in draining the lake, that portion of their fishing ground will be destroyed."

Sproat relayed these and other concerns to his superiors in a series of forcefully worded letters. Sproat argued that the provincial government lacked the authority to grant Crown land to Derby until the Indian Reserve Commission completed its work, and he called on the federal government to disallow the 1878 Sumas Dyking Act. The reserve commissioner protested against Derby's plans to encroach on Sumas land and demanded that the developer be made to stop immediately. He also wrote Derby directly, telling him work could proceed only after Ottawa assessed "the effect of draining lakes and diverting the course of streams touching or near the Indian reserves." Sproat's missives landed on the desk of Prime Minister John A. Macdonald, who fired off a confidential telegraph to BC premier George Walkem: "I fear [the Sumas] Dyking Act interferes with the Indian reserves and obligation to Indians. Would prefer not to disallow. What would you suggest?" Naturally, Walkem suggested that Ottawa do nothing, which it did. Throughout the long, sorry saga of the Derby scheme, the federal government sat conspicuously on the sidelines. As drainage proposals came and went over the following decades, Ottawa failed to fulfill its constitutional responsibility to protect the interests of the Sema:th and other Sto:lo.[119]

Even as the drainage project moved closer to being realized through the early 20th century, officials and drainage proponents did not consider it necessary to consult the Sema:th or other Sto:lo. They casually assumed that any drainage and dyking efforts that, in their eyes, "improved" reserve land would be supported by reserve members. In 1907, Indian Agent R.C. McDonald told Ottawa that the L.M. Rice and Co. drainage scheme "would be a great benefit" to the Sema:th by increasing the market value of their reserve land tenfold, conveniently forgetting that reserve land could not be sold. In fall 1918, the *Chilliwack Progress* reported on the flooding of Sema:th burial grounds on upper Sumas Prairie. The Sema:th, the paper asserted, "like the Whites, have been anxiously longing for government protection of the land from floods, and the Sumas dyking scheme has for years kept them hoping for protection."

The Sema:th hoped no such thing. If White residents and officials had cared to listen, they would have heard Chief Selesmlton's answers in front of the 1915 Royal Commission on Indian Affairs:

Q: Could there be land reclaimed here by dyking?

A: I could not say. I am against the dyking because that means more starvation for us.

Q: Why do you think you would be starved out if this land is dyked?

A: Because the lake is one of the greatest spawning grounds there is, and this dyking would cut it off and it would cut off our fish supply.

Four years later, when informed that the Land Settlement Board's drainage scheme was going ahead, the Sema:th shook their heads in disbelief. After a visit from LSB officials, Sema:th and Chilliwack elders convened at the home of Chief William Sepass. They agreed that, given all the failures in the past, the project could never be done and that "the Whites were foolish to try." Since the scheme would fail on its own, as so many earlier schemes had failed, there was no need to mobilize opposition to it. Then, with surprising speed, the waters of Sumas Lake began to disappear. "It was too late then," Ray Silver concluded. "People realized that they were not BS-ing, they drained the lake."

The draining of Sumas Lake did bring some new economic opportunities for Sema:th, most notably in the hop yards that sprouted up on the lake bed. But these opportunities paled in comparison to what the draining of Sumas Lake cost the Sema:th. The lake's abundant fish population retreated with its waters. The mammoth sturgeon for which Sumas Lake was known disappeared completely, and the salmon that used to migrate through the lake were diverted up Vedder Canal. Then government officials restricted Sto:lo access to Vedder Canal, saving the runs of salmon and trout for White sportsmen. In this way, one of the Sema:th's most important resources was transferred into White hands. With the ready source of fish gone, the upper Sema:th were forced to rely more on Fraser River fishing sites, including that at Devil's Run.

There was nowhere the Sema:th could go to replace the once-abundant waterfowl that had migrated through Sumas Valley. Here too the actions of government officials and White hunters had already thinned the formerly boundless flocks; the lake's draining depleted them even more. Decades later, elders still lamented the loss of Sumas Lake's rich food supply. "We lost our lake and that killed our people," Ray Silver explained with emotion.

"The lake was the lifeline of our people....The lake was so full of fish, sturgeon, ducks, geese, everything. All of a sudden there was nothing left."

Also gone were the annually flooded grasslands along the edges of Sumas Lake, which Sema:th and White farmers had shared as a "commons" for feeding their livestock. The Sema:th were particularly dependent upon these commons, as they could not produce enough forage on their limited reserve land, much of which was rocky hillside. To make matters worse, the Sema:th effectively lost the Aylechootlook reserve, a crucial source of hay and pasture land. The reserve sat at precisely the point where the new Vedder Canal flowed into upper Sumas River. The canal and dykes occupied more than half of the 49-acre reserve. In 1923, with the reserve already eaten away, the Sema:th signed the papers ceding those 27 acres to the dyking commission. In exchange, the Sema:th were paid $189, or $7 an acre; officials justified the low price because draining the lake "greatly increased [the] value of the remaining 19.83 acres." The meagreness of this sum stood in sharp contrast to the $74,852 spent by the commission to acquire White-owned properties it needed to build on. Approximately 750 acres of land were purchased; the average cost of $100 per acre was 14 times that paid to the Sema:th for their reserve land.[120]

For the Sema:th, the draining of Sumas Lake compounded and magnified the forces of dispossession that had assailed them for decades. In the face of depopulation, the loss of most of their land and restricted access to traditional resources, the waters and wetlands of Sumas Lake provided a lifeline. With the lake gone, the Sema:th struggled mightily to build an economy that could sustain them. They persevered as a people, but they sorely missed their lake.

CHAPTER 11:

AFTERMATH

If we ended this book at the 25th anniversary of Sumas Lake's draining, it would be easy to conclude that the grand project was an environmental and human failure. The bill for the works had soared to $10 million, large agricultural companies dominated local industry, family farms were failing, and cleanup operations were still under way after the second worst flood on record. At the same time, the Sema:th were robbed of the one resource essential to their way of life. But the story does not stop there. Through the second half of the 20th century, the tragedy continued to afflict that lake's first peoples, but they refused to accept the fate and rallied to challenge the way they had been treated. Meanwhile, White farmers and residents benefited, as many of the promises originally made by drainage proponents were being met: the landscape of corporate estates and struggling family farms was transformed into an approximation of the family farm model envisioned by planners.

World War II pulled Canada out of the Great Depression; after the war, the country was transformed by unprecedented economic growth, fuelled by a baby boom, rising immigration and freer-flowing international trade. The national and international demand for agricultural products soared, and Sumas farmers profited. Meanwhile, government policies and technological advances made it possible for the family-owned farm to be a competitive economic operation. Marketing boards and quotas; easy farm credit; co-operative stores and banks; and more affordable and efficient farm machinery all brought the dream of the prosperous family farm within reach. By the 1950s, the large tobacco companies had left the valley, and Buckerfield's had decided to divide up and sell its vast Sumas holdings. The total number of Sumas farms rose while the average size of them stayed more or less the same. By the 1960s, the family farm was the dominant mode of land ownership and production in Sumas Valley.

Dairy farming was the biggest contributor to Sumas's economic boom, as the valley belatedly lived up to its billing as "pre-eminently the land of the cow." With the draining of Sumas Lake, farmers made the shift from extensive pastoral practices to more intensive agricultural ones. The growth of the greater Vancouver market and better transportation now made this pay. The lush fodder crops that could be grown on the former lake lands— which after several decades were living up to earlier promises of fertility— made intensive farming possible. Through the mid-1940s, Sumas farmers devoted about 14,000 acres of cropland and pasture to feed nearly 5,000 milking cows. By 1961, the acreage given over to dairy remained the same, but the amount of cultivated cropland grew while pasture land shrank, increasing the amount of feed produced. Meanwhile, the number of milking cows rose by 50 percent.

After early failures, the berry industry grew into another success story for the family farm. Beginning in the late 1930s, and continuing through the war, Mennonite farmers from Yarrow moved onto the sandy lake bed, acquired compact lots of five acres or so and planted them to berries. Raspberries proved the best growers; whether preserved or in jam, they found a ready market in food-rationed Britain. By 1948, some 240 farms comprising 900 acres were producing raspberries; another 10 farms spread over 100 acres grew strawberries. Taken together, this represented one-fifth of Sumas Valley's agricultural earnings. The following year, a bumper crop was met by the collapse of the British and European markets, as the continent restarted producing its own food. By the 1960s, the industry had rebounded as domestic markets grew and frozen-food technologies spread.[121]

The postwar turnaround was heralded by White residents and officials as proof of the drainage project's ultimate triumph. Long-time resident Fred Zink stated in 1963, "The reclamation of Sumas is one of the greatest assets to the lower mainland...[and] to the whole province." Fred Toop agreed, adding, "It reclaimed 10,000 acres of the finest land you can find anywhere in this continent." In 1967, the provincial government erected the historic marker we first encountered at the start of this book. The marker celebrating the lake's "reclamation" concludes: "Produce of the mixed farming on this deep lake-bottom land is an important factor in the economy of our mountainous province."

The common refrain in this triumphant chorus was the claim that man had taken what nature gave him—an unproductive wasteland the *Chilliwack Progress* dismissed as a "water blister"—and remade it into fertile agricultural land. Yet the new landscape was not completely new. Industries that succeeded relied on the same types of plants that for centuries had grown naturally around Sumas Lake. Fields of raspberries—and more recently cranberries and blueberries—flourished where original berry bushes once thrived. Dairymen relied on two to three cuttings of grasses and grass-like alfalfa planted in soil that once sprouted lush expanses of indigenous grasses. And nurseries grew row upon row of familiar cedar trees and hedges in the valley's wet soil.

Among Sumas's White residents, a few voices expressed regret at what had been lost. Myrtle Ferguson recalled the summers of her youth, which she and her cousins spent on the shores of Sumas Lake. "We thought of it as the most beautiful spot you could imagine"—from every window in the farmhouse was "the beautiful lake, every day, that we looked out on." The picturesque view was gone, as were the carefree days of swimming, sailing and picnicking. Barbara Beldam fondly remembered the "privileged isolation" of White settlers around the lake. After the lake was drained, "most of the ducks disappeared...and the open prairies were cut into small farms. The peaceful leisurely times were gone." But these dissenting voices were more nostalgic than angry; even they concluded that losing the lake was the price that had to be paid for the sake of progress and prosperity.

There were no mixed feelings among the Sema:th. Of all the people of Sumas Valley, the Sema:th have continued to be the hardest hit by the lake's draining. From the end of the last century on, as official channels for Indigenous land and resource claims opened up, the Sema:th have launched claims for their losses to be compensated. In the 1990s, the Sumas band pressed two cases in front of the federal Indian Claims Commission. One claim concerned the 31 acres of the Upper Sumas reserve that was granted as a right-of-way to Vancouver, Victoria and Eastern Railway. The Sema:th argued that when the railway abandoned its line through the reserve in 1927, that land should have reverted back to the band, instead of being sold to the Kilgard Fire Clay Company: the sale was illegal, and the Sema:th were owed compensation. Another claim challenged the validity of the surrender of the Whatcom reserve (Sumas 7) in 1919, and demanded restitution for it.

Within the last few years, the Sema:th have been investigating a specific claim, which asserts that the federal government failed to protect their rights and interests when Sumas Lake was drained. "If they were going to reclaim the land, then I think we should have had all the say so in the world," elder Lester Ned told the *Vancouver Sun*. "They never did talk to us....If they were going to claim the land back, then I think we should have got some of it." The band's lawyer added that the claim was unusual because the land around Sumas Lake was not static, but changed as the lake grew and shrank with the seasons. Indeed, current laws and government policies share much of the same difficulty that White settlers of Sumas Valley historically faced—the tendency to define natural environments (lakes, valleys, prairies) as either land or water. But Sumas Lake and Valley were wetlands, neither wholly land nor wholly water. The Sema:th made full use of these in-between zones; any just decision would compensate the Sema:th for the destruction of these wetlands.[122]

The issue of Sema:th rights and compensation is further complicated by the historical status of the lake bed itself. When the Sumas reserves were set up, this was not dry land but water, and thus reverted to the Crown. Sumas Lake and Valley fell within the Railway Belt, so the Crown in this case was the federal government, which then and now is constitutionally obligated to protect the interests of Native people. The federal government permitted the provincial government to destroy a lake under federal jurisdiction; then, in 1923, Ottawa sold the exposed lake bed to Victoria for one dollar. The Sema:th were never consulted, and Indian Affairs did nothing to protect the band's interests. From the historical perspective at least—and quite possibly in legal terms—the federal government did not fulfill its obligations.

The recent claims of the Sumas band show us that the story of Sumas Lake is not over, that we are still living with its presence. The waters themselves tell us this as well, for the environmental conditions that created and sustained the lake are still there. Twice each year, spring and winter, the waters of the Sumas and Fraser River watersheds try to return to their natural place on the Sumas Valley floor. The machinery and technology used to keep these at bay have become more effective with each passing decade, and the flood threat has receded in the local imagination. This sense of security is faulty. A study released on the anniversary of the 1894 flood concluded that there is a one-in-three chance that a flood at least as big will occur by the year 2045—and it may even be bigger. The 1894 flood was not the perfect storm of legend; it would have been higher if the Fraser and Thompson Rivers had peaked at exactly the same time, rather than a few days apart. All bets will be off if and when the perfect flood does happen, for not even the experts can predict whether the defences guarding the Sumas and Fraser Valleys will stand firm or not.

The only sure way to end the threat of flooding that still hangs over Sumas Valley would be to dismantle the Sumas drainage works altogether. Prior to its draining, sediments deposited by the yearly high waters had been raising the bed of Sumas Lake. Geologist Valerie Cameron notes that if Sumas Lake had not been drained, the area would have eventually filled to the same level as the Fraser River floodplain. Because the Vedder canal was built before this was achieved, much of the Sumas Valley has an elevation close to sea level and still floods periodically due to rising groundwater levels.[123]

Nobody knows how many decades or centuries it would have taken for the Sumas bed and Fraser River to level off. At that point, Sumas Lake would disappear as a lake, but live on in the fertile wetlands and valley it left behind.

Appendix A

Original Plants and Animals of Sumas Lake and Valley

Grasses

cattail
grass, blue-joint
grass, brome
grass, common reed
horsetail, common
horsetail, giant
horsetail, scouring rush
sedge
thistle, Indian
thistle, montane

Bushes, Shrubs and Roots

blackberry, wild trailing
blackcap
blueberry, bog
camas, blue
carrot, wild
cranberry, bog
currant, red flowering
devil's club
dock, western
dogbane
fern, bracken
fern, licorice
fireweed
gooseberry, swamp
hardhack
huckleberry, red

Jerusalem artichoke
kinnikinnick
Labrador tea
lily, chocolate
mahonia
nettle, stinging
ocean spray
onion, wild
Oregon grape
parsnip, cow
parsnip, water
raspberry, red
rose, common wild
salmonberry
saskatoon berry
skunk cabbage
soapberry
strawberry, wild
swordfern
wapato
yarrow

TREES

alder, red
alder, Sitka
balsam
birch, western white
cedar, western red
cherry
cottonwood, northern black
crabapple, wild
dogwood, Pacific
fir, Douglas
hemlock, western
maple, broadleaf
maple, vine
oak, Garry
pine, shore
spruce, Menzies

willow, Hooker
willow, Pacific
willow, Sitka

Fish

bullhead
eulachon
lamprey, Pacific
lamprey, western brook
salmon, chinook
salmon, chum/dog
salmon, coho
salmon, pink/humpback
salmon, sockeye
smelt, longfin
stickleback
stickleback, tiny
sturgeon
sucker, largescale
sucker, Salish
trout, coastal cutthroat
trout, Dolly Varden
trout, steelhead
whitefish, menominee

Birds

baldpate
bittern, American
blackbird, Brewer's
blackbird, yellow-headed
bluebird, mountain
bluebird, western
bobolink
bufflehead
bunting, lazuli
bunting, snow
bushtit
buzzard, red-bellied

catbird
chat, long-tailed
chickadee, chestnut-backed
chickadee, Oregon
coot
cowbird
crane, little brown
crane, sandhill
creeper, California
crossbill
crossbill, white-winged
crow, northwestern
crow, western
cuckoo, California
curlew, long-billed
dipper
dove, mourning
dowitcher, long-billed
duck, canvasback
duck, harlequin
duck, lesser scaup
duck, ring-necked
duck, ruddy
duck, scaup
duck, wood
eagle, golden
eagle, northern bald
eagle, Steller's sea
falcon, peregrine
falcon, prairie
finch (several species)
flicker, northern
flicker, northwestern
flycatcher (several species)
gadwall
goldeneye
goose, cackling
goose, Canada
goose, Hutchins's

goose, snow
goose, white-cheeked
goose, white-fronted
goshawk
grebe (several species)
grosbeak (several species)
grouse, Canada ruffed
grouse, Oregon ruffed
grouse, sooty/blue
gull (numerous species)
gyrfalcon
hawk, Cooper's
hawk, marsh
hawk, red-bellied
hawk, rough-legged
hawk, sharp-shinned
hawk, sparrow
hawk, Swainson's
hawk, western red-tailed
heron, great blue
heron, northwestern
hummingbird, black-chinned
hummingbird, rufous
ibis, white-faced glossy
jaeger
jay, black-headed
jay, Steller's
junco
kingbird
kinglet
knot
lark (several species)
longspur
loon, common
loon, Pacific
loon, red-throated
magpie
mallard
meadowlark

merganser (several species)
merlin
nighthawk
nuthatch
oriole
osprey
owl (numerous species)
pelican, white
pewee, western wood
phalarope
pigeon, band-tailed
pintail
plover (several species)
rail, Virginia
raven, northern
redhead
redpoll
redstart
redwing, northwestern
robin (several species)
sanderling
sandpiper (numerous species)
sapsucker, northern red-breasted
scoter
shoveller
shrike
siskin, pine
snipe
solitaire, Townsend's
sora
sparrow (numerous species)
swallow (numerous species)
swan, Bewick
swan, trumpeter
swan, whistling
swift
tanager, western
teal, blue-winged
teal, cinnamon

teal, green-winged
tern, black
thrush
towhee, Oregon
turnstone
vireo (several species)
vulture, turkey
warbler (numerous species)
waxwing, Bohemian
waxwing, cedar
woodpecker (numerous species)
wren (numerous species)
yellowlegs
yellowthroat

Amphibians and Reptiles

salamander, Pacific giant
salamander, warty
snake, garter
snake, green racer
snake, Oregon bull
snake, Pacific rubber
toad, northwestern
turtle, western pond

Mammals

badger
bat (numerous species)
bear, black
beaver
chipmunk, Townsend's
cougar, Pacific
coyote
deer, black-tailed
deer, white-tailed
dog
elk
fisher

fox, red
hare, Washington
marten, northwestern
mink, Pacific
mole (several species)
mountain beaver
mouse, western jumping
mouse, white-footed
muskrat, Pacific
otter, Canadian river
rabbit, eastern cottontail
racoon, Pacific
rat, Norway
shrew (several species)
skunk, Pacific
skunk, spotted
squirrel, Douglas
squirrel, Pacific flying
vole, creeping
vole, Townsend's
weasel (several species)
wildcat, coast
wolf

These lists were derived from the following sources:

FOR PLANTS

Duff (1952); Galloway (1993); H. Laing (1979); Lord (1866); Lyall (1864); North (1984); Turner (1995, 1998); Upper Stó:lō (1981, 1982).

FOR BIRDS

Brooks (1900, 1917, 1925); Duff (1952); Fannin (1891); Galloway (1993); Kennerly, "Chiloweyuck Depot," *na76/e198*; Kennerly, "Natural History" and "Birds," *sia/kennerly_pprs/bx1*; Laing (1979); Lord (1866); Munro (1947).

FOR FISH, AMPHIBIANS, REPTILES AND MAMMALS

Brooks (1902); Carl (1959, 1960, 1973); Cowan (1965); Duff (1952); Galloway (1993); Kennerly, "Natural History," *sia/kennerly_pprs/bx1*; Laing (1979); Lord (1866); "Mammals" and "North American Salmonidae," *sia/suckley_pprs/bx1-2*.

APPENDIX B

SEMA:TH PLACE NAMES (C. 1860)

Sluch-kéhn	Soomas Mountain
Kéh-ka-la-hun	mountain on Soomass Lake south of above
Mam-ook-wum	prairie between Soomass and Chiloweyuk
See-it-léh-hu	first creek running into Soomass Lake
Tah-ta-lá-o	river entering Soomass Lake from southwest
Shum-mehn	first site on creek coming in from west
Swáh-leh-whai	second site on creek coming in from west
Noos-maāts	small house on See-it-léh-hu
Sháhs-ma-koom	the swamp
Tseh-lehm	stream from mountain into Soomass Lake
Shwum-mut	place of Custer's camp
Seétsh-taun	high peak ascended by Custer
Klāa-lum	creek into Soomass Lake beyond Tah-ta-lá-o
Kwul-stánn	another creek into Soomas Lake
Yuch-wun-néh-ukw	first small prairie on Tah-ta-lá-o
Hoo-mal-so-melp	second prairie on Tah-ta-lá-o
Kwil-tel-lum-un	prairie between Tah-ta-lá-o and Nooksack River
Laā-how-ie	stream on Fraser River above Soomass flat
Ko-méh-litsh	mountain above Laā-how-ie
Yeech-yill	first stream into Fraser River from south
Tsah-mohtl	second stream into Fraser River from south
Tsó-ho-mass	first stream into Fraser River from north
Kwee-áh-matsh	second stream into Fraser River from north
Se-méhn	creek into Fraser River from south, at Cheam
Kwáiss	small lake, Se-méhn's source

Sources: G. Gibbs, "Indian Nomenclature," *na76/e223*, and "Notebook No. II," *brml/gibbs_notebooks/f2*.

APPENDIX C

HALKOMELEM WORDS AND NAMES

Used in Text	Halkomelem
Chehalis	Sts'ailes
Chilliwack	Ts'élxweyeqw
Halkomelem	Halq'eméylem
Kwantlen	Qw'ó:ltl'el
Lakahamen	Leq'á:el
Lekwiltok	Yéqwelhta
Matsqui	Máthxwi
Nooksack	Lexwsá:q
Pilalt	Peló:lhxw
Sema:th	Semá:th
Sema:th Xo:tsa	Semá:th Xó:tsa
Sto:lo	Stó:lō
Swilhcha	Swílhcha
Thompson	Nlaka'pamux
Xwelitem	Xwelítem
Xexa:ls	Xexá:ls

ENDNOTES

Archives cited in the endnotes and sources have been identified by the following abbreviations:

ama	Anacortes Museum and Archives
bca	British Columbia Archives
bcerp	BC Electric Railway Papers, University of British Columbia Rare Books and Special Collections
brml	Beinecke Rare Book and Manuscript Library (Yale University)
ccec	Coqualeetza Cultural Education Centre
cma	Chilliwack Museum and Archives
cpns	Center for Pacific Northwest Studies
cva	City of Vancouver Archives
ltsv	Land Title and Survey Vault (Victoria, BC)
na76	National Archives and Records Administration (Washington, DC), RG 76: Records of Boundary and Claims Commissions and Arbitrations
pffn	Paul Fetzer Field Notes, C. Wellman Collection (Bellingham, WA)
rg10	Library and Archives Canada, RG 10: Department of Indian Affairs Black Series
rgm	The Reach Gallery and Museum (Abbotsford, BC)
sia	Smithsonian Institution Archives
sna	Stó:lō Nation Archives
ubcr	University of British Columbia Rare Books and Special Collections
vpl	Vancouver Public Library

INTRODUCTION

1. Lord (1866), 1:315.

2. In the triumph camp: White (1937); Imus (1948); Smith (1982); Sleigh (1999); K. Foulds, "Land Beneath the Lake," rgm. In the tragedy camp: L. Cameron (1997); Carlson (1997, 2001); Murton (2007)

CHAPTER 1: GLACIERS TO WETLANDS

3. On the geology and glacial formation of Sumas Lake and Valley: Armstrong (1960); V. Cameron (1989); Kovanen (2001).

4. The interviews and oral histories used here and throughout the book are listed in Sources; the list notes in which chapters each interview is used. As a rule, the interviewee is named in the text when quoted.

5. "Fraser River at Mission, Maximum Yearly Gauge Heights," *cma/ am373*; US Army Corps of Engineers (1967). Reports prepared for the Sumas Lake drainage project described the dimensions of Sumas Lake, its watersheds and flooding cycles; see Sources for these. Imperial units · of measurement are used in the book, mainly because they were the ones used in historical records until very recently. This prevents having to constantly convert units back and forth.

6. Lord (1866), 2:64.

7. Jackson (2000), 246–52; E. Robson, "Diary," *bca/h-d-r57*. Appendix A lists the plants and animals native to Sumas Valley; it also cites the primary sources used in the text to reconstruct the valley's natural history.

8. Swindle (2001), 133, 242; Gardner (1857).

9. Langston (2003); Mitsch (2009); Lerman (1951); Lord (1866), 1:313–14.

10. Lewis (2001); R. Wilson (2010); Langston (2003).

CHAPTER 2: FIRST PEOPLES

11. Jenness (1955); Carlson (2001, 2010); "Stalo River Story," *bca/ ms2794/bx2/f3*; Gibbs, "Notebook II," *brml/gibbs_notebooks/f2*. Gibbs's phonetic rendering of S'Hui-yahm appears to match the Halkomelem word Skoyá:m or Skeyá:m, which translate as "a stone like a statue at Harrison Lake"; Galloway (2009).

12. Duff (1952),12; Carlson (2001), 191.

13. On migration theories, see: Suttles (1987); Carlson (2001).

14. The archaeological literature on the lower Fraser Valley is rich. On the Sto:lo: Lepofsky (2000, 2009); Mohs (1992a); Schaepe (2009). On the Sema:th in BC: Bernick (1991), and "Perishable Artifacts from Liyómxe-tel," sna; Kenyon (1953); Lepofsky (2003); Mohs (1991); RRN (DgRm 1, 10, S1–3; DgRn 2, 10, 24). On the Sema:th in Washington State: Emmons (1952); Montgomery (1979).

15. Hill-Tout (1895), 114–18; (1978), 91; *Victoria Colonist* (May 10/1900); Lepofsky (2003), 9.

16. Carlson (2001), 76–77, 170–71; Gardner (1857); C. Wilson (1866). During the 1800s: Mayne (1859); R. Parsons letter (Apr 31/1861), *bca/c-ab-30.6j-5*; McColl (1864); W. Ralph, "Field Book," *ltsv/fb2101*; "Plan of Township 20" (1889, 1892, 1901, 1906), *ltsv/142796, 150308-1503010*.

17. "Devil's Run," *sna/ware_notes*; "Stalo River Story," *bca/ms2794/bx2/f3*; Galloway (2009), 239.

18. J. Launders report (Dec 18/1868), *bca/gr1372/f969*; Duff (1952); W. Sepass [untitled map, c. 1918], *cma/map374*; Wells (1965), 23–24.

19. McColl (1864); A. Smith (1988).

20. Wells (1987), 216, 222; C. Wilson (1970), 60, 63; Lord (1866), 1:315–16; (1867), 279–80; Crosby (1907), 176; Tate (1874–76); Galloway (2009), 605; W. Sepass [untitled map, c. 1918], *cma/2004.052.2871*. In RRN: SN 2001.10.4-19, SN 2001.41, SN 2002.61.1-2.

21. Along with Tom's account, see: Amoss (1978), 120; Richardson (2011), 23–24, 97–99; Kenyon (1953); "T'xwelátse Me t'ókw' telo qás" (2006), sna. In RRN: DgRm:S1-3, DgRn2, DgRn24. Mohs (1992b).

22. Boas (1894), 453; Wells (1987), 216-18; Carlson (2001), 139, 142, 150; Galloway (2009), 189.

Chapter 3: Sema:th Xo:tsa

23. Maclachlan (1998), 42, 113, 148; Jackson (2000), 110–11; Galloway (2009), 1000.

24. Lerman (1951); Lord (1866), 2:254; Gardner (1858). Other sources include: Turner (1995, 1998); *Upper Stó:lō* (1981, 1982); Galloway (1993).

25. Lord (1866), 1:40–77; Kennerly, "Chiloweyuck Depot," *na76/e198*.

26. Lord (1866), 1:177; Duff (1952); G.F. White (1917); Galloway (2009), 325–26.

27. Lord (1866), 1:97–100; Carl (1959), 39–40.

28. C. Wilson (1866); Hawley (1945), 42; Suttles (1955); "Elders' Meeting" (1977), *sna/ware_notes*.

29. Jenness (1955).

30. Lord (1866), 1:316–20; (1867), 279–80; C. Wilson (1970), 62–63; Beckey (2003), 122; R. Parsons letter (Jun 8/1860), *bca/c-ab-30.6j-5*. On mosquito mythology: Lerman (1951); Joe (1979); Sepass (2009).

31. "Nooksack Tribe," *pffn*; Richardson (1974, 2011); Gardner (1857); "Matsqui," *pffn*; C. Kelleher, "Matsqui Indians," *cma/am1/f684*; Carlson (2001), 79.

32. Schaepe (2006); Gibbs, "Notebook II," *brml/gibbs_notebooks/f2*.

33. Kennerly, "Trip up Fraser," *na76/e198*; Fraser (2007), 124–27; Maclachlan (1998), 41–42, 56–57, 148; Carlson (2001), 50–51.

Chapter 4: First Encounters

34. Fraser (2007), 118–35. See the relevant histories: L. Cameron (1997); Oliver (2010); Sleigh (1999); Wells (1987). On the Halkomelem words: Gibbs, "Notebook II," *brml/gibbs_notebooks/f2*, and "Indian Nomenclature," *na76/3223*.

35. US Commissioner (1857), 328. The main sources on Fort Langley are: Maclachlan (1998); McDonald (2001).

36. Gibbs, "Notebook II," *brml/gibbs_notebooks/*f2; J. Work letter (Nov 24/1858), *PRA* (1859).

37. The American commission records are a treasure trove and were used throughout this book. The main body of them is at the National Archives in Washington, DC (referred to here as *na76*). The surveying records include: *e196* (Reports on Surveys); *e198* (Journals of Exploring Surveys); *e199* (Special Survey Books); *e200* (Field Notes); *e201* (Topographical Notes); *e202* (Reconnaissance Books). Official British commission records are limited to correspondence between J. Hawkins and the Foreign Office, published as *CCFO* (1899).

38. Jackson (2000), lvi–lvii, 104–5.

39. G. Gardner and H. Custer reports in *na76/e196*; Jackson (2000), 70–71, 80–83, 93–96; Jeffcott (1949), 8, 353–54.

40. C. Wilson (1866); H. Custer, "Report of Reconnaissances" (1866), *sna*; for Gibbs see Appendix B.

41. [Native Placenames], *na76/cs68/map1*; Carlson (2001), 134–53; Richardson (2011), 28–29.

42. These sketches and paintings are at *na76/e208, e221*.

43. Preliminary Sketch of Reconnaissances and Surveys (1858), *RRNB* (1961) v 1. US commission maps are at *na76/cs66, cs68, cs69*.

44. Hawkins's letters in *CCFO* (1899) v 3; Campbell's letters in *RRNB* (1961) v 1; C. Wilson (1970), 59. Royal Engineer maps published in: *FPRA* (1860) v 3, (1862) v 4; and Woodward (1975). The first civilian survey map: "Roads and Trails: 3," *ltsv/26t1*.

45. "Map of the International Boundary" (1869), *ubcr/map_coll*; "The North West Boundary" (1869), *na76/cs66/map7*.

Chapter 5: Hungry Newcomers

46. See Jeffcott (1949); Marshall (2000); O. Wells, "Chilliwack's Early History," *cma/am1/f152*.

47. The main primary sources on the gold rush were newspapers from that time: *Northern Light* (Jul 10, Sep 4/1858); *San Francisco Bulletin* (Jun 16, 28, July 5/1858); *Victoria Gazette* (Jul 7, Aug 4/1858). Also, see Swindle (2001); Jeffcott (1949). The Northwest Boundary Survey records also provided information.

48. Galloway (2009) 925–26; Gardner (1858); Harris letter (May 20/1858), *RRNB* (1961) v 1; Jackson (2000), 93–96.

49. DeGroot (1858), 22–23.

50. Lord (1867), 17–19; Gibbard (1937), 186; Mikkelsen (1950), 54; Siemens (1968), 105–6.

51. A major source for the 1860s on is contemporary newspapers; those used in this and following chapters are cited in Sources. Also see business directories published by Langley (1867), Mallandaine (1871–74), Hibben (1877), Williams (1883–99), Henderson (1890–1901). Pre-emption records are found in: *bca/gr112/v92-97, v210-11*; *bca/gr1069/bx70*; F. Laing (1939). On pre-emption laws, see: Cail (1974); Mikkelsen (1950).

52. A. Day, "Adam Swart Vedder," *cma/am1/f102;* T. York letter (Oct 26/1858), *bca/gr1372/f1147a.*

53. P. O'Reilly letter (May 6/1861), *bca/gr1372/f1279.*

54. Gibbard (1937), 185; Dept. of Lands and Works (1873).

55. H. Webb, "Chilliwhack Valley and Its Pioneers," *bca/g-c43-w38c;* E. Macleod, "B.C. Centennial Story," *cma/am1/f120*; W. Ralph, "Field Book" (1874–75), *ltsv/fb2125.*

56. "Laura Miller," *cma/pp500063.*

57. "Justine Allard," *ubc.bcmetis.ca*; P. Campbell letters (Oct 23, Dec 20/1868; Mar 26, Apr 27/1871), *bca/gr1372/f266a.*

58. "Printed Family Tree of the Chadseys," *cma/am1/f19*; "Donald Mc-Gillivray," *chilliwackmuseum.ca.*

Chapter 6: A Second Eden

59. "Sumas Land Declarations," *bca/gr312.*

60. F. Toop, "Introduction" (1960), *cma/am362/f32*; Riggins (1991), 53; C. Wells, "Excerpts," *cma/am1/f123*; Orchard (1983), 75.

61. Wells (2003), 101; Bosselman (1996); J. Donnally et al. petition (Dec 9/1869), *bca/gr1372/f1355*; Mikkelsen (1950), 132, 138.

62. E. Stephens, "Field Book," *ltsv/fb2071*; Hendrickson (1980), 159.

63. Sumas Municipal Council (1919); Cook (1979), 30.

64. H. Webb, "Pioneer Life," *bca/g-c43-w38p.*

65. H. Webb, "Chilliwhack and Its Pioneers," *bca/g-c43-w38c*; Cook (1979), 25.

66. Brooks (1902), 240.

67. Carl (1959), 100–102.

68. Orchard (1983), 35; Wells (2003), 147.

69. Brooks (1917, 1925); H. Laing (1979); "Biography of Major Allan Brooks," *cma/am404.*

70. Orchard (1983), 7; W. Hall letter (Jun 30/1894), *cma/am510*; "Biography of W. Hall," *cma/am1/f36*; H. Laing (1979), 51, 62-63.

71. Crosby (1907), 191; Sleigh (1999), 47–51.

72. On picnicking: Sleigh (1999), 187. Swimming: Orchard (1983), 21. Boating: I. Bowman, "Log of the *Argo*," *ama/bowman_papers*. Skating: C. Wilson (1970); Orchard (1983); "Skating on One of the Sumas Lake Swamps," *cva/p841*.

73. Tate (1876–78).

74. Fraser (2007), 121–22; Maclachlan (1998), 151–52; C. Kennerly, "Chiloweyuck Depot," *na76/e198*.

Chapter 7: Peoples Displaced

75. On the impact of diseases, see: Boyd (1999); Harris (1997); Carlson (1997, 2001, 2010); Mohs (1990).

76. Along with interview sources named in the text, see: Jenness (1955); statements of H. Uselick, A. Martin and J. Jimmy, *cma/am1/f684*.

77. Letters and reports from the following officials were published in *PILQ* (1875): J. Douglas (Mar 14/1859); R. Moody (Mar 6/1861); C. Brew (Apr 6/1864); A. Howse (Apr 25/1864); W. McColl (May 16/1864); J. Trutch (Aug 28, Nov 19/1867); B. Pearse (Oct 21/1868); J. Launders (Dec 18/1868). Also see: R. Parsons letter (Apr 31/1861), *bca/c-ab-30.6j-5*; J. Trutch letter (Dec 19/1865), *bca/gr1372/f943*. Reserve maps include: McColl (1864); J. Launders, "Indian Reserves (Fraser R. and Sloughs)," *ltsv/26t1a*. On White reaction: *British Columbian* (Apr 27/1864); Hendrickson (1980), 237.

78. P. Ayessik et al. petition (Jul 14/1874), *LASP*; Carlson (2001), 170–74.

79. "Somass River Indians–Decision" (1879) and "Summary of Year's Work" (1879), *rg10/v11028/fSRR2*; "Plan of Sumass Indian Reserves" (1882), *cma/d_cook_fonds*.

80. Selesmlton and Lewis testimony (Jan 12/1915), in RCIA (1916); Harris (2002), 228–48.

81. The primary sources on the lynching of Louie Sam are: "Coroner's Inquest" (Mar 1, 3/1884), *bca/gr1327/inquest#1-84*; the Dept. of Indian Affairs file on it, *rg10/v3674/f12061*; Jeffcott (1949).

82. Crosby (1907), 225; Tate (1874–75); Carlson (2001), 80–81; Kennerly, "Chiloweyuck Depot," *na76/e198*.

83. Carlson (2001), 175–78; Harris (2002), 203.

84. Letters from Selesmlton and government officials in: *rg10*: *v1453* (Aug 18/1899; Mar 6/1902); *v1462* (Apr 29, May 1/1905); *v1472* (Mar 24/1910); *v1474* (Mar 14/1911).

85. Letters from Selesmlton and officials: (Aug 8/1910; Jul 25/1918; Dec [nd]/1927; Jan 23/1928), *rg10/v8086/f987*.

86. F. Pedley letter (Mar 18/1903), *sna/rg10_index*. In RCIA (1916): Women's Institute testimony (Jan 11/1915); P. Byrne testimony (Feb 8/1915). In *ccec/f8394*: letters from F. Stacey and P. Byrne (Apr 16, Jun 4, Jul 16, Nov 1/1919).

87. Sleigh (1999), 99–100.

CHAPTER 8: REDEEMING SUMAS LAKE

88. On these views of nature, see: Merchant (2004); Worster (1977). Again, newspapers cited in Sources were a major source for this and the next chapters.

89. Letters from Mohun, Pearse and Edmonds: (Jun 22, 23, Jul 4/1871), *bca/gr1372/f1147a*; (Dec 9/1872), *bca/gr983/f2*; (Jul 27, Sep 5/1873) *bca/gr868/bx2/f6*.

90. E. Dewdney report (Nov 27/1876), *bca/gr868/f2987-76*.

91. D. McGillivray et al. petition (Aug 29/1877), *bca/gr868/bx3/f21*.

92. Cail (1974), 136 n 31.

93. Petitions in *LAJ* (Jan [nd]/1891; Mar 17/1892).

94. In *LAJ*: "Sumas Dyking Act, 1894"; petitions (Feb 19, 23/1894).

95. Orchard (1983), 61; C. Cartwright, "Report on Sumas Reclamation Project" (1919), *bca/gr929/bx48/f5*.

96. "Regina vs. Edwards et al." (1895), *bcerp/bx182/f9*.

97. On the history of drainage schemes, including SDC and BCER plans, see works cited in Sources. Numerous petitions (Feb 2, 16, 17, 27, Mar 3/1905), *LAJ*, voiced opposition to the SDC.

98. Letters to R. Sperling (Mar 26/1907), *bcerp/bx147/f9*, and (Oct 3/1907), *bcerp/bx38*. Also: "Reclaimed Area and Proposed Line" (1907), *bcerp/bx183/f1*.

99. Letters from Hill, Mead and Kidd in *bcerp* (Jun 5/1908), *bx171/f13*; (Apr 15/1908), *bx183/f5*; (Jul 10/1909), *bx175/f7*.

Chapter 9: A Lake Dewatered

100. L. Rice, "Report on Reclamation Works" (1913), *bca/gr1569/bx10/ f3.*

101. F. Sinclair, "Preliminary Report on the Sumas-Chilliwack Reclamation Project" (1913), *bca/gr1569/bx10/f3.*

102. Hearle (1926).

103. For LSB plans and detailed reports on the four years of drainage construction, see material cited in Sources. Also Murton (2007), 37–42, 119–21.

104. "Minutes of Sumas Dyking Meeting," *bca/gr929/bx50/f8*; "Instructions to Bidders," *cma/am646/f8.2.*

105. "Memo—Minister of Agriculture" (Sep 4/1924), *cma/am646/f8.2.*

106. A. Van Meter, "Marsh Construction Company" (1982), *cma/am692*; C. Power and D. Mathers interviews.

107. *Vancouver Province* (Jul 2/1924); *Chilliwack Progress* (Jul 9/1924).

Chapter 10: New Land

108. Sumas Drainage, Dyking and Development District (1926); C. Tice report (Mar 5/1925), *cma/am646/f8.2*; *Abbotsford, Sumas and Matsqui News* (Aug 1/1924). L. Frank photographs: *rgm/p5657-60* (1922); *vpl/p12357, p12532, p12532a-b* (1928).

109. "Sumas Lake Area" (1923), *bca/cm-a1847*; Land Settlement Board (1924); Sumas Dyking District (1926) [map]; S*umas Reclaimed Lands* (1926).

110. Fell and Scharfe (1930); Sumas Dyking District, "Fraser Valley" (1936), *cma/am646/f8.3.*

111. "Amount of Land Sold" (1930), *bca/gr1569/bx9/f3.* Newspapers cited in Sources describe post-drainage development. Also, on tobacco see: A. Mann letter (Feb 24/1936), *rgm/sam9/f7.* On Buckerfield's: Imus (1948), 83–87, 128; Sleigh (1999), 74–75.

112. B. Smith (1982), 10; Murton (2007), 110, 134. Financial statements in: *bca/gr1569/bx/f2*; *LAJ* (1945); Sinclair (1961). In today's dollars, the construction bill for the Sumas Lake drainage works comes to about $90 million. This figure was calculated using the non-unionized construction labourer's wage then (50 cents per hour) and now ($15 per hour) to get

a relative multiple between 1924 and 2017 dollars. Similarly, the website measuringworth.com pegs the real value (calculating what it would cost to buy the same goods and services) of 1924's $3 million at $93 million today. Or to take another perspective: the construction of the Pattullo Bridge—which took two years to build and opened in 1937—cost $4 million.

113. R. Davies letter (Jun 20, Aug 9/1922), *cma/am646/f8.1-2*.

114. BC Water Board, "Report on the Causes of Flooding" (1935) and "Supplementary Report" (1935), *bca/gr1569/bx13/f7*.

115. Baird (1998); Watt (2006); Sewell (1965).

116. L. Cameron (1997), 68–69. Letters between J. Motherwell and LSB (Aug 11, [nd]/1922), *bca/gr919/bx51/f1*. On the perspective of drainage planners, see: Langston (2003); Evenden (2004).

117. Macleod (1974), 103; "Elder's Meeting" (Oct 5/1977), *sna/ware_fn*; Foerster (1931, 1936).

118. Orchard (1983), 21; Boyle (1997), 193; R. Wilson (2010), 11, 23–34, 65.

119. A. Farwell letter (May 16/1879), *rg10/v11028/fSRR2*; J. Macdonald letter (Feb 24/1879), *bca/gr429/bx1/f8*. In *rg10/v7538/f27150-8-20*: Sproat's letters to Derby (Dec 26/1878), to Dept. of Indian Affairs (Jan 25, Jul 27/1879), to Indian Reserve Commission (Mar 17, Apr 18/1879).

120. W. Ditchburn letter (Apr 7/1922), *sna/rg10_index*; L. Robertson letter (Jun 9/1922), *ccec/f8395*. In *rg10/v7886/f36153-13*: "Plan Shewing Right of Way, Sumas IR" (1923); F. Lewis et al. letter (Nov 29/1923); W. Ditchburn letter (Dec 11/1923).

CHAPTER 11: AFTERMATH

121. On the postwar economy, see: Imus (1948), 74–90, 126–28; Siemens (1968), 182; Klassen (1976), 68–70; and "Continental Farmers in British Columbia," *cma/yarrow_binder*.

122. Indian Claims Commission (1994–98); *Vancouver Sun* (Apr 29/2013).

123. Fraser Basin Management Program (1994); V. Cameron (1989), 111.

SOURCES

INTERVIEWS AND ORAL HISTORIES

Beldam, B. ([nd] 1974), in *Making History*. Ed. M. Lindo. Victoria. [used in Ch. 6, 11]

Bolen, S. (Mar 7/1978), *R. Ware Notes, sna*. [Ch. 3]

Boyd, J. (Jan 10/1978), *rgm/ah82*. [Ch. 10]

Commodore, A. (Dec 17/1977), *R. Ware Notes, sna*. [Ch. 7, 10]

Cooper, A., (Nov 24/1964), *cma/am362/f257*. [Ch. 1, 7]

—, (Jan 18/1966), *cma/am362/f260*. [Ch. 3]

Cromarty, S. (Aug 26/1983), *cma/am416*. [Ch. 7]

Douglas, A. (Dec 6, 15/1994), *sna/96.04/bx2*. [Ch. 2]

Edwards, H. (Oct 8/1964), *cma/am362/f258*. [Ch. 4]

Ewen, F. [1945], *bca/ms2794/bx2*. [Ch. 3]

Ferguson, M., (Oct 24/1983), *cma/am435*. [Ch. 6, 11]

—, [nd], *rgm/ah96*. [Ch. 6, 11]

George, J. [1950], *pffn*. [Ch. 2, 3]

George, L., et al. (Apr 27, May 1/1973), *Northwest Tribal Oral History*, cpns. [Ch. 3, 4]

Guiterrez, T. (Dec 6, 15/1994), *sna/96.04/bx2*. [Ch. 3]

James, A. [1950], *pffn*. [Ch. 3]

James, S., et al. (Apr 27/1973), *Northwest Tribal Oral History, cpns*. [Ch. 2]

Joe, B., [1945], *bca/ms2794*. [Ch. 2, 3, 7]

—, (Feb 8/1962), *cma/am362/f256*. [Ch. 1, 2, 7]

—, (Jan 16/1964), *cma/am362/f257*. [Ch. 2, 4]

—, (Dec 5/1964), *cma/am362/f258*. [Ch. 3]

—, [nd], *sna/96/04/bx2*. [Ch. 2]

Kelleher, C., (Mar [nd]/1963), *bca/ms3268/f705*. [Ch. 2, 3, 5, 7]

—, (Sep 11, Oct 6/1966), *cma/am362/f261*. [Ch. 2, 3, 5, 7]

Kelly, E. (Aug 20/1987), *rgm/ah97*. [Ch. 3, 6, 7, 10]

Kelly, F., (Jun 3/1976), *rgm/ah24*. [Ch. 3, 7, 10]

—, (Oct 5/1977), *R. Ware Notes, sna*. [Ch. 7]

Lamson, E. [nd], *rgm/community_history*. [Ch. 10]

Louie A. (Aug 5/1965), *cma/am362/f259*. [Ch. 3, 7]

Louie, J., (Jan 4/1967), *bca/ms3268/f437*. [Ch. 3]

—, (May 1/1973), *Northwest Tribal Oral History, cpns*. [Ch. 3]

Malloway, R. (Sep 28/1976), *R. Ware Notes, sna*. [Ch. 10]

Malloway, S. (May 19/1995), in I. Johnson, "History of the Chilliwack Tribe," *sna*. [Ch. 10]

Mathers, D. [1971], *rgm/ah1*. [Ch. 9]

Milo, D., (Nov 15/1957), *sna/96.04/bx2*. [Ch. 2, 7]

—, (Jan 8/1962), *cma/am362/f256*. [Ch. 2, 3, 7]

—, (Apr 2/1963), *cma/am487/f719*. [Ch. 2, 3]

—, (Jul [nd]/1964), *cma/am362/f256*. [Ch. 2, 6]

—, (Dec 4/1964), *cma/am362/f257*. [Ch. 2]

Mussell, B. (Mar 2/1978), *R. Ware Notes, sna*. [Ch. 7]

Ned, L. (Jul 16/2015), *indigenousreporting.com*. [Ch. 11]

Peters, Mrs. V. [1945], *bca/ms2794/bx4/f11*. [Ch. 7]

Power, C. (Jun 28/1983), *cma/am401*. [Ch. 6, 9, 10]

Selesmlton (Chief Ned) Testimony: (Jan 12/1915), in RCIA (1916). [Ch. 3, 7, 10]

Sepass, W. [1935], in D. Jenness, "Coast Salish Mythology," *sna*. [Ch. 1, 2, 3, 6]

Silver, R., (Nov 30/1992), *sna/96.04/bx2*. [Ch. 2, 7]

—, (Jun 3/2002), in E. Scott, "They Lost Their Refrigerator," *rgm*. [Ch. 3]

—, (Jun 26, 29/2007), in "Ethnohistory Field School," *sna*. [Ch. 2, 3, 7, 10]

—, (Jul [nd]/2008), *First Nations Collection, rgm*. [Ch. 2, 3, 7, 10]

Sinclair, F. (Apr 4/1963), *cma/am487/f307*. [Ch. 9]

Sorenson, R. (Feb 8/1978), *rgm/ah79*. [Ch. 6]

Sparrow, Rose and Ed [1975], in L. Sparrow, "Work Histories of a Coast Salish Couple" (1976), *sna*. [Ch. 1, 3]

Stromberg, F. (Nov [nd]/1972), *rmg/ah100*. [Ch. 1, 6, 10]

Swanaset, G. [1950, 1951], *pffn*. [Ch. 2, 3, 7]

Tom, L. [1950], *pffn*. [Ch. 2, 3]

Toop, F., (Mar 15/1963), *cma/am487/f717*. [Ch. 11]

—, [1973], *cma/am110*. [Ch. 6]

Zink, F., (Mar [nd]/1942), *cma/am1/f154*. [Ch. 6]

—, (Apr 1/1963), *cma/am487/f722*. [Ch. 1, 6]

NEWSPAPERS

Abbotsford Post
Ch. 6: (Jun 4/1920).
Ch. 7: (Mar 26/1920).
Ch. 8: (Aug 1/1919).
Ch. 9: (Oct 3/1913); (May 7/1915); (Apr 6/1917); (Sep 13/1918); (May 16/1919).
Ch. 10: (Apr 27, Nov 16/1923).

British Colonist (Victoria)
Ch. 5: (Dec 20/1859); (May 15, Sep 26/1860); (Aug 28/1863); (Aug 28/1868); (Nov 20/1870); (Feb 5/1898); (May 5/1860).
Ch. 6: (Jan 20, Apr 3/1867); (Jan 5/1873); (Mar 9/1889).
Ch. 7: (Feb 17/1897).
Ch. 8: (Mar 15/1873); (Jun 30, Jul 19, Sep 14/1876); (Mar 29, Sep 15, 25, Nov 13/1877); (Sep 27, Nov 13, 16/1877); (Jan 19/1878); (Jun 1/1879); (Jun 8, 11/1882); (Apr 11/1883); (Jan 20, Feb 1/1887); (Jan 14/1894); (Sep 21/1899); (Mar 14/1908); (Apr 8/1909).

British Columbian (New Westminster)
Ch 5: (Jul 25/1861); (Jan 16, 23, 30, Feb 13, Nov 1/1862); (Jan 31, Sep 19, 23/1863); (Mar 18, Jul 4/1865); (Apr 25, 26, May 9, Dec 15/1866); (Apr 27, May 6/1867); (Aug 8, Nov 21/1868); (Jun 10/1876).
Ch. 6: (Sep 29, Nov 26/1864); (Mar 18/1865); (Jun 22, Oct 16/1867); (Aug 8, Oct 3/1868); (Jun 13/1869).
Ch. 7: (Apr 27/1864).
Ch. 8: (Nov 13/1867); (Nov 10, Dec 1, 7/1892); (Apr 2/1893); (May 25/1894); (Feb 27/1895).

Chilliwack Progress
Ch. 5: (Feb 24/1904); (Oct 26/1910); (Apr 30/1914); (Jul 22/1936).
Ch. 6: (Aug 11, Sep 8/1892); (Jul 26/1911); (May 5/1912); (May 7/1913); (Jun 25/1958).
Ch. 7: (May 2/1894); (Feb 24, Mar 2, 16, 24/1904); (Apr 26, May 3/1905); (Apr 25/1918); (Jul 10/1919); (Dec 23/1926).
Ch. 8: (Apr 23, Sep 24/1891); (Sep 8, Nov 3, Feb 4/1892); (Jun 6, 13, Jul 11, Aug 29/1894); (Apr 3/1895); (Apr 13/1898); (Mar 4/1903);

(Jun 13/1904); (Aug 30, Sep 5/1905); (May 23, Aug 29, Sep 19, Nov
28/1906); (May 25, Jun 15, 22, Sep 11/1907); (Aug 5, 18/1908); (Feb
2/1910).
Ch. 9: (July 21, Aug 18, Sep 1–29, Oct 6/1909); (Jan 22, 29/1913); (Jun
11/1914); (Sep 5, Dec 23/1918); (Apr 10, Aug 14, Nov 27/1919);
(Mar 11, 25, Apr 1/1920); (Jul 9/1924).
Ch. 10: (Sep 19/1918); (Nov 27/1919); (Mar 8, Apr 5, Sept 20, Oct
11/1923); (Feb 3, Jun 2, Jul 14, Sep 8/1926); (Sep 29/1927); (Mar 15,
May 10/1928); (May 9/1929); (Mar 20, Apr 3, Dec 4/1930); (Apr
27/1933); (Jan 24, 31, Feb 7, 14/1935); (Aug 13/1941); (May 27, Jun
2, 9, 16, 23/1948).

Mainland Guardian (New Westminster)
Ch. 5: (Mar 27; Jul 10/1872).
Ch. 6: (Nov 13/1869); (Nov 26/1870); (May 13, Aug 9, Nov 22/1871);
(Jul 10/1872); (May 17/1873); (Oct 7, 14/1874); (Sep 1/1875);
(Jun 27/1877); (Nov 6/1878); (Sep 24/1879); (Nov 17/1880); (Nov
13/1886).
Ch. 7: (Jul 10, Dec 12/1872).
Ch. 8: (June 19, 30/1875); (May 31, Jun 28, Jul 5, 19/1876); (Nov 7,
14/1877); (Jan 16/1878); (Jun 14, 17/1882); (Oct 28/1885); (Mar
16/1887).
Ch. 9: (Apr 13/1889).

SUMAS LAKE DRAINAGE PROJECT RECORDS

History of Drainage Project Schemes and Construction

Davies, R., "Record of Land Settlement Board" (1923), *bca/gr1569/bx14/
f4*.
Land Settlement Board, "Report on Sumas Reclamation Project" (1922),
rgm/sam9/f2.
Latta, W., "Record of Events" (1926), *bca/gr1569/bx15/f3*.
"Minutes of Sumas Dyking Meeting" (1919), *bca/gr929/bx50/f8*.
"Old Minute Book" (1919), *rgm/sam9/f1*.
Sinclair, F., "Report by Chief Engineer" (1923), *bca/gr929/bx49/f6*.
"Skeleton Outline—Sumas Dyking Project" (1919), *bca/gr929/bx5/f8*.
"Sumas Report" (1923), *cma/am646/f8/1*.

SUMAS DEVELOPMENT COMPANY PLANS

Hill, S., "Sumas Dyke: Explanation of Engineering Features" (1906), *bcerp/bx183/f11*.

Mead, D., and S. Hill, "Map Showing Proposed Works and Lands Benefited" (1906), *bcerp/bx38*.

Mead, D., to Sumas Development Co. (1906), *bcerp/bx182/f11*.

BRITISH COLUMBIA ELECTRIC RAILWAY PLANS

Hill, S., "Report—Reclamation of Lands within Sumas Dyking District" (1909), *bcerp/bx38*.

LeBaron, F., "Report on Reclamation of Sumas Prairies and Drainage of Sumas Lake" (1908), *bcerp/bx38*.

—, "Final Report—Sumas Development Co." (1909), *bcerp/bx182/f7*.

Mead, D., et al., "Report—Reclamation of the Chilliwack-Sumas Drainage and Dyking District" (1909), *bcerp/bx38*.

Schuyler, J., "Report on Proposed Reclamation Works" (1908), *bcerp/bx38*.

—, "Review of Various Reports on Sumas Reclamation Project" (1909), *bcerp/bx38*.

LAND SETTLEMENT BOARD PLANS

Brice, H., and C. Smith, "Interim Report on Sumas Reclamation Project" (1919), *bca/gr1569/bx15/f1*.

Cartwright, C., "Report on Sumas Reclamation Project" (1919), *bca/gr929/bx48/f5*.

"Key Map of the Sumas Reclamation Area" (1918), *bca/gr1569/bx50/f3*.

"Key Map of the Sumas Reclamation Area" (1919), *cma/am646/bx1*.

Sinclair, F., "Sumas Reclamation Project: Final Report" (1919) *bca/gr929/bx48/f5*.

Smith, C., "Final Report on Sumas Reclamation Project" (1919), *bca/gr929/bx48/f5*.

Smith, P.M., "Sumas Reclamation Project: Supplementary Report" (1919), *bca/gr1569/bx10/f3*.

BOOKS AND ARTICLES CITED IN ENDNOTES

Amoss, Pamela (1978): *Coast Salish Spirit Dancing*. Seattle: University of Washington Press.

Armstrong, J.E. (1960): *Surficial Geology of Sumas Map-Area*. Ottawa: Department of Mines.

Baird, Carol (1998): "Sandbags and Rubber Boots: Chilliwack and the Flood of 1948." Chilliwack: Chilliwack Museum and Archives.

Beckey, Fred (2003): *Range of Glaciers*. Portland: Oregon Historical Society Press.

Bernick, Kathryn (1991): *Wet Site Archaeology in the Lower Mainland*. Victoria: BC Heritage Trust.

Boas, Franz (1894): "The Indian Tribes of the Lower Fraser River." *Report of the British Association for the Advancement of Science*. 64th Meeting: 453–63.

Bosselman, Fred (1996): "Limitations Inherent in the Title to Wetlands." *Stanford Environmental Law Journal* 15: 247–337.

Boyd, Robert (1999): *The Coming of the Spirit of Pestilence*. Seattle: University of Washington Press.

Boyle, C. (1997): —, et al. "Changes in Land Cover and Subsequent Effects on Lower Fraser Basin Ecosystems." *Environmental Management* 21: 185–96.

Brooks, Allan (1900): "Notes on Some of the Birds of British Columbia." *Auk* 17: 104–7.

— (1902): "Mammals of the Chilliwack District." *Ottawa Naturalist* 15: 239–44.

— (1917): "Birds of the Chilliwack District." *Auk* 34: 28–50.

— (1925): —, and H. Swarth. *Distributional List of the Birds of British Columbia*. Berkeley: Cooper Ornithological Club.

Cail, Robert (1974): *Land, Man and the Law*. Vancouver: University of BC Press.

Cameron, Laura (1997): *Openings: A Meditation on History, Method and Sumas Lake*. Montreal: McGill-Queen's University Press.

Cameron, Valerie (1989): "Late Quaternary Geomorphic History of the Sumas Valley." MA thesis, Simon Fraser University.

Carl, G.C. (1959): —, et al. *Fresh-Water Fishes of British Columbia*. Victoria: BC Provincial Museum.

— (1960): *Reptiles of British Columbia*. Victoria: BC Provincial Museum.

— (1973): *Amphibians of British Columbia*. Victoria: BC Provincial Museum.

Carlson, Keith (1997): Ed. *You Are Asked to Witness*. Chilliwack: Stó:lō Heritage Trust.

— (2001): Ed. *A Stó:lō-Coast Salish Historical Atlas*. Vancouver: Douglas and McIntyre.

— (2010): *The Power of Place, the Problem of Time*. Toronto: University of Toronto Press.

CCFO (1899): Otto Klotz, ed. *Certain Correspondence of the Foreign Office.* Ottawa: Deptartment of the Interior.

Cook, Donna (1979): "Early Settlement in the Chilliwack Valley." MA thesis, University of British Columbia.

Cowan, I.M. (1965): —, and C.J. Guiguet. *Mammals of British Columbia.* Victoria: BC Provincial Museum..

Crosby, Thomas (1907): *Among the An-ko-me-nums.* Toronto: William Briggs.

DeGroot, Henry (1858): *British Columbia: Its Condition and Prospects.* San Francisco: Daily Alta California.

Dept. of Lands and Works (1873): *Report of Explorations.* Victoria: Queen's Printer.

Duff, Wilson (1952): *The Upper Stalo Indians of the Fraser Valley.* Victoria: BC Provincial Museum.

Emmons, Richard (1952): "Archaeological Survey in the Lower Nooksack River Valley." *Anthropology in British Columbia* 3: 49–56.

Evenden, Matthew (2004): *Fish versus Power: An Environmental History of the Fraser River.* Cambridge: Cambridge University Press.

Fannin, John (1891): *Check List of British Columbia Birds.* Victoria: Queen's Printer.

Fell and Scharfe (1930): *Sumas: The Garden of the West.* Vancouver: Fell and Scharfe.

Foerster, R.E. (1931): "A Comparison of the Natural and Artificial Propagation of Salmon." *Transactions of the American Fisheries Society* 61: 121–30.

— (1936): "A Study of Sockeye Salmon Propagation Methods in BC." *Progressive Fish Culturist* 3: 4–6.

FPRA (1860, 1862): British Columbia. *Further Papers Relative to the Affairs of British Columbia.* Vols. 3–4. London: Eyre and Spottiswoode.

Fraser, Simon (2007). *Letters and Journals of Simon Fraser.* Edited by W. Kaye Lamb. Toronto: Dundurn Press.

Fraser Basin Management Program (1994): *Source Book: A Compendium of Information.* Vol. 1. Vancouver: Fraser Basin Management Program.

Galloway, Brent (1993): *A Grammar of Upriver Halkomelem.* Berkeley: University of California Press.

— (2009): *Dictionary of Upriver Halkomelem.* Los Angeles: University of California Press.

Gardner, George (1857–58): "Journal." *brml/g_gardner_journals.*

Gibbard, John (1937): "Early History of the Fraser Valley." MA thesis, University of British Columbia.

Harris, Cole (1997): *The Resettlement of British Columbia*. Vancouver: University of BC Press.

— (2002): *Making Native Space*. Vancouver: University of BC Press.

Hawley, Robert (1945): *Skqee Mus*. Bellingham: Miller and Sutherland.

Hearle, Eric (1926): *Mosquitoes of the Lower Fraser Valley*. Ottawa: National Research Council.

Henderson (1890, 1891, 1897, 1901): *Henderson's British Columbia Gazetteer and Directory*. Victoria: Henderson Publishing Co.

Hendrickson, James (1980): Ed. *Journals of the Colonial Legislatures—British Columbia*. Vol. 4. Victoria: Public Archives of BC.

Hibben, T. (1877): *Guide to the Province of British Columbia*. Victoria: T.N. Hibben and Co.

Hill-Tout, Charles (1895): "Later Prehistoric Man in British Columbia." *Transactions of the Royal Society of Canada*.

— (1978): *The Salish People: The Local Contribution of Charles Hill-Tout*. Vol. 3. Edited by R. Maud. Vancouver: Talonbooks.

Imus, Harold (1948): "Land Utilization in the Sumas Lake District." MA thesis, University of Washington.

Indian Claims Commission (1994–98): *Annual Report*. Ottawa: Ministry of Public Works.

Jackson, C. Ian (2000): Ed. *Letters from the 49th Parallel*. Toronto: Champlain Society.

Jeffcott, Percival (1949): *Nooksack Tales and Trails*. Ferndale, WA: [np].

Jenness, Diamond (1955): *The Faith of a Coast Salish Indian*. Victoria: BC Provincial Museum.

Joe, Sophie (1979): *Mosquito Story*. Sardis, BC: Coqualeetza Cultural Education Centre.

Kenyon, Walter (1953): "An Archaeological Survey of the Lower Fraser." BA thesis, University of British Columbia.

Klassen, Agatha (1976): *Yarrow: A Portrait in Mosaic*. Yarrow, BC: A.E. Klassen.

Kovanen, Dori (2001): "Late Glacial Ice Margin Fluctuations in the Fraser Lowland and Adjacent Nooksack Valley." PhD thesis, University of British Columbia.

Laing, Frederick (1939): *Colonial Farm Settlers*. Victoria: Ministry of Agriculture.

Laing, Hamilton (1979): *Allan Brooks: Artist Naturalist*. Victoria: BC Provincial Museum.

LAJ (1891–1945): British Columbia. *Legislative Assembly Journals*. Victoria: Queen's Printer.

Land Settlement Board (1924): *Farm Lands for Sale*. Victoria: Land Settlement Board.

Langley, H.G. (1867): *Pacific Coast Business Directory*. San Francisco: H.G. Langley.

Langston, Nancy (2003): *Where Land and Water Meet*. Seattle: University of Washington Press.

LASP (1874): British Columbia. *Legislative Assembly Sessional Papers*. Victoria: Queen's Printer.

Lepofsky, Dana (2000): —, et al. "Archaeology of the Scowlitz Site." *Journal of Field Archaeology* 27: 391–416.

— (2003): "Fraser Valley Archaeology Project." Stó:lō Nation Archives.

— (2009): —, et al. "Exploring Stó:lō-Coast Salish Interaction and Identity." *American Antiquity* 74: 595–626.

Lerman, Norman (1951): "Lower Fraser Folktales." Stó:lō Nation Archives.

Lewis, William (2001): *Wetlands Explained*. New York: Oxford University Press.

Lord, John Keast (1866): *The Naturalist in Vancouver Island and British Columbia*. 2 vols. London: Richard Bentley.

— (1867): *At Home in the Wilderness*. London: Robert Hardwick.

Lyall, David (1864): "Account of the Botanical Collections made by David Lyall." *Botanical Journal* 7: 124–45.

Maclachlan, Morag (1998): Ed. *The Fort Langley Journals*. Vancouver: University of BC Press.

Macleod, Earl (1974): "Early Flying in B.C." *Aviation Historical Society Journal* 12: 100–13.

Mallandaine, E. (1871, 1874): *First Victoria Directory and British Columbia Guide*. Victoria: E. Mallandaine.

Marshall, Daniel (2000): "Claiming the Land: Indians, Goldseekers and the Rush to BC." PhD thesis, University of British Columbia.

Mayne, Richard (1859): —, et al. *Sketch of the Upper Part of the Fraser River*. London: Admiralty.

McColl, William (1864): "A Rough Diagram Shewing the Position of the Reserves Laid Off from Government Purposes etc. on the Fraser, Chillukweyuk, Sumass & Masquee Rivers," *ltsv/31t1*.

McDonald, Archibald (2001): *This Blessed Wilderness*. Edited by J. Cole. Vancouver: University of BC Press.

Merchant, Carolyn (2004): *Reinventing Eden: The Fate of Nature in Western Culture*. New York: Routledge.

Mikkelsen, Phyllis (1950): "Land Settlement Policy on the Mainland of British Columbia." MA thesis, University of British Columbia.

Mitsch, William (2009): —, et al. *Wetland Ecosystems*. Hoboken: John Wiley and Sons.

Mohs, Gordon (1990): "The Upper Stó:lō Indians." Alliance of Tribal Councils.

— (1991): "1990 Stó:lō Heritage Project." Sto:lo Nation Archives.

— (1992a): "Excavations at Hatzic Rock." Sto:lo Nation Archives.

— (1992b): "Sumas Lake Golf Course Development Proposal." Stó:lō Tribal Council.

Montgomery, Keith (1979): "Prehistoric Settlements of Sumas Valley, Washington." MA thesis, Western Washington University.

Munro, J.A. (1947): —, and I.M. Cowan. *Review of the Bird Fauna of British Columbia*. Victoria: BC Provincial Museum.

Murton, James (2007): *Creating a Modern Countryside*. Vancouver: University of BC Press.

North, M. (1984): —, and J. Teversham. "Vegetation of the Floodplains of the Lower Fraser, Serpentine & Nicomekl Rivers, 1859–90." *Syesis* 17: 47–66.

Oliver, Jeff (2010): *Landscapes and Social Transformations on the Northwest Coast*. Tucson: University of Arizona Press.

Orchard, Imbert (1983): *Floodland and Forest*. Victoria: Provincial Archives of BC.

PILQ (1875): British Columbia. *Papers Connected with the Indian Land Question*. Victoria: Richard Wolfenden.

PRA (1859): British Columbia. *Papers Relative to the Affairs of British Columbia*. London: Eyre and Spottiswoode.

RCIA(1916): Royal Commission on Indian Affairs. *Evidence Submitted: Vol. 9, New Westminster Agency*. Victoria: King's Printer.

Richardson, Allan (1974): "Traditional Fisheries and Fishing Sites of the Nooksack Indian Tribe." Nooksack Tribal Council.

— (2011): —, and B. Galloway. *Nooksack Place Names*. Vancouver: University of BC Press.

Riggins, Loretta (1991): —, and L. Walker. *Heart of the Fraser Valley*. Clearbrook, BC: Matsqui Centennial Society.

RRN: Reciprocal Research Network, rrnpilot.org.

RRNB (1961): United States. *Records Relating to the First Northwest Boundary Survey Commission.* Washington: National Archives.

Sandwell, R.W. (1999): Ed. *Beyond the City Limits.* Vancouver: University of BC Press.

Schaepe, David (2006): "Rock Fortifications." *American Antiquity* 71: 671–705.

— (2009): "Pre-Colonial Stó:lō-Coast Salish Community Organization." PhD thesis, University of British Columbia.

Sepass, Chief William K'HHalserten (2009): *Sepass Poems.* Mission, BC: Longhouse Publishing.

Sewell, Derrick (1965): *Water Management and Floods in the Fraser River Basin.* Chicago: University of Chicago Press.

Siemens, Alfred (1968): Ed. *Lower Fraser Valley.* Vancouver: Tantalus Research Ltd.

Sinclair, Frederick (1961): "A History of the Sumas Drainage, Dyking and Development District." *cma/am12.*

Sleigh, Daphne (1999): Ed. *One Foot on the Border.* Deroche, BC: Sumas Prairie and Area Historical Society.

Smith, Allan (1988): *Ethnography of the North Cascades.* Pullman, WA: Washington State University Press.

Smith, Bob (1982): "The Reclamation of the Sumas Lands." Chilliwack, Fraser Valley College.

Sumas Drainage, Dyking and Development District (1926): *Choice Farm Lands for Sale.* Chilliwack: Sumas Drainage, Dyking and Development District.

Sumas Dyking District (1926): *Map Showing Lands for Sale.* Chilliwack: Sumas Dyking District.

Sumas Municipal Council (1919): *Sumas, British Columbia.* New Westminster: Columbian Company Printers.

Sumas Reclaimed Lands (1926): British Columbia. *Sumas Reclaimed Lands.* Victoria: Sumas Dyking Commissioner.

Suttles, Wayne (1955): *Katzie Ethnographic Notes.* Victoria: BC Provincial Museum.

— (1987): *Coast Salish Essays.* Vancouver: Talonbooks.

Swindle, Lewis (2001): Ed. *The Fraser River Gold Rush of 1858.* Victoria: Lewis Swindle.

Tate, Charles (1874–80): "Diary." *bca/ms303/bx2/f3-6.*

Turner, Nancy (1995): *Food Plants of Coastal First Peoples.* Vancouver: University of BC Press.

— (1998): *Plant Technology of First Peoples in British Columbia*. Vancouver: University of BC Press.

Upper Stó:lō (1981): *Upper Stó:lō Fraser Valley Plant Gathering*. Sardis, BC: Stó:lō Sitel Curriculum.

— (1982): *Upper Stó:lō Ethnobotany*. Sardis, BC: Stó:lō Sitel Curriculum.

US Army Corps of Engineers (1967): *Sumas River Supplement: Flood Plain Information Study, Nooksack River*. Seattle: Army Corps of Engineers.

US Commissioner (1857): United States Commissioner of Indian Affairs. *Annual Report*. Washington, DC: Department of Indian Affairs.

Watt, K. Jane (2006): *High Water: Living with the Fraser Floods*. Abbotsford: Dairy Industry Historical Society.

Wells, Oliver (1965): *Vocabulary of Native Words*. Vedder.

— (1987): Ed. *The Chilliwacks and Their Neighbours*. Vancouver: Talonbooks.

— (2003): *Edenbank: the History of a Canadian Pioneer Farm*. Madeira Park, BC: Harbour Publishing.

White, George (1937): "A History of the Eastern Fraser Valley since 1895." MA thesis, University of British Columbia.

White, George F. (1917): *Fish Isinglass and Glue*. Washington, DC: Government Printing Office.

Williams, R.T. (1883, 1885, 1889, 1891, 1892, 1894, 1898, 1899): *British Columbia Directory*. Victoria: R.T. Williams.

Wilson, Charles (1866): "Report on the Indian Tribes." *Transactions of the Ethnological Society of London* 4: 275–322.

— (1970): *Mapping the Frontier*. Edited by G. Stanley. Toronto: Macmillan of Canada.

Wilson, Robert (2010): *Seeking Refuge: Birds and Landscapes of the Pacific Flyway*. Seattle: University of Washington Press.

Woodward, Frances (1975): "The Influence of the Royal Engineers." *BC Studies* 24: 3–51.

Worster, Donald (1977): *Nature's Economy: A History of Ecological Ideas*. Cambridge: Cambridge University Press.

INDEX